NORMAN
MACLEAN

.

NORMAN MACLEAN

A Life of Letters and Rivers

Rebecca McCarthy

UNIVERSITY OF WASHINGTON PRESS

Seattle

Norman McLean was published with the support of the Robert B. Heilman Endowment for Books in the Humanities, established in honor of the distinguished scholar who served as chair of the University of Washington English Department from 1948 to 1971.

Published by the University of Washington Press

Design by Katrina Noble
Composed in Freight Text Pro

28   27   26   25   24   5   4   3   2   1

Printed and bound in the United States of America

UNIVERSITY OF WASHINGTON PRESS
uwapress.uw.edu

LIBRARY OF CONGRESS CATALOGING-IN-PUBLICATION DATA
Names: McCarthy, Rebecca (Freelance writer), author.
Title: Norman Maclean : a life of letters and rivers / Rebecca McCarthy.
Description: Seattle : University of Washington Press, [2024]. | Includes bibliographical references and index.
Identifiers: LCCN 2023055125 (print) | LCCN 2023055126 (ebook) | ISBN 9780295752488 (hardcover) | ISBN 9780295752495 (ebook)
Subjects: LCSH: Maclean, Norman, 1902–1990. | McCarthy, Rebecca (Freelance writer)—Friends and associates. | Authors, American—20th century—Biography. | College teachers—Illinois—Chicago—Biography. | Teacher-student relationships —Illinois—Chicago.
Classification: LCC PS3563.A317993 Z55 2024 (print) | LCC PS3563.A317993 (ebook) | DDC 813/.54 [B]—dc23/eng/20240208
LC record available at https://lccn.loc.gov/2023055125
LC ebook record available at https://lccn.loc.gov/2023055126

♾ This paper meets the requirements of ANSI/NISO Z39.48-1992 (Permanence of Paper).

FRONTISPIECE: Joel Snyder took this photo of Norman in Jackson Park on a crisp fall day in 1975, after the University of Chicago Press had accepted *A River Runs Through It and Other Stories* for publication. Norman is standing on the Clarence Darrow Bridge. Photo courtesy of Joel Snyder.

CONTENTS

Introduction   1

1   Meeting Maclean and Chicago   3

2   Light and Shadow   19

3   Seeley Lake Summer   27

4   Walking the City Through Stories   37

5   Finding Montana   55

6   Western Friends   67

7   Tragedy Was Inevitable   77

8   Creating the Committee   93

9   Searching for a Story   117

10   Student and Teacher   125

11   A Choice Soul   133

12   Tragedy and Accident   149

13   The Crux of It All   159

14   The Work Never Ends   167

15   Loose Ends and Long Friendships   179

16 No Time to Tarry 189

17 Honors and Unfinished Work 205

Acknowledgments 213

Notes 217

Index 251

Illustrations follow page 108.

NORMAN MACLEAN

Introduction

AS A COLLEGE STUDENT at the University of Chicago, I spent four years in a friendship with Norman Maclean. I met him at the beginning of my adult life and toward the end of his, when he had been harrowed by disease and despair. His wife, Jessie, had endured a long decline and excruciating death from emphysema and cancer. Decades of smoking had brought him heart disease. His teaching career was over. Hyde Park, his Chicago neighborhood of more than forty years, was changing, and not for the better. Many other people would have simply succumbed to depression and drink and faded away. But when I was with Norman, I didn't think about his age—his mind and sense of humor remained youthful, and his curiosity buoyed him.

He was happy talking to me and meeting my friends, and he was generous, introducing me to his many favorite ethnic restaurants around the city, walking with me in city parks and outside forest preserves, treating me to Crock-Pot dinners in his Hyde Park condominium, sharing his friends with me—nurturing me, my mother would say. He had been a lonely, homesick boy while in college, and he didn't want me to experience the same isolation, so he remained supportive and consistent throughout my college years. Besides, one condition of my going to Chicago was his promise to my mother that he would look after me. He kept his promise.

Before he retired from teaching, Norman began putting down on paper stories he had heard and told. He was also coming to grips with a challenge that had long preoccupied him: untangling the strands of his brother Paul's life and weaving them into a work of art. It took Norman decades to come to terms with what had happened to his family and to himself and then to write the story. He said he didn't cry for his brother until the 1970s, after reading aloud the last few pages of the story to his daughter and son-in-law. But he had been grieving for Paul his whole life.

1

Meeting Maclean and Chicago

ON THE CUSP of turning seventy, Norman Maclean did what many people facing retirement want to do. He launched a successful second career. He became a writer, though he preferred to call himself a storyteller. And in this career, he did what anyone, at any age, wants to do when they start putting thoughts on paper: he wrote a popular book. *A River Runs Through It and Other Stories* has sold close to two million copies, with five different editions and numerous translations. There are two illustrated editions of the title story, which was also made into a beloved movie. That story centers on Norman's version of losing his glittering, doomed younger brother, whom he loved but couldn't help and who was murdered.

Published posthumously, *Young Men and Fire* also focuses on dead young men: elite, parachuting forest firefighters who died in a conflagration near Helena, Montana. "For the second book I wanted to do something very different from the first," Norman wrote. "Something objective, apart from me, not 'spots of time' out of my own life. I thought it would take me a year, but things slowly went wrong." He set the manuscript aside in 1987; Alan Thomas, then the humanities editor at the University of Chicago Press, assembled its different parts into a book years later. In telling that story, Norman expanded the limits of compassion, wrestling with questions of immortality as he tried to make art out of a tragedy, contemplating his own mortality as he searched for what he called "the consolation of explanation." His second career could not have happened without his first, in which he was also successful. And he couldn't have written either book as a young man.

Norman was celebrated as a formidable English teacher at the University of Chicago long before the publication of *A River Runs Through It and Other Stories*, before Robert Redford released his movie of the title story, and before he received an avalanche of awards and honors. He was an intellectual but, unlike his colleagues, was not a prolific scholar. For almost forty years, he focused his considerable energy on engaging and educating college students. He lavished attention on them, helping them improve their writing, penning letters of recommendation for graduate schools, professional schools, jobs, and fellowships. He remains the only faculty member to win the prestigious Llewellyn John and Harriet Manchester Quantrell Award for Undergraduate Teaching three times, an honor bestowed by the student body itself.

I met Norman in 1972, while he was working on "USFS 1919," one of the stories in his first book, *A River Runs Through It and Other Stories*. He had started the story the previous year. The book includes two stories and a novella, the celebrated "A River Runs Through It." Through roundabout family connections, one of my aunts had learned that Norman was an English teacher who was trying to write about his early years in Montana, before he had moved back east, and he was staying at his family's cabin on Seeley Lake. I was a teenager at the time and had flown to western Montana to spend a few summer weeks with my oldest brother, John, and his family in Seeley Lake. John worked full-time as a professional forester with the US Forest Service (USFS), and he was in charge of recreation. My sister-in-law Marilyn was being treated for breast cancer. My job was to drive her to Missoula, fifty-two miles away, for radiation treatments. I was also expected to babysit my niece, Meg, who was two, when Marilyn needed to rest, which was daily.

On my second Saturday in Seeley, we were going out to dinner with Norman. Marilyn told me he was a widower who knew a lot about poetry. I read and wrote poetry. "How should I address him?" I asked. The casual western practice of children referring to adults by their first names didn't extend to me. My brother and sister-in-law insisted I call him "Dr. Maclean."

In the Forest Service compound where we lived, word of our dinner plans spread. Though he would have hated the term, Norman was considered a "summer person." Most year-round Montanans in Seeley didn't mix with the summer people, an affluent group who arrived in June and stayed until early fall. But my brother did. Part of his job as a recreation officer was making sure all was well with these temporary residents, some of whom, like Norman, were older and lonely. Norman and John swapped stories, talked about alpine wildflowers, and shared a dislike for the "loud bastards" who took over the lakeside campground near Norman's cabin on weekends, leaving the trash cans overflowing and the outhouses a mess.

That Saturday, we waited in the living room of John and Marilyn's cabin, ready to drive to the Seven-Up Ranch restaurant in Lincoln, fifty-seven miles away. Logging at least one hundred miles for a good meal was typical in Montana, where at the time there was a speed limit only at night. Norman arrived promptly at six, driving a boxy Volvo sedan. Holding my niece on my hip, I watched through the window as Norman got out of his car. He was a compact older man, about five feet eight, my mother's height, with high cheekbones and a slight scowl. His dark hair was parted in the middle. He hiked up his pants and smoothed his hair as he looked around the yard at Meg's upturned tricycle and scattered toys. He wore brown corduroy pants, a denim shirt, a plaid tie, and a beige windbreaker. My brother opened the front door as Norman climbed the porch steps. He smiled up at John, who towered over him, and they shook hands. Norman kissed Marilyn on the cheek as he walked through the door. I stood behind her, jiggling Meg to quiet her. I smiled.

"Rebecca, darling, this is a great pleasure," he said. I wasn't sure it was a pleasure. I thought it was a trial. His voice had music in it, with emphasis on *bec* and *dar* and *great*. He nodded at me, and I nodded back. Something about the way he spoke was intimidating.

Norman suggested we take his Volvo. John, Marilyn, and Meg could have the front seat, Norman said, and he and I could sit together in the back and talk. John held open the door for Marilyn, and Norman held the door for me. As I climbed in the car, I wondered what we would talk about. Would he quiz me on nineteenth-century Romantic literature? On Shakespeare? We didn't say anything until John turned onto the highway.

"What's on your great mind, dear?" Norman began.

What was on it? What mind? I was blank.

He drew some papers out of a pocket in his windbreaker. There was writing all over them. Most of the writing was mine. I felt nauseated when I realized these were my poems I had sent to Marilyn, the traitor in the front seat. Norman laid the papers in his lap and began to talk to me about my poems, telling me things I had never noticed about their imagery and language. While John and Marilyn entertained Meg with songs, Norman and I talked about poetry. The questions he asked were ones I could answer, and the poems he talked about were poems I had read. I had never had an adult take me so seriously.

At the Seven-Up Ranch, John, Marilyn, and Norman sipped scotch before the meal. I asked for a Tom Collins. In those days, I believed a good drink was multicolored, sporting little umbrellas, orange slices, and cherries on swords, the more colors and weaponry, the better. Norman glanced at the tall glass, raised his eyebrows, and pursed his lips like he might whistle, but he didn't say anything. I didn't drink much of the fruity concoction, but I saved the little umbrella. After we had eaten salad and steak and potatoes and ordered ice cream, Norman leaned across the table toward Marilyn, who was sitting next to me. He frowned. "Are those bastards killing you to cure you, darling?"

Marilyn smiled. "No, Mac, they're not. I'm just tired, that's all."

He raised his eyebrows and gestured with his head toward me. "God, darling, rely on your sister-in-law there. She's young and tough, and she can help out."

On the way home, Norman asked me about college. Where would I go? What did I want to study? I didn't know where I wanted to go, I said, or if I wanted to go. Maybe to the university in Missoula. Marilyn and I had eaten lunch there after one of her doctor visits, and it seemed like a comfortable place. He ignored this idea and suggested I think about Chapel Hill, Duke, or the University of Chicago, where he had taught for decades. "Fuck it, Rebecca," he said, then he told me I should leave the South. I was glad it was dark because I was blushing. "Chicago's the big leagues, darling, but I think you could handle it. You're a strong, powerful woman." Until then, no one had ever referred to me as a woman, much less a strong, powerful one. I felt older just hearing it and decided I would think of myself as a strong, powerful woman from then on.

"You haven't met her mother," Marilyn said from up front. She held a sleeping Meg on her lap and leaned against my brother. "You'll have to get past her."

Late one afternoon a week or so later, John and I were riding around Seeley Lake when we turned down the narrow driveway to Norman's cabin. John made a habit of checking regularly on the older summer people, and today was Norman's day. The cabin was on a knoll overlooking the water. There were tamaracks all around it. As we approached the door, I could hear someone inside humming. Before John could knock, Norman opened the door, smiling, inviting us in. He stepped into the kitchen, took the lid off a Crock-Pot, and stirred whatever was cooking. A delicious, meaty aroma enveloped me. He herded us onto the screen porch, then disappeared, humming. A few minutes later, he returned with two tumblers half-full of something amber colored, handed one to John and one to me, then went back inside for his glass. He sat down in a chair near me and began to talk. Norman had a way of speaking in which he paused, a millisecond, before an important phrase and then drew out words, his voice rising and falling for emphasis.

"Rebecca, darling, this is bourbon on the rocks." Pause. A sip. "Before dinner, you can drink scotch or bourbon or whiskey, with ice or water or club soda." Pause. "With a twist of lemon in the scotch if you like. Or you can have a glass of sherry." Long pause. Another sip.

"A Tom Collins, a gin and tonic, those are drinks for you and your boyfriend after a game of tennis. Not before a meal." Pause. "With food, you can have wine. And after a meal, you can have another glass of scotch or bourbon." Pause. "Or a sherry. Or a cordial, maybe brandy." Long pause. A sip. "That's it, darling, those are your choices."

I looked at the liquid in my glass. I was sixteen, and I had never had a real drink. The bourbon smelled and tasted like lighter fluid, but I managed to swallow a little without choking. It went straight up my nose, setting my nasal passages on fire. Norman was complaining to John about some clear-cutting bastard who needed his testicles removed. From my brother's response, I realized the bastard was the ranger who lived next door to us, who I had thought was a nice man. I looked around the porch. There were two beds against one wall and a few chairs and tables. I drank some more bourbon and closed my eyes tight, then opened them and gulped down the rest of the drink. Norman had told me what to drink, but he forgot to tell me to sip liquor as if it were boiling hot. To savor it. Still, I managed to swallow all of it.

Noting my empty glass, Norman said, "Rebecca, darling, I'll get that," and he took my glass away. He soon returned with a full glass. I made it about halfway through the second drink before getting up and making for one of the porch beds. A couple of hours later, I woke up. I smelled wood burning. Far away, I could hear John and Norman talking about the early days of the Forest Service. I shivered and tucked my legs under a blanket someone had draped over me. I opened my eyes and saw that dusk was dwindling into dark, so it must have been close to nine. Loons were calling. They sounded too hysterical to get their songs out. My mouth felt full of cotton, and my temples were pounding.

"John?"

He appeared at the bedside and handed me a glass of water. I drank and felt better. He said it was time for supper. He had decided we'd stay and eat with Norman.

"How do you feel? Did you have a nice nap?"

I could feel myself blushing, but my brother ignored it. He helped me sit up and led me to the table where Norman was sitting. There was stew on each of the three plates and glass tumblers at two. Smaller plates held pears and cherries. A fire was burning in the fireplace. Norman looked up at me. "Your big brother here has promised to warn me of your next visit so I can have enough bourbon on hand." Norman grinned and shook his head. "God, woman, I tell you the proper way to drink, and you drink. I'm just glad I didn't tell you about rock climbing or grizzly hunting."

By then, I was convinced strong, powerful women could drink liquor without feeling woozy.

"Sit down, dear, and eat." He pointed to the place with no glass tumbler. "We have stew and some wonderful bing cherries for dessert. But I'm not giving you any wine."

Everything seemed to slow down with Norman. Maybe he and John had continued drinking whiskey after I went to sleep and were a little tiddly. Maybe he always ate bite by bite. Whatever the reason, we were at that table for two hours, listening to Norman tell stories about a book he was writing about his time in the Forest Service and about his own decision to go east to college.

At his mother's kitchen table, he had completed exams that colleges had sent him. He mailed them all back. Weeks passed. Several schools, including Harvard and Yale, accepted him, but he eventually chose Dartmouth. It seemed to him like an "outdoorsy" school. When it came time for him to go, he cleaned his best shotgun, packed his clothes and fly rod, and got on the train with his father. At Dartmouth, once he had found his footing, he had edited a humor magazine, boxed, and befriended Theodor "Ted" Seuss Geisel, the creator of the Dr. Seuss books and "the craziest guy I ever met, darling." Norman had also taken money from "a lot of rich bastards" at the poker table. He smiled from ear to ear at the memory. Right then, I made up my mind to shine up my poker strategies.

"But the East isn't the place for you, Rebecca. The Ivy League is filled with rich men's sons and daughters. Old money. Secret societies. Joe College. Bastards." He shook his head and hissed, "Ssssttt." The sound was a cross between a punctured tire and an angry rattlesnake and one I would come to know well. "No, Chicago's the place for you, darling. A strong, powerful woman like yourself, a poet, they would love you." The part about the school blew right over me. What I heard was that Norman considered me a poet. When an adult names you, before the wax is completely dry, the name becomes part of who you are.

"I don't know what our mother will say about my baby sister going to Chicago, Mac," John said, repeating Marilyn's warning. He leaned back in his chair. "Could be a hard sell."

"You can handle her, John. I have confidence in you. You don't want any small-town provincialism wrecking Rebecca's chances just as she's starting out. And neither do I." Norman drained his glass.

"You can't stay here, Rebecca." He turned to look at me. "You would end up married to some piss-fir willy with too many children and no time for poetry. I decided to leave Montana by asking myself, 'Who would you talk to if you stayed here? And what would you talk about? Fishing?' I would have died. I needed to live in the world of ideas, and so do you."

He had given me a lot to think about. If Norman despised the East as much as he seemed to, why did he choose to go there? I would later learn he had a lifelong hatred of New York, but he loved Chicago. My sister-in-law was determined that I leave the South, at least for a while. A native of Idaho, she had been put off by southern manners and mores when she visited my family, and she was having none of it. Chicago, she said, would show me "just what big teeth my grandmother had." My brother was anxious for me to have "a first-rate education" because he felt he hadn't had one.

Later that summer, before I returned to South Carolina, John, Marilyn, and I heard Norman read part of "USFS 1919," which talks about Norman's experience as a teenager in the early Forest Service. "It tries to say directly how I feel about the mountains of Idaho and Montana and to make these feelings a dramatic part of the story," Norman said. We thought the story was great—it was thrilling to me that the narrator in the story was roughly my age. I knew what Norman meant by "spots of time" because sometimes I, too, felt I was playing a character in my own life's story.

Norman liked getting an unvarnished review from a teenager, but he also wanted advice from an expert woodsman. John suggested Norman write William R. "Bud" Moore, a career forester who knew something about the early Forest Service and who also knew many of the characters in Norman's story. Bud was a native Montanan who had run a trapline in the Bitterroots as a kid and landed as a marine at Normandy. And who, without a college degree, had risen in the ranks to become chief of the Division of Fire Control and Air Operations for the US Forest Service's Northern Region, which included Montana. Bud made both suggestions and corrections to Norman's manuscript. His wife, Janet, and he became Norman's lifelong friends.

In the fall quarter of 1972, I know Norman was teaching, probably Shakespeare or the Romantics, something he had taught long and well, but he also had taken on another challenge. After hooking me in Seeley Lake, he spent months landing me during my last year of high school. Almost as soon as my plane touched down in Augusta, his letters—and ones from my sister-in-law—started arriving. They worked together as a tag team, bent on persuading me, and my mother and father, that I should attend college at the University of Chicago or another school Norman approved of, such as Duke or Chapel Hill. He had friends and former students at both schools and at the University of Texas as well. He would slip one or two of my poems in an envelope, add a note of endorsement, and mail it to his friends, then copy the whole shebang, including their replies, and send it to me. I was flattered.

What I didn't know then was that only the previous year, Norman had been hospitalized a few months for depression. I had no knowledge of depression and its debilitating effects, and I doubt either of my parents, or John, did either. In looking back, I think I helped Norman continue to feel healthy because I was an eager young person he could encourage and influence. I was a project. As a naive sixteen-year-old, I knew Norman wanted me to come to Chicago, without his ever saying so, but I wasn't sure about being in such a metropolis. I had grown up in a city of fifteen thousand people and had family in small towns in Alabama, Pennsylvania, and Delaware. The city of Sister Carrie, of painted women luring farm boys, the city of Al Capone, machine-gunning gangsters, the City of Big Shoulders, butchering hogs and playing with freight trains—the idea of living in Chicago scared me. Did I have the moxie to live there? When in October, Marilyn became too sick to write her weekly letter, Norman took up the slack, firing off two or sometimes even three missives each week. I wrote back, usually including a poem.

Just as he had become the writing coach and guide for generations of students, so Norman became, for me, a critic of my poetry, gently suggesting changes, praising words and lines he liked, and teasing me about my shortcomings. I once sent him two poems in a letter, a short poem and a sonnet. He responded that he liked my free verse poem a lot while slamming my feeble attempt at a sonnet as doggerel, with rhythm that "walks all over its partner feet." My lines reminded him of Wordsworth's couplet: "The horse galloped down the street / On all four feet." At least he mentioned Wordsworth, whom I admired. He ended with a zinger, as he often did: "So I won't have to write such long letters (except to women more my own age), you had better come to the College of the University of Chicago where I can teach you something about rhythm and harmony."

Norman had learned about rhythm first from his mother. Whenever one of his high school English assignments involved reading Shakespeare or poetry, he would sit at the kitchen table with his mother, and she would read the plays or the poems aloud to him. She held his hand and touched it to the table and beat time to the words she was reading, stressing the syllables so he could hear iambs, anapests, trochees, and dactyls. He said he could feel the words reverberating in his body, along with his mother's voice. For Norman, the way his mother read went to the heart of things. He often said his writing was more affected by poetry than prose, and indeed, much of what he has written can be scanned.

In November, Norman sent me a copy of a letter he had received in October from my brother John, who had written: "The larch needles slowly turned to gold and stayed on the trees for a few days longer than in any of the past years since I've been here. Now the needles are starting to fall and beginning to cover the ground with a golden yellow mat. None of the roads in Seeley Campground are visible because of the mat. It is so pretty that I park on the road outside the campground and walk in so as not to disturb the covering of needles." Norman asked me, "Did you know you had a male poet in the family?" I did know my brother took lovely photographs and had an eye for beauty.

In early December, Norman and I began to strategize about where I should apply to college, and he wondered if I would like Chapel Hill and whether I had my ducks in a row. His former student and friend Bill Harmon was the chairman of the English department at the University of North Carolina, and Bill liked my poetry. Norman wrote to me: "Today is the anniversary of my wife's death, which I spend always in trying to be of some help to others. I am sure my wife would have liked you and would have been happy if we could have helped you in any way to realize the best that is within you." It was the same philosophy that guided his teaching as well as his interactions with people he cared about. I wished Jessie were still alive. She had been diagnosed with emphysema in 1950 and had rarely been seen without a cigarette in her hand. When she was in Billings Hospital, Norman said, she would take a hit of oxygen and then puff on a cigarette. Esophageal cancer finally killed her in 1968.

Even as he was planning to get me into college, he was planning on leaving it. On January 1, 1973, Norman wrote Stuart Tave, then the head of the Department of English at the University, and told him he would be retiring at the end of the academic year. He had winter quarter off and had time to think. Norman had been teaching at Chicago since beginning graduate school there in 1928 and had lasted five years longer than almost all other professors. "I would rather not teach at all than not to teach well—and to be too damn old to know it," he wrote to Tave. He then explained that the University of Chicago was one of the loves of his life, along with his family and friends, America, and especially Montana. "To me, the University is a way of life, a way of thought and feeling. It is so much a part of me that I do not think I could ever live far apart from it," he wrote. His Woodlawn Avenue condominium put him four blocks from the main library and two blocks from the Quadrangle Club, the campus faculty club. Instead of teaching in a classroom, he would spend the rest of his life writing, researching, and talking about writing. A few weeks after he wrote to Stuart Tave, as word of his decision circulated through campus, University of Chicago president Edward Levi wrote a note saying: "I don't believe for a moment you teach less well. You are still one of the great teachers among the select few."

In one of my letters to Norman, I added a postscript asking, "What type of place is Chicago?" After pondering my question, Norman replied: "Chicago is a rather large place that was incorporated as a village in 1833 for the primary purpose of plucking the down off young chicks from the western edge of South Carolina. Why don't you come up and see for yourself?"

So I did. One Thursday in January, I boarded a flight in balmy Augusta, Georgia, and headed to Chicago. Norman met me at my gate, and I know I was grinning like a cat with a mouth full of briars. The plan was for me to stay in a residence hall, tour the campus, and attend classes on Friday, hang out on Saturday with students, eat dinner with Norman, and fly home. Norman wanted me to see if I could picture myself at the university. I got off the plane with a backpack stuffed with a second sweater, a second scarf, and a pair of gloves my mother had worn when my father and she lived in Kansas. I had on good hiking boots—a gift from Marilyn—and what I thought was a warm coat.

As soon as I stepped outside, I realized my thin wool coat was inadequate. I had never been so cold—even my eyeballs were freezing. Norman wore a hooded, industrial-strength parka, wool pants, boots, and a watch cap. He looked ready for Antarctica. The sky was gray, there was gray snow on the ground, and the cold wind took my breath away. We piled into his Volvo and headed into the city. The Thursday evening traffic on the four-lane highway was heavy. Norman asked about my brother John and his family, saying he had gotten a cheery letter from them.

We passed a factory topped by a giant Morton Salt box, with the words "When it rains, it pours" on it, just like the salt box in my mother's kitchen. I felt as if I had stepped into a picture book I read to my niece, Meg, and was now in a city designed by Richard Scarry, with factories and tall buildings, trains and planes, goofy policemen, and distracted drivers in pickle cars. Farther on, I saw near the highway a mass of onion-shaped domes and church towers and two-story brick buildings extending in rows for miles to the west. Norman told me only Warsaw had more Poles than Chicago. Only Israel had more Holocaust survivors. The city had almost as many ethnicities as countries and as many corresponding neighborhoods, with markets and restaurants giving them a taste of home. I felt as if I had landed on another planet. My hometown in South Carolina didn't divide into ethnicities—just into Black or white. Everyone was southern.

Norman turned east and made his way to Lake Shore Drive. We passed lights shining on a giant fountain spread across the center of a big park. Even without jets of water, it looked like something that belonged on a giant's birthday cake. Buckingham Fountain. Norman drove along a narrow causeway toward a domed building that seemed to float in the lake. He found a parking place and got out, fighting the wind to open the door. I pushed open my door and leaned against the car, wondering what in the world we were doing there, other than freezing to death. Had he lost his mind? We walked toward the building, leaning into the wind, passed the trees, and stopped. A sign said Adler Planetarium. Norman withdrew a handkerchief and dabbed at his nose. A distant red light on the lake blinked on and off.

"Turn around, Rebecca."

Like a sparkling bracelet, the light from the skyscrapers was reflected in the lake. The buildings were immense—I had never seen anything like them—rimmed at the bottom by the headlights of passing cars. They were different shapes, some with more than one tower, but they all stretched up as high as they could go. A giant child could have stacked those blocks. For a few seconds, I forgot the cold.

"I think it's the most beautiful skyline in the world," Norman said. "London, New York, they can't hold a candle to it. The rise and fall of the buildings—God, it's just beautiful. Not like the Missions, darling. It shows the power and genius of the people who built it. The Sears building"—he pointed to one stacked with antennae—"is the tallest in the world. The Standard Oil Building, my best friend worked there."

For a few seconds he was silent. "This is it, darling, the Big Leagues."

What I most remember about that weekend is being cold and eating delicious food. Thursday night, Norman dropped me off at a co-ed residence hall, a block from his home, where I spent three nights in a shared room on the women's floor. A young biology major from Michigan welcomed me; her obliging Massachusetts roommate slept elsewhere. The next day, my female host escorted me to a class taught by one of

Norman's friends and colleagues, a humanities course required of all first-year students. The students were talking about Emerson and beauty, and they sounded smart. I went to another class as well and came away with the same opinion. Friday night, my temporary roommate and two of her friends took me on the elevated train, the L, to the Loop. We got off and walked north on Michigan Avenue, stopping to look at the different stones embedded in the Tribune Tower, before making our way to Uno's for deep-dish Chicago pizza, then we took a late-night bus back to campus.

Saturday evening, Norman and I went to the Parthenon, a Greek restaurant on Halsted Street, where the waiters all seemed to know him. He ordered most of the menu—dishes I had never heard of, much less tasted, like gyros and spanakopita—and then, always the teacher, explained what I was eating and how it had been prepared, ending with baklava and custard. I was so busy thinking about the food that I wasn't even cold when we walked back to his car. The next morning, I flew back to Augusta. On the way home, I decided if I could get in, Chicago was the school for me. The students I had met were people I wanted to have as friends. And I wanted to get to know Norman's Chicago.

2

Light and Shadow

A WEEK OR SO after my visit to Chicago, Norman went to Florida
to spend ten days with Larry Kimpton on his boat. A former president
of the university, Kimpton had been close friends with Norman and his
late wife, Jessie, since the early 1940s. The two friends traveled down
the Atlantic Coast to Key West, Norman wrote, "and even out to the
sign that says it is the southernmost point in the United States (but I
don't think it is). We ate fish at every meal and always lime pie at night.
I'll have to sober up on my own cooking." As soon as he returned, he
wrote another letter of support to the admissions officer at another
college. In addition to writing letters for me, Norman was working on
his USFS story, corresponding with Bud Moore about possible changes.
With my college applications completed, Norman suggested I finish a
series of poems I had been working on. "I'll try to finish my story on
the good old USFS, when I was 17 and it was 14. *Pax vobiscum*. When you
have done your best, there isn't much left to do but to wait," he wrote.

At times, I was surprised by the attention Norman gave my poetry,
but I was thankful for the way he was steering me out of shallow water,

believing I could navigate in a deeper sea. I knew he wrote stories, but I didn't know at the time that he, too, had written poetry when he was young and that, like me, had won prizes for his work. Here's his poem "The Joke of the Stars," which appeared in the *Bema*, a Dartmouth literary magazine:

> A red star smolders between two purple mountain tops.
> And a night-cloud is between the white moon and a white star.
> Can it be such a long way? Is it so very far
> To three low stars where the sky haze stops?
> Night skies and heavens, you are holy lots
> Where buried worlds repose. Light shafts jar
> You imperceptibly. A falling star
> Unspools a thin thread of gold . . . Is it far?
>
> Below, the lights from the city flicker and peep
> Through the night that is between me and the city.
> The lights blink an hour, and then go out . . . Pity,
> But is there reason to bow to the stars and to weep?
> It is all a softly told joke; on the lights of the city is the joke,
> For the stars span the heavens eternally—a high arched yoke.

The poem won a prize in a contest sponsored by the *Dial* magazine, with first place going to T. S. Eliot. The award was mentioned in a story in the Missoula newspaper, to the delight of the Maclean family and the First Presbyterian congregation. Norman also won sixth place in the 1923 Witter Bynner poetry contest, sponsored by the Poetry Society of America. Carl Sandburg was one of the judges. Vassar student Martha Keller and Countee Cullen of New York University—both later had books of poetry published—won first and second prize, respectively.

Another poem that appeared in the *Bema*:

Dream a bit with me—
Our worlds are made of dreams
Empty valleys, echoless
Shadows without themes.

Close the eyes a moment—
Hopes that ne'er shall be
Rise in silent tumults
Like waves on a quiet sea,

Waves that roll for a moment
And then are lost in the flood,
Dreams that rise in the dream time
Blossoms that never bud.

Sleep not in your chamber
When the moon is waning low;
Gaze at the stars above you,
Though your world be full of woe.

Stars are not in the heavens
To hold with the naked hands;
Stars are for evening watches
Dreamings—for midnight lands.

So—dream a bit with me—
Our worlds are made from dreams,
Empty valleys, echoless,
Shadows without themes.

But at the time, Norman talked only about my poetry, my future, my decisions, and his emerging stories about Montana. I think he had stopped writing poetry, or at least, he had stopped sharing it. As Edward "Ned" Rosenheim, Norman's longtime friend and colleague told me, "To be loved by Norman was to have expectations set on you." Norman had set expectations on me: "You know, I am picking you to be an extra fine woman, and I don't settle on every chick that comes flapping through the coop," he wrote. As a teenager, I wondered if I could measure up. As an adult, I still do.

In March, Norman was preparing for his last quarter of teaching and was continuing to revise "USFS 1919." A poem I had entered in the National Scholastic Creative Writing contest had advanced in the competition. He knew the poem, he said, because "it was the first poem of yours I saw that I thought was a poem all the way through." My mother flew out to Montana in late March to take care of my niece, Meg, and to nurse Marilyn. And while she was gone, I did an end run a few weeks later. After I learned I had been accepted, I committed to attending the University of Chicago with no input from her or from my father, believing things would work out.

In Seeley Lake, Marilyn smiled when my worried mother told her I was going to Chicago, but that was one of her last smiles. When Marilyn couldn't walk to the bathroom, Mother carried her; when morphine couldn't touch her pain, Mother would take Marilyn into her lap and rock her. Norman advised me to write about Marilyn, so I wrote three poems. I kept Norman apprised of what was happening in Seeley Lake, telling him in a phone conversation that Marilyn was going to have more radiation. His response was a sharp intake of air and a hiss. I told him I was praying it helped her. His wife, Jessie, had undergone radiation for cancer—"a great sickness—so great that it eats away at everybody's courage"—and he said: "Do not pray for things worse than death. You also have to pray for the life of John and Meg."

During the last week of April, Marilyn's mother came from Idaho to be with her through the final days. Knowing she had done everything she could do, my mother flew home to South Carolina with Meg in tow, changing planes in Chicago. Norman took time from his busy teaching schedule to meet them at O'Hare, where they had a long layover. Mother and he spent a few hours talking—about John and Marilyn, about Meg, and about me. My beautiful and charming mother was worn out from weeks in Montana, and she wasn't at all happy that I was leaving the South for college. Norman promised her that he would take care of me in Chicago, and she thawed. A bit.

The next day, the last of April, Marilyn died. She was twenty-nine. When I called Norman, he asked, as he usually did, "Rebecca, dear, what's on your great mind, darling?" I couldn't speak for a few seconds. I managed to say Marilyn had died. There was silence and then a hiss. He said, "I didn't want anything like this to touch you." He paused. "To lose someone so young." Another pause. "May God bless her. Good night, dear." A few days later, I called to tell him I had won the National Scholastic Creative Writing Award for Poetry.

"The poets are always talking about the lights and shadows playing simultaneously in life, and at least the talk of poets turns out to be true about one young poet, for through the darkness surrounding Marilyn's death came the news that you had won the National Scholastic prize in poetry," Norman wrote. "In the darkness, I am also very happy. And very proud of you."

He then cautioned me about becoming "fatheaded," his term for *conceited*. I knew he had described me to friends in Chicago as being "six feet tall with a seven-foot ego" (even though I am not six feet tall). In other letters, he teased me mercilessly about being the editor of my high school literary magazine, *Pine Needles*, and filling said magazine with many of my own poems and essays. On the day I was graduating, Norman was going to be attending a retirement barbecue his many students were having for him. He told me about his plans for the coming months in Montana, which included going hunting with my brother John and Kenny Burns, Jessie's brother, "and the three of us will get our deer and maybe our elk or at least we'll have a hell of a good time." He then said he had gotten a note from my "beautiful mother" and ended his letter saying, "In her coming time, Meg will win her share of medals, and already not being short of ego, she will probably edit some southern literary magazine almost entirely written by herself." I loved getting his letters, but at times, I wondered what he was really saying.

In June, at the University of Chicago's college convocation, Norman received his third Quantrell Award for Excellence in Undergraduate Teaching. An English major writing to support Norman told administrators that "[Mr. Maclean] is a man who loves literature, which is not an uncommon thing, but he is also a man who can convey that love and create a similar love within his students without pretense or affectation."

Not only did Norman get the award; he also received a one thousand–dollar check "and an ovation in the [Rockefeller] Chapel, where there are supposed to be no ovations." He wrote to me: "Not great, my dear, but better than being threatened at the end with impeachment— although not so good as being editor of *Pine Needles* and being able to publish everything you ever wrote. My love to you and Meg and your mother and father." A few days later, a postcard of Seeley Lake arrived from Norman that he said was "beautiful and the photograph for it must have been taken right in front of my cabin, but I thought maybe the adjectives for the copy came from *Pine Needles*." The copy says: "SEELEY LAKE, a spectacular sapphire on a jewel necklace of lakes which dot the wooded valleys east of the Mission Mountains, dazzles its many visitors with its deep-blue, translucent depth."

If another adult had said something similar to me, I'm not sure how I would have responded, but Norman seemed to consider me "a strong, powerful woman," capable of handling his comments. I learned it was his nature to pass judgment on, well, everything and everyone, without worrying about the fallout. According to Norman's friends, the only two people immune from his criticisms were Larry Kimpton and Norman's daughter, Jean Maclean Snyder. I think his compulsive judging sprang from the Calvinist training of his Presbyterian minister father. Everyone had fallen short, not just bait fishermen. Former students told me Norman gave the business only to those he felt could take it. I decided always to take it, even if it was crushing.

Throughout my friendship with him, as long as I met his expectations, as long as I was developing "the best that was within me," things were fine. But when I was in my early twenties, heartbroken and at loose ends, Norman was not kind or supportive. He wasn't capable of showing me empathy, of listening to my problems without judgment, because he was always judging. It was a habit of being. I learned that in 1980 he had written to a friend who was recovering from surgery that after a visit from me, he himself had been disabled, "engaged in what her friends refer to as 'Recovery from Rebecca.' I'll trade her to you for an infected kidney." I'm glad the friend kept that letter to himself and that I read it many years after Norman's death.

3

Seeley Lake Summer

ALL OF THAT was to come. When my mother brought my niece
to South Carolina after Marilyn died, my father and she had assumed
they would be keeping Meg and rearing yet another child. There were
no daycare facilities in Seeley Lake and nothing like pre-K or even full-
day kindergarten. I overheard tense phone conversations between my
parents and John about where Meg should grow up and with whom.
Ultimately, my brother won. My mother and John decided I should fly
out to Montana with Meg and spend the summer taking care of her. I
was happy to think I would be in Seeley Lake, mostly because Norman
would be there, but apprehensive about keeping house for my brother
and a three-year-old. Shopping. Cooking. Cleaning. Tending to Meg.
Knowing I would leave that routine in late September and go back to
South Carolina before heading to college was a great relief—I hoped I
could bring my niece back south with me.

A friend from my hometown decided to come along and help out, and
the three of us flew to Chicago in late June. Norman met us at O'Hare,
where we learned we had missed our connecting flight. My brother would
be leaving Seeley and heading to Great Falls—a two-and-a-half-hour

drive—to meet us, only to realize we wouldn't be there for six or seven hours. Norman knew whom to call in the federal hierarchy to inform John we were delayed. He somehow got the airline to call the regional Forest Service office in Missoula, and a clerk then relayed the message to John in Seeley Lake. With that settled, Norman talked about what he was writing, bought us food, and sat with us for hours. He wasn't especially happy that Meg was going back to Montana, but he was glad I would be in Seeley Lake for the summer.

Once we knew our departure time, Norman then called the regional office again to tell them when we would arrive. Then he escorted us to the end of a distant Northwest Airlines terminal. I carried my exhausted niece, Norman brought her giant baby doll, and my friend toted a bag stuffed with Meg's toys and books. When we reached the gate, Norman kissed each of us goodbye and we left for Billings, where we would change planes one more time and then land in Great Falls. Meg slept most of the way. There weren't a lot of people leaving with us off the plane, which was continuing on to Seattle. The Billings airport had saddles and Charlie Russell paintings on the walls. We trudged to the end of a deserted hallway toward the check-in desk for our next flight. It was close to nine-thirty but not yet dark. The sky was smeared purple and blue, and I stared into it, trying to see what was in the distance.

* * *

After Marilyn died, I learned, my brother had invited three Forest Service employees to move in with him. He didn't want to be alone in a silent house. They stayed for six weeks, but the day before we arrived, the "boys" had taken their things and returned to the bunkhouse, one of several Forest Service buildings in the district compound. We cleaned the chaos left in their wake. When John's cabin was back in order, it was my job to go through my sister-in-law's belongings, mostly her clothes, still hanging in closets and folded in dresser drawers. I called

Norman and told him what was being expected of me, and I could hear him hiss. He felt John was shirking his own duties, then told me to do what Marilyn would have wanted.

I found Pendleton sweaters that smelled like her. Strands of her dark hair were in her brush. I put aside a sweater to keep for myself. My friend and I wrapped the Hummel figurines my sister-in-law had collected in newsprint and filled a box with them. Marilyn's mother drove from Idaho to Seeley Lake in early July and, much to my dismay, took Meg home with her for a few weeks. She also took the jewelry, the box of Hummels, clothes to give away, a sterling silver tea service, and the sterling silver flatware my brother and sister-in-law had received for their wedding. John didn't care. He didn't care about much of anything, except riding his new motorcycle. You can't think about your dead wife as you're rocketing one hundred miles an hour on a winding mountain road.

When Norman arrived in July, I was working at a girls' sleepaway camp on the lake and couldn't see him as often as I wanted to. He was following his Chicago schedule—writing in the morning, stopping for lunch, putting something in the Crock-Pot for supper, and getting out in the afternoon to fish, take a walk, chop firewood, or run errands. His in-laws from Helena—Jessie's brother Kenny Burns and his wife, Dotty—were with him. They more or less ran the house for Norman. I met them when the camp's water skills instructor and I paddled a canoe to the lakeshore one evening for a surprise visit. Through John, I learned Norman was beginning to write another story, longer than the one about the Forest Service or the one about the pimping sawyer. It would become the title story of *A River Runs Through It*. George Jensen and Heidi Skurat, scholars at the University of Arkansas at Little Rock, spent years analyzing the structure of the many manuscripts of "A River Runs Through It," line by line and, in places, word by word. As teachers of rhetoric and writing, they wanted to figure out how Norman had created such a beautiful story. In so doing, they learned how Norman wrote himself into being a writer. His only other foray into fiction I know of had burned to ashes in a Hanover rooming house fire in the mid-1920s, and he had never created another—or at least, had never seen it published.

Surrounded by larch trees, in a cabin on a sapphire-colored lake where so much of his early life had unfolded, Norman sat with the ghosts of his father, mother, and brother. Writing in longhand, he placed the people he loved and longed for in scenes, titling the manuscript "Fly Fishing." He kept the pages in a three-ring binder. He wrote what he called "throwbacks" to provide background information but then told himself there were too many of these and started to arrange the scenes in chronological order, according to Jensen and Skurat. On the first draft, he criticized his work, saying it was "too long and sappy" and "not well-written."

My South Carolina friend left in August, after my job with the camp ended. An older female cousin arrived from Pennsylvania; she had grown up with John and had met Marilyn a few years after she and John married. She knew something about grief and loss and was both tender and tough with my brother. He no longer spent his evenings in the local saloon, and he adopted a healthier routine. She was also a dynamo, shopping, cooking, and cleaning much more efficiently than I could. When Meg's room was all arranged, my cousin and I drove to Priest River and picked up my niece. During a supper at Norman's cabin, my cousin charmed Norman as well as Kenny and Dotty.

As my departure date drew closer, John became more agitated, worrying about how he would handle being a single father. I know he wanted me to stay with him and to eventually attend the University of Montana, when Meg started first grade. Norman repudiated that notion—I heard him arguing with John outside our cabin. I loved my brother and wanted to help him, but I really couldn't picture myself staying in Seeley Lake. And then, barely four months after my sister-in-law's death, I realized John was hunting for a new wife, afraid of having to care for a three-year-old. He told me he couldn't be alone with a three-year-old every evening. He ignored pleas from our parents to move with Meg back to

South Carolina and find a Forest Service job there or at least to send Meg to them. Though Montana law prohibited it, Norman and I hoped John would marry our cousin, but that didn't happen, and she returned to Pennsylvania.

I remember waking up on my last Saturday in Montana and finding a strange woman sitting at the kitchen table. I had seen her serving drinks behind the bar in the Seeley Lake saloon, and now here she was in our cabin, wearing my brother's Forest Service shirt and drinking coffee from one of my sister-in-law's Franciscan coffee cups. She didn't see me as I backed out of the room, or if she did, she didn't say anything. While I was waking Meg, I heard the door to John's bedroom open and close. The woman wasn't in the living room when I rushed from the cabin with Meg. I had to talk to someone and decided the someone was Norman. I found him puttering around his kitchen, waiting for water to boil for tea. He was clearly surprised to see us, but he invited us in. I apologized for barging in on him, but I told him about finding the woman at our table. His eyebrows went up, and then he frowned and hissed, saying John was a goddamn fool. He also said he felt bad for John but worse for Meg.

In South Carolina, in early September, I got a letter from Norman spelling out his further frustration and disappointment. My brother, he wrote, was spending his evenings courting women in the Swan Valley, all along the Swan, Clearwater, and Blackfoot Rivers. My mother was also upset with John—I could hear her on the phone pleading with him not to do anything so rash as remarrying for at least a year. I wondered how he would find someone as accomplished and capable and funny as my sister-in-law. Marilyn could sew and knit, could cook any cuisine, play bridge, and play the piano and organ. She was a graceful swimmer and a good volleyball player. She had taught business math at Seeley Swan High School. She had insisted I read *Catch-22*, *Slaughterhouse 5*, and *The Catcher in the Rye*. No one could replace her.

Norman knew, as I did, that John wouldn't be hunting deer or elk with Kenny and him. My brother was interested in hunting only one thing—a cure for his loneliness. And someone to take care of his daughter. There would be no man-to-man talks with Norman about how to deal with grief and how to rebuild a life while missing an outstanding woman. There would be no hikes to the glacial lakes in the Missions or into the Bob Marshall Wilderness, no throwing a line in Holland Lake. There would be no searching for alpine wildflowers and no transplanting a few sacrificial specimens into Norman's lakeside garden. It was as if Norman felt John was cheating on Marilyn, and that was something he couldn't stomach. I think Norman also felt John was abandoning their friendship, and that surely stung. There weren't a lot of people for Norman to talk with in Seeley Lake.

I later learned from Norman's numerous friends, students, and colleagues from the University of Chicago whose marriages had ended or whose careers had crumbled that Norman had been disappointed and even disgusted with their failures. Sometimes the split was irreparable and he cast them out of the tribe forever. The Calvinist in him hated failure. When he failed at something, he was mortified. Divorce—from a partner, from a job—meant you had failed at something that was likely more than half your fault. In chasing women, John wasn't showing Marilyn, or at least her memory, the respect Norman felt she was due. His friendship with my brother cooled considerably. I don't know if he saw John again before he left for Chicago, but Seeley Lake was small enough for him to have heard about John's further romantic exploits.

Norman was back in Hyde Park before the fall quarter classes began in October. He was giving a talk at the end of the month, he told me, at the rededication of Harper Library. It was named for William Rainey Harper, the university's visionary first president, who had badgered John D. Rockefeller into funding a university, not a college. Norman spoke about the art of teaching, something I would learn, firsthand, at which he excelled.

It was no coincidence I ended up with a room in Pierce Tower, a multistory residence hall only a block from Norman's condominium—

the same dorm I had visited in January. His friend Kenneth Northcott lived in Pierce Tower with his family, and he held author receptions and other events for the hundreds of students living there. He was very kind to me, arranging for me to have a small poetry reading in his apartment. Only a handful of students, and Norman, were there. Before classes began, I also visited Norman in his Woodlawn Avenue home, a cozy two-bedroom condo with a giant begonia in the front window. The heavy furniture dated from the late nineteenth century. He said many pieces had come from his parents' home.

I needed a campus job, so Norman suggested I apply at Regenstein Library, the biggest library on campus—where he knew the director, of course. I got a job in the circulation department and kept it the four years I was in college. It was no accident that I ended up in a humanities class in which both the teacher and the graduate assistant were friends of Norman's—unbeknownst to me, both of them gave him regular reports about my classwork and essays. He handpicked my advisor, a warmhearted guy who was one of his former students. Norman told me that at the University of Chicago, one should take teachers, not courses. (After finishing my Common Core courses, I did just that.)

Norman described his writing ritual to me. He would draw a hot bath in the evening and relax in the water, thinking about the day's work and planning what he would write the next morning. When the water grew cold, he would get out and know what he would write and then rise the next day and do it.

He finished the first, very rough draft of "A River Runs Through It" in late October, but he didn't share it with anyone. According to Jensen and Skurat, he started immediately writing another iteration, incorporating a few scenes from the first draft while jettisoning others. Norman's son-in-law, Joel Snyder, called the first draft one of Norman's "finger exercises." He worked on his manuscript through the holidays and completed it early the next year. In a letter to Bud Moore, Norman told him he had finished the first draft of "a long story (longer by ½ than

USFS 1919) that I have been working on since last summer. I think parts of it are beautiful but I can't allow myself to think of how much more work I have to do on it. Another six months, and there are faults in [it] that I don't know whether I can work out."

The problem with "A River Runs Through It," said his friend and university colleague classicist Nick Rudall, director of the Court Theatre, "was that Norman felt totally constrained. He was in some sense an Aristotelean and he had no plot. What mattered to him was character, and that's what drives the story."

The talk Norman had given in late October at the rededication of Harper Library subsequently appeared in the university's alumni magazine as "This Quarter I Am Taking McKeon: Some Notes on the Art of Teaching." McKeon was philosopher Richard McKeon, one of Norman's longtime friends, who was revered and feared on campus. When I read that essay, I realized I knew very little of Norman's early life—my knowledge of him began in Seeley Lake, when he was hitting his seventh decade. I now wish Norman had devoted part of his second career to writing about the early days of the university, which was only ten years older than he was, but he had other plans. As soon as the alumni magazine arrived, former students and alumni from around the country wrote to Norman about the essay, congratulating him and sharing memories. University friends and colleagues knew Norman was structuring his retirement around his writing. The essay was an indication of how serious he was.

Since he hadn't been writing his entire life, Norman felt writing "is all hard and tortuous." "To get it done," he said, "I have to live almost a monastic life and take the oath of poverty, obedience and chastity, so I live in Chicago and Montana and live alone and work a great deal of nearly every day."

Norman's confidence in his writing had grown since the spring of 1972. Then he had tested the waters by reading a version of "Logging and Pimping," a story that was later included in *A River Runs Through It and Other Stories*, to a group of Chicago faculty members called the

Stochastics and many of their wives. It was a university club of both scientists and humanists, then all male, who would meet monthly at the Quadrangle Club, a Gothic Revival multipurpose building at the edge of campus, for drinks and dinner, followed by a member's talk about, say, dental pathology or Jonathan Swift and satire. At the end of the year, the members' wives attended the last meeting. The promotional flyer for Norman's story—"'Logging and Pimping,' by Norman Maclean, noted authority"—undoubtedly increased the number of attendants. The talk was a big hit with both men and women, according to those in attendance.

* * *

The Quadrangle Club was very busy at lunchtime, serving faculty and staff members who filled the large main dining room. Whole departments took over private rooms for presentations. Some faculty members had long-standing reservations and could be seen talking and arguing every noon. A few people would drift in for dinner, as Norman and I did occasionally. Once, as we were leaving the dining room, Norman nodded to an older man wearing Coke bottle lenses who was sitting by himself, leaning over a bowl of soup, and reading a book. Norman said he was a scientist of some note. The man smiled as he nodded at Norman and then went back to his soup and his book. Norman said: "I saw a famous man eating soup. That's what Sandburg might say." I didn't know the poem, but I did think the man looked lonely, and I was glad I was with Norman.

4

Walking the City Through Stories

DURING MY FIRST YEAR of college, I saw Norman often during the winter—he no doubt remembered his promise to my mother to look after me. I had grown up with blue skies in winter. In Chicago, the sky was gray. The sun had disappeared. On many weekday afternoons, we took walks in Hyde Park. The walks were really moving lectures—on the people who had made the university and city great; on the buildings, the trees and flowers; on different friends, events, and moments in Norman's life. The stories made things less foreign for me. Norman had worked hard to be comfortable in Chicago, to make it feel like home, and he wanted me to find the beauty in it as he did. When Jessie and he were in Hyde Park in the 1920s, they had often spent Sunday afternoons on open double-decker buses, riding all over Chicago, exploring neighborhoods, learning the streets, and making the city their own. With friends, they ventured south of Sixty-Third Street to clubs to hear jazz and blues and went to beer gardens and taverns. Norman wanted me to love the university and neighborhood that had welcomed him so many decades earlier.

The center of the university campus was beautiful. Mature elms on the quadrangles led to Gothic buildings that looked as if they had dropped out of the sky from Oxford University. Gargoyles perched on the pitched roofs. There was the small, elegant Bond Chapel near a classroom building, Cobb Hall. I found the old part of campus mysterious and imposing. The nearby streets were narrow, with trees erupting near the sidewalk and cars squeezed one behind the other. Architect Frank Lloyd Wright's Robie House—I was astounded to see a real Frank Lloyd Wright building—was on Woodlawn and Fifty-Eighth Street.

The north edge of campus, where I lived in Pierce Tower, was a different story. The ho-hum building was like a project created by a fourth grader, with a massive tower rising from a flat rectangle that squatted next to Fifty-Fifth Street. Strips of concrete ran top to bottom, outlining the windows. A dining hall was on the first floor, along with an attendant's office and mailboxes. Stairs and elevators led to our dorm rooms. It was stark. From the ninth-floor windows, I could see Fifty-Fifth Street, which reminded me of a *Ligustrum* branch whose leaves had been stripped away. I later learned that before urban renewal in the 1950s and '60s, Fifty-Fifth Street had been one of Hyde Park's major areas for shopping and entertainment. There were few signs of life, just another massive building, McCormick Seminary, across the street and, a block away, Jimmy's Woodlawn Tap, the only bar around. It was usually packed after midnight, when students left the library to have a drink.

Walking toward Lake Michigan on Fifty-Fifth Street wasn't pleasant—it was a four-lane wind tunnel. The buildings that had gone up in the late 1950s and early 1960s during urban renewal were to me strange and unnatural—I. M. Pei designed a multistory apartment building in the middle of Fifty-Fifth Street at Blackstone Avenue, with traffic parting like water around it. We called it Monoxide Towers. A shopping center near Fifty-Fifth and Lake Park had a Soviet feel.

The first few weeks of school, I found many of my classmates odd and intimidating and wondered if I had picked the right school. Like a guy in my Political Order and Change class who was reading *The Republic* in Greek while I struggled to understand Plato in English. A fifteen-year-old math genius who couldn't toss a tennis ball for a serve without throwing his racquet as well, no matter how I tried to help him. The professors who seemed not to care if students swam or sank. The students on my dormitory hall who opened their doors and emerged trailing clouds of marijuana smoke. For me, Norman was the University of Chicago. He kept me from being homesick because he had known me before I became a student, and he knew and loved some of the same places and people in Montana I loved. He was the only person in Chicago who had known my sister-in-law. It was reassuring to me to hear him say, "I wonder just who the hell I am, darling," because if someone who had lived as long and knew as much as Norman was still trying to understand himself, then I was in good company in wondering about myself and my place in the world.

It must have been warm on some of our outings, but in my mind, it was always cold: the wind howling off the lake, Norman stopping to wipe his eyes and nose with a bandanna, the feeling in my toes disappearing until I was walking on shards of glass. Norman usually had on wool pants, a flannel shirt, and a tartan necktie, over which he wore a cardigan, a scarf, a parka, gloves, and a watch cap that was rolled above his ears. He enjoyed explaining his clothes, most of them from L. L. Bean, the New England company he loved. Compact and comfortable, he looked like a man with the right gear for taking on the cold. I looked like a walking yard sale, with two sweaters, a hat, mittens, a parka, and two scarves, one wrapped around my neck, the other covering my lower face. I pulled my hat so low that only my eyes were visible, and they were watering. We usually walked in late afternoon, after I had finished working in the stacks at Regenstein Library.

Coming around the corner of a building, I would feel myself being blown backward. Norman would squint at me and chortle, "You don't have that kind of wind in South Carolina, do you, darling?" Often we walked through the Gothic main campus to the Midway Plaisance, a marshy area drained in the 1890s during the World's Columbian Exposition to connect Jackson Park on the lake, the fair's site, with Washington Park to the west. Norman told me Frederick Law Olmsted had designed the parks. I remembered everything he told me, expecting to be quizzed later on the material. The Midway had housed the entertainment side of the exposition: the first Ferris wheel, restaurants, displays from around the world, girlie shows, and ethnological exhibits. Under construction during the same time, the university opened in October 1892, months before the Columbian Exposition did, Norman told me with a wry smile.

There had been plans by Olmsted to have a series of lagoons and bridges along the Midway, Norman said, but those had never materialized. What was left were scooped-out patches of defeated grass pocked with clumps of weeds where we could see students kicking soccer balls and swinging field hockey sticks. On the far side of the Midway, on East Sixtieth Street, were two modern structures, the law school designed by Eero Saarinen and the social services school designed by Ludwig Mies Van der Rohe. Norman pointed out the beauty and power in both buildings, the horizontal lines, the way Van der Rohe's glass exterior brought the outside in. He wasn't one to eschew modern architecture or art, and he would stop and stare at the buildings as if he had lost something inside them. I didn't walk on Sixtieth Street with other students—we were told it wasn't safe, but Norman had missed that bulletin. He and I would sometimes drive to Sixty-Third Street, where a favorite Chinese takeout restaurant crouched under the tracks of the elevated train.

I liked hearing about the World's Fair from Norman—some of his own teachers, members of the original University of Chicago faculty, had ridden on the Ferris wheel—but I didn't much like walking on the Midway. There was nothing to block the wind when you were up high on the sidewalks. If we headed west, walking was easier with the wind at our backs. If we headed east, we leaned forward, turning our heads as the wind snatched away our words. The wind off the lake would usher us to the edge of Washington Park. It seemed a lonely and scary place to me, but Norman managed to find something to love in all of Hyde Park. Across South Cottage Grove Avenue was one of Norman's favorite sculptures, *Fountain of Time*, a dingy concrete masterpiece by Lorado Taft. It was massive and, to me, a little spooky. Rising from the primordial gray concrete were couples, lovers, children, men, women, soldiers, and old people. They passed in front of Father Time, a twenty-foot-tall robed figure holding a scythe. A dry reflecting pool separated the two, a few weeds poking up through the cracking concrete.

"That's it, darling, from cradle to grave," Norman said. He dabbed at his nose with his bandanna and then pursed his lips as though he might whistle. He told me how Taft had worked out of Midway Studios, a few blocks away on Ellis Avenue. Installed in 1922, the sculpture predated Norman's arrival in 1928. He had known and admired Taft and was concerned that the studios, like the sculpture, weren't in good shape. One of the figures in the work was Taft himself, complete with a smock, Norman said with a smile. "Art imitates life, darling. And sometimes, rarely, life imitates art."

After a few minutes of studying the people, each on his or her way to death, and feeling as cold as concrete myself, I was happy to start moving again. We would turn north on South Cottage Grove, walking along the sidewalk bordering Washington Park. It was always about 5:00 p.m. when we left the Midway—and overcast, the sunlight fading as the day dimmed into darkness. Drivers heading home from Billings Hospital had turned on their headlights, and streetlights were coming on. Often, as we followed a path through the park, Norman took me by the elbow and didn't let go until we had reached East Fifty-First Street, a mile away.

When I told friends in my dormitory where Norman and I walked, they were alarmed because Cottage Grove was the extreme edge of the campus, and everyone knew it wasn't safe. Norman didn't know or didn't care. Or maybe he did know and he didn't care. He had been walking around his neighborhood for decades, and he wasn't going to avoid certain streets or parks, even if the demographics had changed, the buildings had deteriorated, and statistics suggested walking around there wasn't prudent. I felt safe with him. Both of us had walked in the Missions, where encountering a grizzly or a black bear wasn't that unusual. There were no bears in Hyde Park. We would pass young men wearing hooded sweatshirts and high-top sneakers, their hair in Afros, braids, and ponytails, their wallets chained to their jeans, who would look at us and laugh in disbelief, a tall skinny girl with a fuzzy orange hat and a shorter old man who talked the entire time.

"Hey, old man crazy!" they would say. "What you doin' out here, man?"

Norman just kept walking. People had been mugged and shot at Cottage Grove and Fifty-Fifth Street, but I think Norman was too annoyed by the many changes to be afraid.

On the return home, we would turn onto Ellis Avenue and walk by Regenstein Library, where there was a sculpture that looked to me like a giant skull. Norman told me Henry Moore had created it to commemorate the first sustained nuclear reaction, which happened in 1942 in an underground lab where Joseph Regenstein Library sits today. Norman talked about the power of the negative space in the sculpture and about the loss of the handball courts where the reaction happened. But he didn't tell stories that placed him at the university in the 1940s.

From others, I learned while the 1930s had been the giddy days of working with the fiery head of the English department to knock down old tenets about literature, the next decade saw Norman juggling family duties in Montana and Chicago with overwhelming work responsibilities. That time for him was marked by constant fatigue. In 1940, he received his PhD. The next year, World War II started. His father died. Jessie and he had two children fourteen months apart. He helped prepare thousands of recruits to fight in the war, working at night and on the weekends. He took on enormous administrative and teaching duties for the university. As an older man, what Norman remembered about the war years was being "exhausted all the time, taking more things on and scheduling more," he told an interviewer. "I didn't have any time." He also regretted not spending time with his children when they were little.

* * *

In the late 1930s, everyone on the University of Chicago campus knew the United States would enter the war sooner or later, according to Norman Dolnick, an undergraduate student at that time. "It was an unreal life on the campus. We indulged in poetry and abstract thought while a war was shaping up. We knew that, but we sought the time before our reckoning with reality." Aware of the threat of war, the university began offering preinduction military training to volunteers in September 1940, believing that unless "they established Chicago as a center of military learning and research, the university's considerable assets [particularly in cartography and linguistics] might be hauled off in army trucks, 'to be returned torn and soiled, if at all.'" Since Norman had learned as a child from his father how to handle firearms, he taught rifle marksmanship to the volunteer recruits. After completing his eight-hour course, many participants received a high ranking for accuracy. Norman told Chicago student George McElroy that he used the same method in teaching men how to use a rifle that he followed in teaching literature, indicating the objective and then giving participants the means to reach it.

By December 1940, Norman received his PhD, writing a thesis titled "The Theory of Lyric Poetry in England from the Renaissance to Coleridge." Ronald Crane was his major professor. The dissertation embodies the neo-Aristotelian methods of analysis, focusing as much on what the critics had to say about lyric poetry as on the poetry itself. Norman's degree meant he was teaching courses more of his own choosing, and it also meant a slightly larger salary as an assistant professor.

He was earning an annual salary of $3,150 as of March 19, 1941, according to university records. During the spring quarter convocation in 1941, Norman received his second Award for Excellence in Undergraduate Teaching, which came with a welcome $1,000. His teaching load was different from what one might find in a typical twenty-first-century university. Instead of fifteen students in an undergraduate class, he had thirty, each of them writing two papers a week for ten weeks. Norman was expected to critique each paper. He usually taught three classes a quarter. No doubt, students wrote more than just one paper. Imagine the time he spent reading and making comments on roughly eighteen hundred papers.

Among the students taking a class in lyric poetry from Norman during that time was John Paul Stevens, who would become a justice of the US Supreme Court. "The study of English literature, especially lyric poetry, is the best preparation for the law," Stevens later said. A native of Hyde Park and a graduate of the University of Chicago Laboratory Schools, Stevens was always a top student in any setting, and he must have thrived in Norman's class. "He taught me to read every word of a poem," Stevens said. "That training helped me later, when trying to decipher Law statutes."

For much of 1941, the University of Chicago was celebrating its fiftieth birthday, reaching out to local business leaders and alumni to invest in the school and to recognize its importance to the city. The effort to have Chicagoans donate to the university had begun in the early 1900s, when benefactor John D. Rockefeller stopped the seemingly endless flow of money to the school he had helped found. Celebratory events culminated in September 1941 with ten days of lectures and seminars, informal and formal dinners, parties, banquets, and processions. There were festivities and attractions mimicking those of the Midway of the 1893 World's Fair. Attending were 450 scholars and researchers from North and South America and Europe, but for Norman, the star was Canadian Charles Best, codiscoverer of insulin, who received an honorary degree.

"When they called his name, he stood up in some fantastic gown of red and yellow, crossed his arms, and let the world look at him, handsome and self-possessed," Norman wrote to his Canada-born parents. "He was something, more than you can say by far for scholars in general." Participants talked about new discoveries and advances in subjects ranging from archaeology and geology to literature, medicine, and chemistry.

Norman said his own presentation "went very well." It took place in Mandel Hall, where he had given many lectures to humanities students during his first years at the university. Among those packed into the hall was President Hutchins, who was there solely to hear Norman. "I feel alive a thousand times more talking before a big crowd than to one or two people—then I feel very self-conscious," Norman wrote to his Canada-born parents. His talk generated a round of questions. "I think I did better on them than on the prepared paper," he noted. "I think the audience got a kick out of seeing some hair fly rather than the customary back-slapping that followed most of the symposia." After all the events surrounding the fiftieth anniversary had ended, Norman settled into teaching his courses for fall quarter. Life went on, the country teetering on the brink of war until December 7, 1941.

Two weeks after the bombing of Pearl Harbor, Norman wrote President Hutchins, outlining a list of proposed courses for the Institute of Military Studies and possible course instructors drawn from the university's faculty. Included were cartography, electricity and radio, mathematics of navigation and artillery, military hygiene, military photography, and rifle marksmanship, which Norman planned to continue teaching. He wanted the courses to start in January. Hutchins agreed, and the instruction began on schedule.

A letter to Norman late that December from the Reverend John Norman Maclean said that he and Clara, Norman's mother, were concerned because Norman had told them he had never been so busy in his life. "We weren't quite pleased to hear that you were, as the Scotch say, so *thranged*," the Reverend wrote. "In these dreadful days, there is no end to the sort of extra work you are undertaking. You must fix your limits, and let others do their part. But we are proud of you."

Two days letter, on December 30, Norman's father died of a stroke. He was seventy-nine. It must have been a shock to everyone who knew him—in his last letter the Reverend did not sound like someone who was ailing. Six years earlier, he and Clara had moved from Helena, where church work had taken them, back to Missoula and had renewed their friendships with old friends and First Presbyterian members, hosting dinners and get-togethers. Both were loved and admired. The death of his younger son, Paul, in 1938 had aged the Reverend, who "never walked very well again," Norman wrote in "A River Runs Through It."

Norman traveled alone by train to Missoula, leaving a very pregnant Jessie in Chicago. In Ringling, Montana, the conductor stopped the train and told Norman and other passengers to step outside for a moment. It was so cold—forty-five degrees below zero—that Norman's spit froze before it hit the ground. The funeral was held on New Year's Day in 1942, the first day in weeks that the temperature rose above zero. The Reverend E. R. Cameron of First Presbyterian eulogized John Norman as "princely in those things of God. . . . He was dedicated to the proposition that all men have come short of the glory of God, but that all men may measure up to the fulness of the glory of God in Christ." Reverend Cameron said John Norman had advocated for others only those things he had tried for himself. He was remembered as being generous toward others, firm in his teaching, keenly intellectual, finely emotional, sharp in humor, "and he was deep, very deep in sympathy." His body was buried in Missoula Cemetery next to Paul's.

With Jessie in her last weeks of pregnancy, her mother, Florence, came to Chicago to help with the new baby. The loss of his father must have been devastating to Norman, who said he "felt closer to him than any man I have ever known." I imagine that just as he had tamped down his emotions after his brother's death three years earlier, Norman did the same after his father's death.

So much was happening at once. Daughter Jean was born in late January, and both Norman and Jessie adored her.

A month after the funeral, Norman registered for the draft. At thirty-nine, he would have been considered old for military service, but he was determined to do his part, hoping to join the US Navy, along with his many university friends, including Heisman trophy winner Jay Berwanger. Norman longed to serve his country. In a letter two months later to President Hutchins, he said that when he taught literary criticism and lyric poetry, "they are so much hay in my mouth. There are others not fit for military service who can teach my courses. In these circumstances, I feel by day and by night that I am not fit for academic service." He applied to be a gunnery officer in naval aviation, but he hadn't heard back before Hutchins appointed him in June to be the liaison agent between the US Navy and the University of Chicago. The appointment must have made him feel more "useful."

He was offered a commission in the naval reserve in August 1942, as long as the position didn't "interfere with procurement of officer candidates at the University of Chicago." Norman was then acting as the university's military liaison officer as well as teaching courses in the English department and rifle marksmanship and orienteering for the Institute of Military Studies. Where could they find someone so versatile? The university requested he stay on campus. He became the director of the Institute of Military Studies and the dean of students in the college. At the same time, he and Jessie were dealing with a new baby and making plans to return to Montana to spend part of the summer with Clara in Seeley Lake. In the midst of all that "thranging," Norman, ever the teacher, cowrote with Everett C. Olson *Manual of Instruction in Military Maps and Aerial Photographs*, which was published in 1943. That May, Jessie gave birth to their second child, son John Norman. No wonder Norman was tired.

As part of the military training course, Norman taught recruits how to read maps and aerial photographs. Once a week, he took them to the Palos Park forest preserve to show them how to use a map to learn to locate themselves. Once, on a dark day, he turned them around and around to confuse them and told them he wanted to show how a map can help when you don't know where you are. A young man "who had never been farther west than Midway Airport" assured Norman that he knew where he was. Norman asked, "Then where are you?" The contented recruit said, "We are here," and pointed to the ground at his feet.

Gordon McTeague was a fifteen-year-old ROTC cadet when he enrolled in the Institute for Military Studies. He returned to the institute as a high school junior and again the next year, becoming an instructor responsible for a training company. One evening at the institute, Norman approached McTeague and gave him a copy of his manual, with an inscription that says: "To Gordon, who is a man among men. Norman." Throughout his career, Norman would take students under his wing if he thought they showed promise. Norman also helped McTeague qualify for special military training and, after the war, supported him as an entering University of Chicago student. "His letter must have been most persuasive as I was accepted with an academic background below U of C students at that time," McTeague wrote.

As dean of students in the college, Norman gave an impoverished Herbert J. Gans a scholarship that allowed him to stay in school long enough to complete his first year at the university. He was beyond grateful for the encouragement and support Norman gave him. Gans was drafted, but after the war, he returned to Chicago on the GI Bill and finished his degree. After the publication of *A River Runs Through It and Other Stories*, Gans wrote to Norman that "his investment paid off" because a poor young man had become a sociology professor at Columbia University. Norman responded with a gracious letter.

But Norman didn't like being dean of students. In the early 1940s, with the war raging, a former student, on leave from the US Army, stopped by to see him. As the man sat down by his desk, Norman told him: "There are just two kinds of students who sit in that chair. Crooked students with straight faces, and crooked students with crooked faces." The soldier said Norman had "no sympathy for anyone trying to manipulate his university record to avoid the draft."

University alumnus Edward Muir first encountered Norman as a student in an English class in the fall of 1940. Two years later, Muir signed up for a US Navy program that let participants earn an AB degree before beginning midshipmen's school. He flunked a course and had to visit Dean Maclean, who chewed him out, saying, "Your nation has given you extra schooling time on the assumption that it would aid our war effort, and you have betrayed your nation." Muir opted to join V-5, the navy's flight program, and left school. Two years later, he visited the university and was wearing gold navy wings and an ensign stripe. Norman, he recalled later, "was clearly glad and proud to see me, and as I left, he said, 'When this mess is over, we'll get you back in here, Ed,' and punched me in the shoulder, just like in the movies."

Muir did return to campus after the war to complete his undergraduate degree and took several courses from Norman, which his colleague Napier Wilt called "Maclean 1, 2, 3." Whenever Muir offered a comment, Norman responded, "Well, Muir, more news from The Light of Nature?" In winter quarter of 1947, as Muir was completing his master's degree, the two men bumped into each other on campus. "So that's what's wrong with you," Norman shouted. "You're a Goddamn poet!" He then proceeded to tell Muir that he had won the Fiske Poetry Prize.

During the summers in the 1940s, Norman and Jessie took their two young children to Montana to visit friends and relatives in Helena, Missoula, and Seeley Lake. The Seeley Lake cabin presented its own challenges for Jessie. Jean Maclean Snyder told me Norman and his mother, Clara, were so tight, "there wasn't much room for my mother in that relationship." Norman treated his mother like a goddess, she said, and his mother revered him. They looked alike, with high cheekbones and dark hair, and had similar sensitivities to poetry and literature. For Clara, the cabin was "a big deal," a place where all her men had been happy together. Little had been moved since Norman was a teenager, not the cribbage board where Paul and he had played games, not two pairs of boxing gloves flecked with dried blood—Norman liked to tell visitors the blood was Paul's, not his—not the books, dishes, or bamboo rods and fishing reels. An accomplished cook and baker, Clara would prepare most of the meals, just as she always had, while Jessie contributed salads and desserts. Norman and Jessie stayed in a guest cabin—where they could smoke and drink—while Clara slept with her memories in the main building.

It must have been a relief for Jessie to spend time with her Burns family in Helena, where houses had electricity and hot running water and where there were cousins for the children to play with. In the Seeley Lake cabin, Jessie had to boil water on the cabin's woodburning stove in order to wash diapers and clothes—with a washboard, her daughter said. She had to heat an iron on the stove. Electricity didn't come to the cabin until the mid-1950s, after Clara had died. In Seeley Lake, Jessie was the main caretaker of the children. Norman spent the morning working on university matters and writing letters. In the afternoons, the entire family would go hiking or have a picnic.

Letters from the 1940s reveal the friendly relationship Norman had with University of Chicago president Robert Maynard Hutchins, another son of a Presbyterian minister. Hutchins had become chancellor of the university when he was thirty. He was known thereafter as "the boy president." Three years older than Norman, he had embraced R. S. Crane and the neo-Aristotelian English department, and he had often dropped in on Norman's humanities lectures. He valued Norman's contributions to the university before and during the war years and fondly addressed him as "Normal" in letters. Colleagues said Norman was "always political," serving on the faculty senate and mingling with faculty members from other departments. "The other day I heard you say in tones not untouched by manly sorrow that you would deliver an address of welcome to each of the entering College classes," Dean

Maclean wrote to President Hutchins, who replied, "Dear Normal, Sorrow is just the word."

After the war, Norman, as college dean, welcomed back to campus many young men he had helped prepare for combat and others who had left school early to fight. "I don't remember that very well," he said later. "I guess I was just glad the goddamned war was over. I don't have many memories of it—that wasn't a very important period in my life. When the war was over, I guess I just rested for a while."

* * *

In 1947, Norman's friend Larry Kimpton, who had been working for the university, moved to Palo Alto to become dean of students at his undergraduate alma mater, Stanford, a position he held for a few years. In a letter to Norman from California in 1947, he wrote, "There are only a few people who have ever made a hell of a lot of difference to me, and I begin to run out of names after you & Dick [Richard McKeon] and Jess [Jessie]."

Friends mattered to Norman and Jessie—they provided most of the social outlets for the Macleans, who didn't have tickets for the lyric opera or the Chicago Symphony, didn't frequent fancy restaurants or attend art openings. They invited friends over for drinks and conversation and sometimes dinners or parties or went to their houses. Besides Larry, who preferred Charlie Russell to Bertrand Russell, Norman's close friends weren't high-powered academics. He and Jessie saw a lot of Joe Dunham, one of Norman's childhood friends from Missoula, and his wife, Joyce. Joe worked as an editor at Baxter Labs, while Joyce was the secretary for Earl Bush, Chicago mayor Richard J. Daley's press secretary. A lifelong Democrat, Norman called Daley "our mayor."

In August 1949, Norman was in Seeley Lake, where he learned that thirteen Smokejumpers—the US Forest Service's elite parachuting, fire-fighting unit—had died on a fire in Mann Gulch outside Helena. As he writes in *Young Men and Fire*, he felt compelled to visit the site of the fire, and he went there with his brother-in-law Kenny Burns, who lived in Helena. They saw a landscape of ashes and dead trees and smoke rising from the still smoldering fire. The firsthand account of their visit anchors his introduction to *Young Men and Fire*. Norman said he never forgot the dead young men.

*   *   *

In late November 1949, after Norman had returned from Montana, he picked up a copy of *Time* magazine and saw, as expected, Robert M. Hutchins on the cover. The accompanying story about his life and his career as the Chicago president contained a few statements that Norman found odd. One was that Hutchins enjoyed "baked cucumbers and cheese," and another was that though he had at one time eschewed exercise, he currently enjoyed fishing. Norman responded to the story with a six-page letter, circling the egregious parts of the *Time* story and gently mocking Hutchins, including two question marks after the mention of fishing: "Naturally I am very touched, but I guess that I was preconditioned to be confused. For instance, when I was four years old my father told me, 'Don't forget to cast on a one-two-three-four <count> xxxxxxx, allowing two counts at the top of your back stroke; check your forward cast at ten o'clock so that your flies won't splash when they hit the water; and remember when you have a big fish on, no matter what happens, keep your damn line tight—and don't bake cucumbers.'"

Later in December, Norman got a letter from Larry Kimpton, who was complaining about life in California, where "Christmas sneaks up on you because the goddamn ranges bloom and it's about 70 degrees outside." He also complained about the new Stanford president, J. E. Wallace Sterling, whom he didn't respect but found harmless.

"This guy Sterling . . . doesn't know an idea from six bits, and strenuously and successfully resists education," Kimpton wrote. You can sense how restless he is. "I don't know how long I can stand it but I have to work at it to become acutely unhappy." The next year, Kimpton was installed as the University of Chicago chancellor, and Norman's best friend was living near him again.

5

Finding Montana

UNLIKE THE UNIVERSITY of Chicago campus, Jackson Park had no grand, evocative sculptures. Rimming Lake Michigan, it was a different walking experience, filled with pleasant memories for Norman. I had no memories: its lakeside location made it feel ten degrees colder than Washington Park. Norman never reacted to the cold, even when the wind roared out of Canada and hit us full force. But we stopped often, so I could rewrap my scarves and Norman could wipe his nose and so he could tell me the about the park. I now think he stopped so often because he was a tad winded—he was, after all, a heart patient, as he told everyone. Him? I didn't believe someone so indestructible could have a heart condition. We rarely saw anyone else walking there, but we did see hungover or strung-out people wrapped in newspaper, sleeping under the trees. They seemed to be part of the landscape. Once when I asked Norman about the men, he shook his head, and we walked on.

The Wooded Isle was one of Norman's favorite places—it was surrounded by lagoons—and walking in it was like walking in the woods. He pointed out the only remaining building from the Columbian Exposition, the Palace of Fine Arts, which had been converted into the Museum of

Science and Industry. One evening in the 1930s, Jessie and he had spread a picnic on the grounds at the back of the museum while the Chicago Symphony played Handel, Norman told me, "and 'Water Music' floated over the lagoon, dear, and it was, well, you just have to imagine how lovely it was." He liked to walk in Jackson Park because the trees there reminded him a little of Montana. He told me how he had made Chicago a place where he could thrive by finding enough pieces of Montana to nourish his soul. He was the only person I knew, other than a minister, who talked about caring for one's soul.

We looked at the murky lagoons. In 1924, he told me, police had found typewriter keys and a typewriter in one lagoon, clues that led to the arrest of Nathan Loeb and Richard Leopold, "cold-blooded bastards who killed a boy just to see if they could do it." Norman hissed. The great defense attorney Clarence Darrow saved them from the gallows, "giving one of the greatest speeches of his career." An underpass led to Lake Michigan, a paler gray than the sky, and we would watch the waves crashing on the shore. Looking north from Fifty-Seventh Street, you could see, far away, the skyscrapers of downtown. "The lake saves Chicago and Hyde Park in the summer, darling, keeping it cool," he said. "What other great city has a clean lake where people can swim?"

Walks around Hyde Park were often spontaneous. Norman would show up at the library as I was heading back to my dorm, and away we would go. But trips to the forest preserves on the edge of the city took some planning because they involved an afternoon and evening. He would dump the ingredients for dinner into his Crock-Pot before leaving. Usually at noon on a Sunday, Norman would pick me up outside my dorm and we'd head to Lake Shore Drive and then down the Stevenson Expressway. It was named for Adlai Stevenson, he told me, an Illinois politician he had hoped would be president, one he admired almost as much as he admired FDR. The drive took maybe forty-five minutes, during which Norman would sometimes talk about the Committee on General Studies in the Humanities' annual lamb roast in Palos Park, a tradition that he and Jessie had started. He had also started the committee itself in the 1950s. The roasted lamb feast was strictly for faculty and their families and general studies students. They would drink, cook, drink some more, talk, play softball, and drink some more, he said, making it a kind of wonderful, boozy day of softball and talking among friends. I wished I could have gone. I had grown up playing softball. When I asked if I should apply to the committee—thinking that membership could gain me access to the picnic—Norman told me that the English department was the place for me.

On our excursions, there was no food. We'd park and get out slowly, our boots crunching the snow-crusted ground, every exhale clouded around our mouths. Everything Norman did was deliberate. He would lock the car and tuck the keys into his pants pocket. After he patted his pocket a few times to make sure the keys were there, we'd start out across a meadow, the sun blinding us as it hit the snow. Norman liked to lead, mostly because he liked to stop and point out an animal's tracks or the beauty of a bare tree's bark. The start-and-stop meant I couldn't ever go fast enough to warm up, but I wasn't about to speed away from him, though I was sure my feet were facing frostbite. We would walk three or four miles, across the meadow and into the trees, hearing only our breathing and the wind scuttling leaves on the ground. Sometimes when we stopped, Norman would say, "Look." And I would turn and take in the landscape, a white expanse bordered by black trees, illuminated by the sun, broken only by two sets of footprints.

A few hours later, back at Norman's Volvo, he would unlock the doors and the trunk, then crank the engine and turn on the heater. From the back seat, he would take a thermos of hot tea and, from the trunk, a Mason jar of whiskey. We would then move to the hood of the car, where he would unscrew the red cup that topped the thermos, pour in steaming tea, fill another plastic cup with tea, place the cups on the hood, and add some alcohol. The preparation had the feel of a religious ritual, and I guess it was. It was the favorite drink of his minister father, he said, and was an absolute necessity when you were out in the cold. We would then get in the car and drink.

Norman would offer a few random but interesting comments, telling me the Twenty-Third Psalm "has only 118 words, and only two adjectives," *green* and *still*. "So when you write, write with nouns and verbs." I would nod as the hot tea scalded my mouth and the alcohol burned my throat and warmed my stomach, then spread to my fingertips and toes, suddenly prickling with the flow of blood. Norman told me about duck hunting with his father on chilly mornings, falling into a frozen stupor, and then coming back to life when the tea and whiskey touched his lips.

"You know, Rebecca, for all of its problems and perils, it really is a beautiful world, isn't it?" he would say. The sun would be disappearing behind the trees, its rays casting long shadows, and I would nod. Because it was.

After sharing two cups of spiked tea, we would drive back to Hyde Park. There would be puddles pooling on the passenger floor as the heater melted the ice and snow off my boots. Though the traffic was usually heavier in late afternoon, the drive home always seemed shorter, probably because the whiskey had made me drowsy, and I was suddenly warm and contented and a bit tiddly. Norman drove well no matter how much we drank.

A walk in the forest preserve would be followed by dinner at Norman's Woodlawn Avenue condominium. The apartment was on the first floor of a three-story building, set back far from the street, with trees and a garden in front. There were two bedrooms, a bathroom, dining room, living room, and kitchen. It was very comfortable. In the living room were a built-in bookcase and a large cabinet with glass doors that had come from Norman's parents as well as a black recliner, a loveseat, and a couch with down-filled cushions. Plants filled the large front window. A small television set was in one corner. His mother's sewing cabinet was against one wall. The view from the front window was of trees and plants.

His daughter, Jean, had given Norman his Crock-Pot, and he used it to great advantage. Almost everything we ate featured a cut of beef, a few vegetables, sour cream, and maybe noodles, all of it very tasty. Norman liked to take me into the kitchen and tell me what he planned to serve for dinner—say, a beef stew—with a handful of good crusty rolls and some canned bing cherries and ice cream for dessert. While he puttered around in the kitchen, he would hum a few low bars of a song I didn't recognize. It sounded like contentment. Somehow Norman had gotten it into his head that I love canned Oregon fruit in heavy syrup, and we had it with almost every meal he ever served me. I couldn't tell him it was cloying. I usually made a green salad and toasted the rolls while he poured us a drink, humming a song that never seemed to progress past the first few bars. I sometimes felt as though I were an acolyte in church.

Norman was adamant that I not become a poor drinker—someone who didn't know a Tom Collins from a bourbon and branch. After my initial experience in Seeley Lake, I was determined to improve my ability to imbibe. I copied how he paced himself, sipping the drink slowly and holding it in my mouth for a second before swallowing. If I went out with friends to Jimmy's, a local bar, my scotch or bourbon order would be met with whistles—everyone else got pitchers of beer. I came to like both scotch and Jack Daniel's, but I never did develop a taste for beer.

Over our meal, Norman and I would talk about my family in Montana and South Carolina, and he would tell me stories about his early days in Montana and why he couldn't live there. He told me what he told others: one had to leave Montana to survive. He counted the exodus of its ambitious young people the state's greatest loss. Later he told others: "If you didn't kiss the ass of the Anaconda Company, you were a dead duck. Anyone who had any independence was just dead. We got the hell out of there. It was a great loss for generations."

He told me he had been miserable at Dartmouth, and getting a little huffy, he said he would never give them "a goddamn dime." When I pressed him, Norman clammed up, miffed. I learned he had had an uneasy transition to college life. The social aspect of the school, the arrogance of his entitled classmates, was what Norman abhorred. He nevertheless appreciated his teachers, saying that Dartmouth was long celebrated for the quality of its teaching, "some of the finest teaching I would ever see."

* * *

When Norman and his father stepped off the train in Hanover, New Hampshire, they found themselves in a small New England village of clapboard buildings and white picket fences. A walk around town confirmed that Hanover was a fraction of the size of Missoula. Where Hanover ended, Dartmouth College began. Its buildings bordered a long, open expanse called "the Green" that had been part of the school for more than 150 years. It was a small, all-male college in an isolated town. The winters were sure to be long, cold, and dark.

A notation in his high school yearbook shows Norman had listed as his college choice Washington and Jefferson, a small liberal arts college south of Pittsburgh founded by Presbyterian missionaries in the late 1700s. But he changed his plans. Norman told me Harvard had accepted him and that he thought about going, but he eventually decided not to, a decision his father seconded. Norman chose Dartmouth, he told his interviewers, because it was "the only outdoor college in the country," and he assumed the woodsy setting would remind him of Montana. All too soon, he learned he was wrong. In Missoula, which sits at the confluence of five valleys, he had been able to see mountains wherever he went. In Hanover, elms and maples hid the vista. The White Mountains were far away. Most of his father's family was in Boston, more than an hour south on the train.

At Dartmouth in the 1920s, the majority of students were privileged, white, wealthy young New Englanders. Some of their fathers and grandfathers had attended Dartmouth. They knew little about the Rocky

Mountains and less about Montana, other than childhood tales about George Armstrong Custer and history lessons on Lewis and Clark's expedition. Norman felt they looked down on him because his family wasn't rich. I later learned that the clubby atmosphere had choked Norman, who told his friend Gwin Kolb that he felt "like an uncouth kid from Montana." While many of his classmates were learning to sail and play polo, Norman had been fighting forest fires and leading pack mules in the Bitterroot Mountains. And though he spoke and wrote well, he was constantly having to explain himself, his hometown, his lineage, and his reasons for coming to Dartmouth. Doing so had exasperated him.

Even in his later years, Norman failed to resolve his antagonistic attitude toward the affluent. "He had a hatred of big money in the abstract," said his son-in-law, Joel Snyder. "He could be very difficult, but at the same time, he could be very gracious with wealthy people." Jessie's attitudes were clearer. She had been a fan of the International Workers of the World, the radical Wobblies, and she later became and remained, like Norman, an unreconstructed Roosevelt Democrat.

The most memorable figure in college for Norman was former Dartmouth student Robert Frost, then in his late forties. The poet was an occasional teacher at the college and had a free hand in instructing his students. Norman said Frost "talked straight to you, and often poetry was there, or something close to it." Classes met once a week, in the evening, in a "great big basement room with a wonderful fireplace." The subject was creative writing, but Frost apparently never bothered to read his students' papers. Instead, he would pace back and forth in front of the class, talking and talking. There were never any questions in Frost's classes, Norman said, and "nobody ever stopped him."

Norman studied hard, later claiming he read a book a day, but he realized he would have to suppress his sardonic sense of humor in class. He became a C student—an accomplishment, given his meager high school education and his many extracurricular activities. He found ways to thrive outside the classroom. He joined Beta Theta Pi and promptly began relieving his fraternity brothers of their money around the poker table. A friend visiting from Montana was astounded that the college boys "didn't know not to draw from an inside straight." In a local gym, Norman boxed with fraternity members and men from the community and enjoyed knocking down opponents. He became a staff member of the *Dartmouth Bema*, a literary magazine, and the *Aegis*, the Dartmouth yearbook. He was selected for Sphinx, the oldest of Dartmouth's many secret societies. He was on the board of governors for The Arts, "a clearing house for the ideas and opinions of those interested in the fields of literature, drama and music." Among the writers coming to campus during his senior year were journalist and critic Rebecca West and poet Edna St. Vincent Millay. How he felt about meeting and hearing these women, we don't know, but I do know he liked Millay's poetry.

Of all his undergraduate extracurricular activities, Norman most valued his time with the *Dartmouth Jack-O-Lantern*, a monthly campus humor magazine. He served as editor-in-chief his last year of college, earning sixteen hundred dollars during the academic year. It was the perfect outlet for him, surrounded by other young men who also appreciated wit and sarcasm. Under his tenure, the *Jacko* was more popular than ever before and was even distributed on other college campuses. It offered jokes and mocking editorials on such topics as the poor quality of the campus newspaper, the *Dartmouth* ("*Jacko wishes to congratulate the advertising manager of* The Dartmouth *for the fine issues he is putting out*") and the injustice of compulsory chapel ("*Christianity vs. chapel: Ye are the salt of the earth: but if the salt have lost its savor, wherewith shall it be salted? It is thenceforth good for nothing, but to be cast out, and to be trodden under the foot of man*").

Another bright spot was his friendship with Theodor Seuss "Ted" Geisel, known today as Dr. Seuss. They had worked together on the *Jack-O-Lantern*. According to Geisel, he and Norman often wrote "practically the whole thing" by themselves, tag teaming the task. "Hunched behind his typewriter, [Norman] would bang out a line of words," Geisel said.

"Sometimes he'd tell me what he'd written, sometimes not. But, then, he'd always say, 'The next line's yours.' And, always, I'd supply it. This may have made for rough reading. But it was great sport writing." Geisel later said his big desire had been to run the magazine in his senior year, saying, "If Mac hadn't picked me as his successor, my whole life at college would have been a failure." Unlike Norman, who eventually thawed about his alma mater, Geisel always had warm feelings for Dartmouth and became its biggest benefactor.

Before Norman graduated, in June 1924, Dartmouth English professor David Lambuth asked if he wanted to return to campus and teach freshman composition. Lambuth had had Norman in a few of his classes and was impressed with his writing ability and his sensitivity to language. Norman accepted the offer, telling an interviewer the class "was full of some poker buddies of mine, and I figured it would be a good way to pay back some debts."

Norman went home to Montana to work for the US Forest Service, gathering some of the experiences he would later turn into stories. He had spent most summers working for the Forest Service, except for part of 1921, when his father, Paul, and he worked on a log cabin on the shore of Seeley Lake, on land leased to them by the federal government. Norman returned to the halls of Hanover in the autumn of 1924 as an instructor of introductory English, and his brother, Paul, went with him to start on his Dartmouth degree. The Reverend couldn't afford to pay for two sons to attend private school at the same time, so Paul had taken classes at Montana State (later renamed the University of Montana) in Missoula for a year before heading east. Bravig Imbs, one of Norman's contemporaries, offers a glimpse of some events in Norman's life while he was an instructor, in *The Professor's Wife*. The professor and the wife are based on Lambuth and his wife, Myrtle. Imbs worked as a butler for the Lambuths, which gave him a bird's-eye view of their lives. Norman makes an appearance in the book as the character Douglas MacNeil, "an exceptional person" with a sensitive and crooked smile, who comes to write in the couple's study. The David Lambuth character says Douglas's poetry "had the streak of genius" and that a novel he was working on was the best poetic prose he had read.

In addition to his own writing, Norman was busy teaching undergraduates how to construct sentences. He told the story of an "observer" visiting his class one session, a redheaded Scotch atheist he admired, Professor James Dow McCallum, whose lectures on Victorian writers were very popular. Weeks passed with no feedback. Norman at last went to McCallum's office. The professor was surprised to see him. Norman asked McCallum how to improve his teaching, and McCallum told him to wear a different suit every day of the week. When Norman said he couldn't afford so many suits, McCallum suggested he wear a different necktie. He followed this advice through his long teaching career at Chicago.

For Norman, the occasional amusement provided by his struggling students—one wrote that the primeval forest was "where the hand of man had never set foot"—failed to compensate for Dartmouth's caste system. Maybe he was struggling with his own writing or tiring of the décor in Mrs. Lambuth's study. The problems Norman had faced as an undergraduate now only worsened. The stratified society of the English department, in which instructors were socially segregated from tenured professors, added to the sense of moneyed clubbiness and made a lonely Montanan long for the West. The feelings of isolation increased when his pal Ted Geisel graduated and left for two years at Oxford. Norman's brother, Paul, had already gone home to Montana, skipping the 1926 spring semester.

Norman squirmed in the dinner jacket he was required to wear to departmental functions. Even the everyday clothes worn by the students set Norman on edge: the pullover sweaters and black-and-white saddle shoes of Joe College.

In June 1926, after two years as an instructor, Norman rode the train out of Hanover to Missoula and back to a job in the woods. In the fall, as the time came to return to New Hampshire, his father helped him realize he wasn't bettering himself by teaching at Dartmouth. Alone, Paul boarded the train, heading east. Norman wrote to Professor Lambuth, telling him that he wasn't coming back and asking if someone else could take his classes. He didn't return to Hanover for decades.

He never wore a tuxedo again.

6

Western Friends

THOUGH SOMETIMES HOMESICK, Norman had thrived as a student at Chicago, where the atmosphere was egalitarian and relaxed, and he wanted me to thrive as well. He named the professors, not the courses, I should take, believing that if you have a great teacher, it doesn't matter what the subject is—you'll learn something. Sometimes before we ate dinner in his condo, while the Crock-Pot was burbling, he would put on his glasses and read aloud Wordsworth or Gerard Manley Hopkins. He loved "Pied Beauty" and "God's Grandeur," explaining that sprung rhythm meant emphasizing different syllables when reading the poems aloud. He didn't need a book—he knew the poems by heart—and he illuminated the words simply by how he read them. He taught me how to read Tennyson and Matthew Arnold, both of whom he loved. He loved Wordsworth's "Ode on Intimations of Immortality from Recollections of Early Childhood." I usually brought one of my poems to share with Norman, who listened to me read with his eyes closed and his fingertips touching as though he were making a tent. He would deconstruct my poem for me, maybe make a suggestion, and ask for a copy of it.

It was no secret among his friends that Norman hated the Vermont outdoor supplier Orvis—for reasons he never explained. It was also no secret that he loved L. L. Bean, another Northeast company selling outdoor clothes and gear. Sometimes when I met him at his home, he would have just opened a package from L. L. Bean. Radiating delight, he would explain the shoes were brogans, the pants were moleskin, and the shirt a heavy, fine-weave wool. Of course, I became a fan as well.

After eating, we would return to the living room with small glasses of Japanese plum wine, which was even more cloying than the Oregon bing cherries he loved. Norman would lean back in his black recliner and read me what he had been working on, usually a scene from one of his stories. His descriptions made me homesick for Montana. We would finish the plum wine, I would rise to leave, and Norman would get up and put on his scarf, coat, and hat, then pull my coat from the closet and help me on with it.

"In or out, dear?" he would ask.

"Out," I said. He would gather my hair to the nape of my neck and lift it out of my coat, then pull the coat up onto my shoulders and walk me home. Intimate and efficient, it was a gesture no one else ever did for me.

I'm sure I could have used the time I spent with Norman for reading and studying, but I figured walking outside and eating a nice meal with him was better for both of us. He enjoyed feeding me. And he especially enjoyed taking me to different restaurants.

One we liked was the Middle East Club on Damen Avenue near Fifty-Fifth Street. My first visit, we parked on a side street, ignoring the sounds of glass breaking and people shouting, and hurried inside a hole-in-the-wall restaurant, long and narrow, with a few tables in front, a kitchen at the back through swinging doors, and a curtain of beads on one side. I removed my gloves, hat, scarves, and coat, settling into the room's warmth. Arabic music played on the speaker system, but over the hypnotic songs, I could hear people talking and shouting from what seemed far away. As I took in the photos of Gamal Abdel Nasser and Anwar Sadat and scenes of Egypt on the walls, Norman grinned at me. "You won't find this in Missoula, will you, darling? The food is wonderful."

I told him I was looking forward to the meal but first needed to find a bathroom. We had had a drink in his apartment before setting out. Norman pointed to the beads. I parted them and stepped into a cavernous room filled with what seemed like fifty pool tables. Around each table were four or five men. They all lifted their pool cues and stared at me, a tall, skinny girl with a short skirt and shoulder-length blonde hair, as I made my way to the bathroom at the back of the room. *Bathroom* is a generous term—it was a storage closet with a toilet from the rule of Ramses the First. As I shut the door, I saw a room of dark eyes staring at me. I tried to pee soundlessly, but as we know, that's not possible. I could hear laughter rippling through the room. When I opened the door to leave, the laughter stopped. But as I hurried toward the beaded curtain, ten, twenty, or thirty men all sucked their teeth, then started laughing again.

I slid into my chair, embarrassed. Norman had ordered hummus, baba ghanoush, tabbouleh, and pita bread, plates of food that covered the tabletop. Norman marveled at what the chef was able to do with vegetables, and he started to explain how each dish was made. I looked up when he said, "It's a pool club, darling, and a restaurant." He tore off a piece of pita and dipped it in the hummus. "I should have told you to use the toilet before we left." I laughed. "They'll be talking about you for weeks, Rebecca."

The next course was lamb stew with rice flecked with saffron. Norman explained how saffron was harvested, "little crocuses, so delicate, so beautiful. I wouldn't want to have to do it." To end the meal, we had knafeh and baklava—the words were as delicious to me as the food—and Turkish coffee so thick you had to stir it with a little spoon before drinking it. I had learned that Norman had a serious sweet tooth—eating with me meant he could always order at least one and sometimes two desserts, supposedly so I could try them. Returning to the car, I followed Norman's lead—I kept walking and ignored people leaning against apartment walls, smoking and calling to us.

*　*　*

When I returned to Chicago after spring break, Norman told me he had sent "USFS 1919" to a publisher. I hoped they would accept it. His Chicago colleague and friend John Cawelti had suggested Norman send the story to Hill & Wang in New York for consideration. That publishing house passed on it. I'm sure Norman was disappointed and disheartened—but he was assured by his friends that others would find his writing worthwhile, as did the Stochastics.

My roommate had family problems that spilled into our tiny dorm room—she was so upset she couldn't sleep—preventing me from studying there, so I asked Norman if I could stay with him for a few days. He said I couldn't do that because even though he was old enough to be my grandfather, people would assume we were "shacking up." He told me, "Nothing can touch me but disease," but he wasn't about to do anything that would hurt my reputation. I was naive enough then to think his precautions were overblown, but of course, he was right. I knew that no matter what others might think, for him to make sexual overtures to me, or another student or a teenager, was ludicrous. It was more likely that he would blow up Harper Library. Norman's attitude was that "the faculty's job is to help young people, not to prey on them," an attitude many in academe would probably consider quaint. I heard a story about Norman from his long-ago students, that a young co-ed had hanged herself in Ida Noyes Hall after Norman told her he was married, he was her teacher, and neither could nor would ever become her love interest.

To give me some respite from my roommate, Norman and I began walking almost every afternoon. Norman saw so much of my girlfriends from the dormitory that he formed friendships with some of them, who took care of his condo while he was in Montana. He often dropped one- or two-line notes at my dorm mailbox, complimenting me on a poem or bemoaning another tone-deaf sonnet. One envelope marked URGENT alarmed me until I opened to read a single sentence: "Rebecca, please, no more sonnets."

In late April, Norman told Bud Moore that he was thinking of giving up his cabin, something he often said he wanted to do. I couldn't image Seeley Lake without him. His list of complaints included: the drive from Chicago to Montana was too far; it took too long to open the cabin and get settled; the campground toilet near his cabin sometimes smelled; it was a huge bother to close the cabin for the winter; the noise of the campers annoyed him; "and the goddamn Forest Service keeps raising the cost of my lease." He felt his children, Jean and John, weren't inter- ested in maintaining the cabin—only his son-in-law from Brooklyn, Joel Snyder, seemed to care for it. Of course, we know Norman kept returning to Montana and his cabin for another dozen years, even as the price of the lease continued to rise. Today his children and their families share the cabin. Contrary to his expectations, they have kept alive their Montana connections.

One May afternoon, Norman appeared in the office doorway of Allen Fitchen, then a humanities editor with the University of Chicago Press. Norman's friend and colleague Wayne Booth, one of the press's authors, had suggested Norman talk with Fitchen, not with the press director, Morris Philipson. Fitchen told me he knew little about Norman at the time, other than he was a revered teacher, and Norman knew only one press employee, publicist Virginia Heiserman, the wife of Arthur Heiserman, a professor in the English department. Fitchen said he was surprised to find Norman "deferential and even shy" as he asked for advice about getting his stories into print.

The editor told Norman what he already knew: unlike commercial houses, the University of Chicago Press didn't publish fiction. Fitchen also told Norman he would be happy to offer an opinion about whatever

Norman had written. Norman gave him "USFS 1919," and Fitchen set it aside for a couple of weeks. Meanwhile, Norman received a laudatory letter from Bud Moore about "USFS 1919" and wrote to thank him, saying, "When we non-writers try to start writing in old age, we have to live pretty much in solitary confinement and a pat on the back reduces some of the loneliness of the self-imposed sentence." I wonder now how solitary he could have been with my friends and me dropping in on him, often unannounced, just to say hello.

The next day, the last Saturday in May, Norman picked up two friends and me, and we drove east around the shoreline to Lakeside, Michigan, to see Larry Kimpton and his wife, Eleanor, and their boat. The town was green and very lush, and so was the manicured estate of the late Harold Swift, where Kimpton's stone cabin was one of several outbuildings. While Eleanor stayed inside—I think she was making dinner—we met outside and walked to the dock. Kimpton was well over six feet tall, and Norman grinned up at him as they shook hands. I remember he had blue eyes, a shock of white hair, black-framed glasses, and laugh lines. "It's a great pleasure," he said as he shook my hand, and then he shook my friends' hands. For a big man, he had a surprisingly soft voice.

We boarded Kimpton's boat, the same one Norman and he had taken to Key West. He started the engine, and off we went, toward Chicago. I remember one scene from that day. Kimpton had shown one of my friends how to steer, and he and Norman were walking around the deck, talking. They stopped, and I watched Norman unbutton Kimpton's shirt to reveal scars across his chest, a red one thick as a piece of rope. Norman touched the scar, near Kimpton's heart, and asked, "Did they hurt you, Larry?" Kimpton shook his head and said, "No, but they cut me from stem to stern, didn't they?" He had had heart problems from years of heavy smoking.

Later, inside the cabin, drinking wine and scotch, we listened to Kimpton read three brief short stories from *Trails Plowed Under* by Montanan Charlie Russell. He was a great reader. He and Norman had read those stories so often, I'm sure the reading for him was like hearing a familiar Bible story. Kimpton told us he got the Legion of Honor "for getting drunk with a Frenchman," which led to another story. When he was the administrator for the Chicago part of the Manhattan Project, the federal program to produce an atomic bomb, a janitor poured two liters of plutonium down the sink, "and it cost $3 billion to produce it. We had to dig up the streets to recover it," he said. Probably because of his heart, Kimpton didn't accompany us as we walked through the gardens and orchards, Norman answering questions about the flowers and trees. He told us that after resigning from the university in 1960, Kimpton had gone to work for Standard Oil of Indiana.

*   *   *

Long after I left the university, after both Norman and Larry Kimpton were dead, I learned just how close they had been. In the early 1940s, chemists and physicists from around the world moved to Chicago to work on secret scientific projects for the federal government. Nobel Prize winner Arthur Holly Compton, a professor of physics at Chicago from 1923 to 1945, headed the collective, called the Chicago Metallurgical Lab—the name was a cover. It couldn't be called the Chicago Nuclear Experimentation Lab. Compton's 1942 reports about research on atomic energy provided the initial, overall guidance for the creation of the Manhattan Project. He recruited scientists like Enrico Fermi and Leo Szilard to the Met Lab.

In December 1942, the team created the first sustained nuclear reaction, in a handball court under the stands of Stagg Field. In 1943, the lab—part of the Manhattan Project—involved hundreds of university employees, scientists and technicians, different government agencies, and private businesses. It needed an associate administrator. Some of the young chemists in the lab had taught at Deep Springs College, an experimental junior college in California while doing postgraduate work at Caltech, and they recommended hiring a former colleague they had known at Deep Springs to manage the lab: Lawrence Kimpton.

Tall, soft-spoken, and charismatic, thirty-three-year-old Kimpton had a PhD in Kantian philosophy from Cornell University and a western charm. He was a practical guy—he had taught at Deep Springs and had operated cattle ranches in Nevada. He soon became the chief administrator of the Chicago Metallurgical Lab, which had moved from the university campus in densely settled Hyde Park to a forest preserve, with no residents, outside town.

"Larry had been brought in," Norman wrote, "when it looked as if the project might end instead in a three-way civil war—between the University business officers who wanted complete inventories of all expenditures in case the project was unsuccessful and a Congressional investigation would follow after the war; scientists like Fermi, Franck, and Urey who could conceive of another world but not of spending any time making inventories of the test tubes of this world; and General Groves, representing the military and representing something of a problem in his own right."

Not one to pass up a chance to pile duties on the competent, President Hutchins named Kimpton the new dean of students for the university and a philosophy professor in the college. The story goes that Hutchins asked Kimpton if he knew anything about student personnel, and when Kimpton said no, Hutchins gave him the job.

Norman met Larry Kimpton in September 1943, a few months after Norman's son, John, was born. He was called into Kimpton's office, where he saw on a desk "the soles of a large pair of shoes. The voice somewhere behind the soles said, 'I hear you come from Montana. Tell me about this place. Does it feel anything like the West?' I said, 'Yes, the people do.' He replied, 'That's what I was thinking. You know,' he said. 'I ran cattle ranches for seven years, and those big cattle ranchers sure believe in academic freedom.' I told him he would get shot around here if he tried to enclose us in barbed wire, but he already knew this." They became friends—in fact, Norman told me Larry was his best friend. Kimpton didn't bond just with Norman—he liked his whole family. In letters to Norman, he would ask after "Jess and the kids." His wife, Marcia, and Jessie grew close.

The two men loved to tell stories, and Kimpton loved jokes and limericks. "Jesus, the tall tales we have told each other over those martinis with orange peel. The woods and the cow country." There were nocturnal phone conversations filled with "colorful" language and nights of drinking that ended with dinner at a colleague's house.

The official record of how, exactly, Kimpton managed to "keep the physicists out of the Army's hair, and the Army out of the physicists' hair," while tending to the university's students, is strangely absent. What we know comes from stories, from the memories of those who were on campus during World War II, several of whom I interviewed, and from Norman's own stories. Colleagues knew that Norman and Jimmie Cate helped Kimpton with his speeches—he would talk about what he wanted to say and they would write a first draft. Often, Norman handled Kimpton's university duties, and sometimes he offered advice about how to deal with the impatient General Groves and the unhurried Enrico Fermi, who was figuring out how to deal with gaseous diffusion.

Though his association with General Groves eventually ended, Kimpton would suffer the remainder of his life from problems created by exposure to radiation. His hero, Fermi, died of stomach cancer.

7

Tragedy Was Inevitable

A FEW WEEKS AFTER our trip to Lakeside, the academic year drew to a close. I was hoping to ride out to Montana with Norman. We planned to stop at Little Bighorn "to have a look around" because he knew "a bit about the battlefield." Only later did I learn he had tried to write a book about Custer before setting that project aside. I was preparing to leave the dormitory and stay in a friend's apartment for a few days until Norman was ready to leave. I found another Norman note in my mailbox that made me feel better about my lackluster academic performance, which included some Cs as well as As and Bs. The note ended, "In coming here, you have made an old man very happy." And that made me very happy.

At the last minute, our proposed itinerary changed. Norman had to stay in Hyde Park a week or two. I had a Forest Service job waiting for me in Seeley Lake, and I needed to get there. Instead of riding shotgun in Norman's Volvo, I had to wedge myself into a packed Datsun B-210 driven by a friend of a friend whom, I discovered, was completely unhinged. He carried a grudge against women because a girlfriend had dumped him, as he told me at least once every hour. At two in the morning, the car started drifting off the road, and I pleaded for him to stop. He insisted we throw our sleeping bags into an open field in North Dakota that turned out to be an airplane landing strip.

I have kicked myself repeatedly since then for taking that ride and missing out on the chance to walk the Little Bighorn with Norman. His "bit" of knowledge could have filled a book. And in fact, years after Norman died, four of the chapters on George Armstrong Custer and the battle appeared in a compendium of his writing.

* * *

For years, en route to the cabin in Seeley Lake, Norman and his family had been stopping at the Little Bighorn Battlefield. There, in June 1876, thousands of Native Americans, mostly Northern Cheyenne and Sioux, massacred Custer and six hundred men from the Seventh Cavalry. During various sojourns, Jean Snyder remembers meeting on the battlefield "strange characters, who weren't academics." Norman "had some pals there who were also interested in Custer. Part of the fun was tramping through the battlefield, looking at the ground and figuring out what had happened," she says. "My dad had his own theories. Custer was like an early version of *Young Men and Fire*, trying to reconstruct what had happened at the moment of a glorious death."

In the summer of 1955, Norman struck up a friendship with historian Robert Utley, who was also fascinated with Custer. Utley had spent his college summers working at Little Bighorn, and in 1955, he was an army officer who wanted to become a professional historian. The two met in person only occasionally but kept up a vigorous correspondence for decades, long after Norman had shelved his idea of writing about Custer. Utley eventually earned a doctorate in history and wrote many books. Their letters from the 1950s reveal Norman's excitement at trying to figure out what had happened when and where—and why—both during the rout at Little Bighorn and afterward. The two men worked together on a 1956 profile of Edward Luce, the superintendent of the battlefield, when he retired from the National Park Service. Utley said he marveled "at how kindly and gently Norman handled our 'collaboration.'" Both Utley and Jean Snyder recall Norman's delight at combing the grounds at Little Bighorn for buttons, shell cases, and other artifacts from the battle.

I do know Custer was never far from Norman's thoughts, even when he returned from Montana. During the 1955–56 academic year, graduate student Michael Fixler, who later became a professor at Tufts University, took two classes with Norman. The first was on William Wordsworth and the second was titled "General Custer and the Battle of the Little Big Horn: A Study in Historiography and Literary Method." "There was a kind of passion in Maclean with this material that wasn't anything like the civil intensity of the Wordsworth class," Fixler told me. Student Marty Roth said, "The Custer segment, offered as an example of using textual evidence, made its way into every course [Norman] taught," whether Shakespeare or Victorian poetry.

For Fixler, taking the Custer course, "was the best thing I did in the whole of my long career as a student, which means of course that for me that the Maclean experience had some memorable highlights." He wrote two papers for the Custer course, one on Col. Frederick W. Benteen. Fixler researched the proceedings of the US Army court of inquiry in Chicago that investigated the conduct of Maj. Marcus Reno during the battle. Benteen had ignored Custer's message to "Come on. Big Village. Be quick. Bring Packs." Rather than join the massacre, Benteen took command of Reno's troops and helped them survive comparatively minor Indian assaults miles from Custer. Fixler concluded that "there isn't any doubt: Benteen screwed Custer both militarily and in terms of the image of utter recklessness Custer thereafter cut." His second paper was a roundup of popular pulp fiction centered on Custer.

A question arose for Fixler during the seminar that he couldn't answer. "Why had not Maclean written this major opus on the obsession of his life with what happened at the Little Bighorn? He had a fire in his gut he wanted to write about. The fire was Custer, or whatever it was that Custer signified and which was to be revealed to him by the work itself. Custer crystallized a personal crux that wasn't academic nor could be strictly resolved in any academic way. Something to do with what used to be called easily enough in those days, manliness."

While his students were wondering about his fascination with George Armstrong Custer, Norman was researching Custer and the Little Bighorn. He had a sabbatical in the spring quarter of 1959, which freed his mornings so he could write. He spent his afternoons attending to administrative duties associated with the Committee on General Studies. For three months in 1959, Norman told Robert Utley, he had focused exclusively on Custer: "I'm getting pretty old to write a book—sometimes I'm not sure I have the physical stamina—and four to five hours a morning morning after morning has me whipped. Also it's very lonely, and I'm glad to get over to the University now and then just to hear a human voice."

*   *   *

In late spring of 1974, before he left for Montana, Norman wrote Fitchen, telling him that if hadn't yet read the story, it was fine, but he wanted it returned, regardless. That evening, on June 9, 1974, Fitchen read "USFS 1919" straight through and was taken with it. The problem was it wasn't long enough to stand on its own, and Norman had only two shorter stories to add to the mix—a piece on his family's hunting dogs and "Logging and Pimping," the toast of the Stochastics. Norman told Fitchen he would have a longer story on trout fishing ready in about six months, and he agreed that while he was in Seeley Lake, Fitchen would be contacting commercial publishers on Norman's behalf.

In the summer, the editor-in-chief of Chicago-based Swallow House found the story "delightful and stunning" but didn't want to publish Norman's work unless it could be classified as memoir, not fiction. That wasn't going to happen. The stories were based on events, stories, and people from Norman's early life in Montana, but they weren't factual. He had played with time in each story, condensing events that could have happened over years into one year, changing some names and locations, keeping others.

I had made my way to Seeley Lake, where everything was tinged with memories of my dead sister-in-law—from the little grocery store, where Daisy Cainan would pat Meg on the head and squeeze Marilyn's arm, to the Post Office, where postmistress Bert Sullivan had always greeted us with a smile, to the Seeley Lake Inn, where John, Marilyn, Meg, and I had often eaten supper. My brother John had promised me a job as a lookout with the US Forest Service, but through a bureaucratic snafu, it had fallen through. I had planned to be living in the Double Arrow lookout tower, not in my brother's cabin. To complicate matters further, during the previous November, John had married a woman—the woman I had encountered at the kitchen table—and she and her five children were crowded into the same two-bedroom cabin where Marilyn, Meg, and he had lived. His new wife turned out to be a wonderful person—even Norman warmed to her—but adding another body to the scrum then wasn't a good idea. I eventually moved in with one of John's elderly friends whose summer lakeside home was a mile from my jobs in town. Meg was in Idaho with her maternal grandmother for the summer.

In the early mornings, I would walk to Seeley Lake's small commercial area and cook breakfast in a small restaurant before becoming a maid in a motel, changing bed linens and distributing towels. And in the evenings, I would dispense soft ice cream and flip hamburgers at a burger bar. The owner believed I should work from four until ten, but I was too exhausted to keep that schedule for long. After two weeks, I quit one afternoon when, with tourists flooding the area, he demanded

I log a double shift. Norman didn't have a telephone in his cabin, and I didn't have a car—the only way to tell him my evenings were free was to leave a message with Bert Sullivan at the Post Office because he went to check his mail there every day.

When he could get away, Norman soon was teaching me to cast on the Swan River, one of his favorite places to fish. The river begins in the Missions and runs about ninety-five miles north before emptying into Flathead Lake, near Bigfork. It's easy to reach—Montana Highway 83 parallels it. And it's a good place for beginners—even if it doesn't have banks. One late afternoon, we left Seeley, heading north, the familiar thermos of black tea in the back seat. He laughed at my stories of the regulars I saw most mornings when I was cooking and at my ridiculous attempt to create a French dip. After a while, he turned off the road near Condon and then parked the car. When he opened the trunk, I saw two Fiberglas rods and fishing reels. We made our way to the water, where he tied a fly on the end of my line and showed me how to position the rod in front, overhead, and slightly behind me. I was to think of myself as part of a clock, with noon overhead, two in front, and ten behind, letting out line gradually as my hand moved forward and back. It made sense.

My first cast, I snagged a bush, and Norman cackled. "God, darling, you're not playing tennis! You've got to use your wrist!" I waded in and unhooked my line. There were overhanging trees and bushes on both sides of the river, and I wondered how someone could avoid them. Back and forth, back and forth, I moved the rod, with Norman telling me to let out the line gradually. There was no one else around. There were clouds of insects on stretches of the water, and I could hear cars passing on the highway. I watched Norman cast, the line whipping over his head before he dropped the fly, leader, and line in the water with only a small ring of rippling water. It was so beautiful, the line falling as softly as a sigh, and I wanted to be able to do that. I know the fish appreciated how he didn't disturb them; he just offered them a little bite of something— with a hook on it. After a few hours, I wanted a little bite of something myself, so we headed back to Seeley Lake and ate dinner at the Seeley Lake Inn. It was a far cry from our Chicago restaurants. Norman didn't have to explain the menu.

For the next week or so, Norman watched me practice casting on the shore of Seeley Lake near his cabin. He thought I was a fast learner, but I wasn't so sure. But I knew he was a good teacher because, after three lessons, I managed to land the fly, leader, and line in the proper order. I never caught anything, but Norman assured me that catching a fish was the easy part. Casting correctly was the hard part.

I liked the flies Norman carried and asked him if he could teach me how to make some since I had done beading and macramé. Norman told me flies were a completely different ball game. We didn't have the supplies or the equipment. He also added that flies were tied, not made, and he would lend me the ones I needed. He gave me the rod and reel I had been using and planned to continue my fly-fishing lessons in Chicago, but that didn't happen. He didn't fish anywhere but in Montana.

One thing Norman did, besides working on his stories, teaching me, and hosting visitors to the cabin, was to ask Bud Moore to write a letter of endorsement for "USFS 1919" to Allen Fitchen and two other people. "I find it somewhat ironical, Bud, that although I have taught books for ½ century, I have no notion of how you would get one published. Being used to thinking of myself as an expert, I find I end up as an amateur with a lifelong hatred of New York." I think he wanted an expert woodsman like Bud to legitimize his story because, on some level, he still lacked confidence in his own work. Bud would provide Norman's Montana bona fides. I thought the story could speak for itself, but Norman wanted outside confirmation.

Norman tried to impart confidence to Bud, who was planning to retire from the Forest Service in June 1974, telling him that he could start on another "life" in Montana when he left Washington, DC. He also said that if Jessie hadn't died, he and she might have tried to live the life Bud and his wife, Janet, were planning for themselves, building a cabin in the

Mission Mountains, far from any city. But Jessie had wanted to travel, her daughter, Jean Snyder, told me—to go to Europe or New England. Jessie had longed to go somewhere, anywhere, besides Montana, but Norman, the Capistrano swallow of Montana, always returned to Seeley Lake. I don't think Norman's picture of distant woodsmoke is realistic. But isn't it pretty to think so?

One evening, John dropped me on Boy Scout Road near Norman's cabin for another Crock-Pot dinner. They weren't speaking, for reasons I didn't know until later—Norman wanted John to stop the ranger's clearcutting, which wasn't possible. After we finished eating, I carried dishes into the kitchen, preparing to wash up, but Norman asked me to sit down and listen. He gathered up some papers and read to me part of what he had been revising, a fictional story about a family and fly-fishing. The fly-fishing part interested me, and I realized I was getting another lesson in how to do it correctly. When I asked Norman about the brother in the story and if that was his brother, he looked at me and said his brother was dead, killed south of the Midway near Sixty-Third Street, where we had often gotten Chinese takeout. This news alarmed me even as it made me sad. The university bordered a rough neighborhood. If a tough guy from Montana could be killed, maybe I was right to be uneasy in Hyde Park. Norman tried to calm my fears by telling me his brother had been in the wrong place at the wrong time, that he was a gambler and a drinker, and I was neither. I told him I was sorry about his brother, and he thanked me and said he had been sorry for most of his life.

*   *   *

Was the Paul who stepped from the pages of "A River Runs Through It" the same man who was Norman's brother? Most readers know little about Paul Maclean other than what they learn in "A River Runs Through It." The Paul we meet is a young man who doesn't suffer fools lightly, who goes his own way, drinks often and heavily, gets into fights, likes to make an impression, and frequents high-stakes poker games. His mother and father adore him, and his older brother admires him, at least as a fisherman, but the older brother and his father wonder if anyone can help the younger sibling change his ways or his life. At the end of the story, Paul is murdered, and Norman and his father talk about whether they ever really knew him or if they could have helped him. In between all the wondering, there's a lot of fishing and drinking.

Norman doesn't tell readers that his brother, Paul, was murdered on the South Side of Chicago because that location would require a much longer story than the one Norman is spinning. And Norman is writing fiction about families and relationships and isolation, not reporting a crime story. Nor does he mention that he was too shattered to cry. Or that, save for a brief conversation with his father, talks with some members of Beta Theta Pi, and some of his students, he didn't mention his brother after his death. Time stopped for Norman during the morning of May 2, 1938. He carried the burden of his brother's unsolved murder, and the guilt for having invited him to Chicago, for almost forty years. In writing "A River Runs Through It," telling the reader how beautiful the fictionalized version of his brother was—while hinting at his troubled side—Norman speaks about Paul's murder for the first time and lets himself publicly grieve.

Friends in Chicago told me that after the book's publication, Norman began to talk about Paul, his strengths and weaknesses, in casual conversation. In the title story, Norman grieves for the man he wished his brother could have been, not for the man his brother was. He had been grieving for that man since they were children, worrying about Paul's self-destructive behavior. Norman doesn't say that he had often feared Paul would commit suicide but that he was afraid to admit that fear. Jean Maclean Snyder told me Norman had urged Paul to leave Montana—and its high-stakes poker games and other gambling opportunities—and move to Hyde Park at the request of their father.

One newspaper story after his death says Paul was planning to return to Montana in September 1938 with a master's degree in English from the University of Chicago, but who knows if he really intended to go home? Or to earn a degree? In a letter he wrote to his father in April 1938, he said he planned to buy new clothes and look for a new job. Maybe in Chicago, maybe elsewhere. If he had listened to his older brother, Paul wouldn't have been walking around the neighborhood south of the Midway on a warm May night with more than fifty dollars—an equivalent of about nine hundred dollars today—in his pocket. Chicago's neighborhoods changed street by street. One block could be safe and the next not. Had he listened, he wouldn't have sustained a crushed skull and ended up unconscious in an alley a few blocks from his apartment, his wallet empty, his pockets inside out. He wouldn't have died in a nearby hospital after Norman arrived.

Like many younger brothers, Paul didn't take much advice from his older brother—by-the-book, Eagle Scout, married Norman, who had cautioned him repeatedly about taking walks in Chicago after dark as he had in Montana. But for Paul, who had been a newspaperman in Helena before moving to Chicago, I'm sure that walking around town at night had been a good way to unwind after the crush of people and politicians he endured as a reporter. Reports of violence in Chicago had little to no effect on his behavior. He was young and tough, taller and broader than Norman, fit from years of street fighting and playing handball, and he believed he could take care of himself. He was in the habit of walking at night. It proved his undoing.

Paul must have thought relocating to Chicago was a good idea; he wasn't one to be bossed around. Maybe he thought that he, too, would earn a doctorate. Paul's brief life—he was thirty-two when he died—reveals a pattern of walking in his older brother's footsteps. Like Norman, he attended Dartmouth, where he joined many of the same college clubs, social groups, and organizations as Norman and added another—the campus newspaper. He also majored in English, but unlike Norman,

Paul contributed money to his alma mater, suggesting he had positive feelings about the school. Like Norman, in high school he had played football and participated in clubs and literary activities. He was movie star handsome, I learned from longtime First Presbyterian members, and fond of flipping cards in the back pew while his father preached.

After earning his Dartmouth College degree in October 1928, Paul took reporting jobs in Montana, first with the *Great Falls Leader* and then the *Great Falls Tribune*. He shared an apartment in Great Falls with two other young men, Einar Stromnes and W. Turner Clack. A few years later, Stromnes entered politics and eventually was elected speaker of the Montana House of Representatives, while Clack worked in his father's petroleum distribution business and became a community leader in Spokane, Washington.

In a letter to Norman, Clack recalled how the three friends had spoofed officials from the Maxwell House coffee company. The company's motto was "Good to the Last Drop." Clack wrote to the company, saying that the last drop was equally as good as the first drop. The company responded that *to* meant "to and including." Stromnes traced legal cases back to English common law, the letter to Norman said, in which *to* meant "that far and no farther" and shared this information with Maxwell House. Paul and Clack searched the literature, from Chaucer to the present, to find examples supporting Clack's position. A file of the back-and-forth letters grew to more than an inch thick. Rather than continue debating the issue, Maxwell House eventually sent the three scholars a case of coffee.

Anyone with access to the internet can find the many stories Paul wrote for the *Helena Independent*, which he joined in December 1932 and for which he eventually covered the Montana legislature. Over the years, he become well known for his reporting, his temper, and his prowess on the handball court, winning community tournaments, according to the *Independent*. In January 1936, in addition to his newspaper duties, Paul became the editor of a monthly magazine, *Montana Fish and Game*

Notes, put out by the Montana Fish and Game Commission. I'm sure the extra money he earned as editor was welcome during the Depression. Because his brother was behind in card games and was drinking too much, Norman encouraged Paul to move to Chicago, work for the university, maybe get a second degree, just get out of Montana for a while. Norman had agreed to ask Paul to relocate at the urging of his father, who told Norman his brother was headed straight to hell if he stayed in Montana. The Reverend asked Norman to help his brother, and he did as he was asked. On March 15, 1937, a story in the *Helena Independent* reported that Paul had left Helena the previous Friday evening on a train for Chicago, where he was to work with William Morgenstern as the assistant publicity director for the University of Chicago.

Sometime in March 1938, Paul met Lois Nash, a 1930 University of Chicago philosophy graduate from Champaign, Illinois, who was working for an insurance company. Four years younger than Paul, Lois was small, attractive, and capable. Her high school yearbook shows she was an intelligent and well-rounded student, involved in honor societies and clubs. After Paul's murder, she told authorities that she and Paul had been planning to marry, though they hadn't yet announced their engagement. In a letter to his mother dated March 31, 1938, Paul was chatty and upbeat, telling her that the suddenly springlike Chicago weather was lovely. He didn't mention Lois to her nor to his father in an April letter.

The life he presented in letters to his parents isn't a complete reflection of what was going on. Paul didn't mention wedding plans. He was used to keeping the details of his life private, so their engagement could have been just another secret. Was he really planning to marry Lois, or was a promise of marriage a convenient route to intimacy with her? He mentioned being in "tip top physical condition" but doesn't talk about his nighttime wanderings through South Side neighborhoods. In his letters, Paul comes across as a dutiful son who attended church and a supportive brother who wanted Norman to finish his dissertation. He wouldn't have mentioned to his abstemious mother that the repeal of

Prohibition gave him easy access to a plethora of Chicago bars, taverns, and beer gardens. If he were gambling again, as Norman believed he was, he certainly wouldn't have talked about it.

On Sunday, May 1, 1938, after a late breakfast, Lois Nash and Paul rode the L to Comiskey Park for an afternoon baseball game—the White Sox played, and lost to, the St. Louis Browns. After the game ended, the couple then stopped at a tavern and visited a friend's apartment, before Paul took Lois home to her apartment at Fifty-First Street and Greenwood Avenue. He left between nine thirty and ten fifteen that night, she remembered, telling her he was tired, presumably heading to his rooms in the Weldon Arms, an apartment hotel at Sixty-Second and Ingleside Avenue, a little over a mile away. She never saw him again. The last person to see Paul alive was a witness who saw him at about one in the morning, scuffling with two other men at Sixty-Third Street and Drexel Avenue, then walking away as the men drove off. About six in the morning, two men found Paul lying unconscious, but alive, in an alley between Rhodes and Eberhardt Avenues, four one-dollar bills, an empty wallet, and a cigarette case nearby, his pockets turned inside out. Paul was taken to Woodlawn Hospital, a few blocks away, where he died a little after 1:00 p.m.

There's a lot of speculation about what happened to Paul Maclean, and why. Some people believe his death was a mob hit, which to me seems far-fetched, given the mob in 1930s Chicago was clannish and either Italian or Irish. What could he have done in a little over a year to motivate the mob to kill an employee of an egghead school like Chicago? It seems ludicrous to believe the high rollers at the "big stud poker game at Hot Springs" would have tracked Paul to Chicago and murdered him in an unfamiliar and heavily policed large city. It could have been, as Norman suspected, that Paul—who had what today would be called a gambling addiction—had incurred gambling debts somewhere in Chicago that he couldn't pay. Another half-baked theory percolating online also says Paul was dating an African American woman. I don't think this is true, but who knows? One Associated Press newspaper story in the *Manchester (NH) Union Leader* says seven women, three of them African American, were questioned in Paul's death. Two Black women and one Black man were seen near the place where he was found. Nothing came of these inquiries. Paul liked to flaunt convention, if we believe Norman's story about his brother dating a Native American woman in Montana, but Chicago in the 1930s was very tribal—the African Americans who settled the South Side by and large had fled the racism of the South, and they weren't likely to mix with whites romantically.

I believe Paul's arrogance and belief in his own street-fighting abilities led to his death. What did good ol' stick-in-the-mud Norman know about late-night Chicago? Or gambling? Paul didn't put a premium on safety—he liked to challenge authority, and charm went a long way. If Paul wanted to walk around different neighborhoods at night, carrying almost fifty dollars in his pockets, he was going to do it. He had punched out a lot of people, and he believed he could take care of himself. He may have been tipsy; some bars in Chicago were open all night.

Norman thought his brother was killed because he owed someone money, and he blamed the death on gambling. Norman never gambled. I believe Paul was the victim of a robbery that morphed into a murder—given what little we know about Paul, I don't believe he would have given up his money willingly. Who knows whether he was targeted or was just another guy who got robbed? It could be the men he fought with on Drexel Avenue a few hours before his death later robbed and killed him. We'll never know. The Chicago police talked to numerous witnesses but never found even a suspect.

I drew a map of Paul's known whereabouts on the night of his death, trying to figure out where he was and when he was there. I was struck by how all the sightings and events south of the Midway happened within a few blocks after he took Lois Nash to her Greenwood apartment. It reminded me of another map, one plotting the deaths of thirteen young men at Mann Gulch, outside Helena. Both events are heartbreaking, leading to an inevitable phrase that must have plagued Norman his whole life: *if only*. If only the firefighters had had a few more minutes and gained a few more yards, likely more of them could have made it to safety. If only they had listened to their foreman. If only Paul had decided to walk on this block instead of that one, or reached his rooms, he might not have been murdered. If only Paul hadn't died in the spring of 1938, the Reverend might not have died three years later. If only the Reverend hadn't asked Norman to bring Paul to Chicago, Norman wouldn't have carried such a burden for so many years, thinking he had failed his brother. I can't imagine the anguish and guilt Norman must have felt and the anger and sorrow at being robbed of someone he hoped was going to accompany him through his life.

Both Norman and Paul had been members of Beta Theta Pi at Dartmouth, and Norman was involved with the fraternity chapter at the University of Chicago. When the members of Beta Theta Pi heard about Paul's death, they walked to the Maclean apartment, intending to tell Norman how sorry they were, member George McElroy told me. But they didn't know what they should say, so they just stood outside the apartment for a while, humming. Fraternity member Gene Davis immediately sent Norman a note about Paul. Norman's replied: "My dear friend, You are wonderfully kind and fine. I know because my brother told me. Norman."

On May 3, Norman took his brother's body by train home to Missoula for burial. Jessie didn't accompany him. If we believe the version in "A River Runs Through It," Norman and his parents didn't talk much about Paul's death, though Norman did tell his father the bones in Paul's right hand had been broken. Norman was so distraught at the funeral parlor that he ran into a plate glass door as he left. Hundreds of people jammed into First Presbyterian in Missoula for the afternoon funeral on May 6. Dr. David E. Jackson, minister of First Presbyterian, and Reverend Everett Top officiated. Church members said that both the Reverend and Clara aged visibly after Paul's death—he had been the favorite child of both. After the funeral, Norman and his parents went to their Seeley Lake cabin, and they took walks among the tamaracks, where yellow and white glacial lilies were blooming. Norman's mother insisted on calling the flowers lilies, and not dogtooth violets as some people did, and his father and he agreed that was the better name. Talking about flowers was a way not to talk about Paul. A coroner's inquest later in May determined Paul was the victim of a robbery "by persons unknown." After talking with the police during their investigation into Paul's murder, Lois Nash stayed in Chicago. She married William Dickson in 1941. They had no children.

Two days before he died, in 1941, the Reverend wrote Norman a letter describing the Christmas celebration he and Clara had enjoyed with friends in Missoula. He told him about a holiday display. In the front room were photos of the two Maclean sons decorated with evergreens. Norman's photograph was surrounded by cone-bearing branches, and Paul's was surrounded "with heavier branches which slightly covered his face," the Reverend wrote. "Mamma objected to having the picture so concealed in any measure, but I contended that although he too was present, he was partially concealed from us, and I had my way."

8

Creating the Committee

IN EARLY AUGUST 1974, I decided I wasn't doing much good in Seeley Lake and decided to return to South Carolina. Norman drove me to Missoula, where I spent the night with Bud and Janet Moore, who took me to the airport the next morning. Except for the casting lessons and getting to know the Moores a little, it had been a disappointing eight weeks, and I was exhausted. For Norman, the summer gave him time to ruminate, revise, and continue working on what he considered a suitable draft of "A River Runs Through It." The past several months, the story hadn't been "gelling," said Joel Snyder.

The version he read to me was one of several. Was he writing fiction or nonfiction? Autobiography? History? Poetry? A combination of all of these genres seems the best answer. He was idealizing his family in order to make art out of the tragedy of his brother's death. We have no clues about his parents' relationship and not much about his mother's role in the family. And from the time he finished a version of each story, until he corrected galleys for the entire collection, Norman was fine-tuning the manuscript, striking and adding phrases and words and then sending out copies to friends and family members, including George Croonenberghs, Kenny and Dotty Burns, and Don Morris, the editor of the *University of Chicago Alumni Magazine*. Suffice it to say that some of his Burns relatives didn't appreciate the character Neal, who was partially based on Jessie's brothers.

Norman had lived the experiences in the stories, but he had not lived the exact stories that unfold in the book. He had worked for the Forest Service as a teenager while older men were fighting in World War I, as does the protagonist in "USFS: 1919." He had worked in the woods as a lumberjack while attending and after finishing Dartmouth, as does the narrator of "Logging and Pimping." He had a minister father who taught him and his younger brother to fly-fish, a younger brother who came to a bad end. And though he often said he had told his children versions of the stories in *A River Runs Through It and Other Stories*, his daughter, Jean Maclean Snyder, says that isn't true. Norman didn't talk about Paul, she said, not even to her mother, who had known Paul well. Norman told friends he was "trying to take old western bear stories and turn them into art": "I am trying to take historical remembrances and reminiscences far beyond memories and yet they are memories, and, usually like this story, say they are memories." I'm not sure what genre, if any, Norman was creating, but the tone is melancholic. He wasn't happy with what he had written; the highlight of his summer had been watching from his cabin as two moose swam from the lakeshore into the sunrise, their antlers "ablaze" in the sunlight.

Undergraduate classes at the University of Chicago started at the end of September. Waiting for the residence halls to open, I briefly stayed at Norman's apartment with friends who had been house-sitting for the summer. There were photos in the hallway and bedrooms that Norman had taken, of a smiling Jessie wearing a necktie and a hat at a jaunty angle and of Paul wearing a sweater and holding a cigarette. I had a hard time imagining such a handsome man had been murdered. Norman was toughing it out in the unheated cabin in Seeley Lake, stoking the fireplace for warmth and writing away. When the temperature dropped below freezing, he secured the cabin and headed back to Chicago, and my friends and I moved elsewhere.

In an October 1974 letter to Robert Utley, Norman wrote: "Shortly before my retirement I began to write reminiscent stories. My children wanted me to, and I also wanted to. I felt it was important as one grew old to clarify himself about his life—to see if it ever took on patterns or forms and, perhaps more important, to clarify one's attitude about life especially his own. . . . To date, I have written 3 such stories—one short and the other 2 long, one 100 pages and the one I am finishing will be 10 or 15 pages longer. . . . The story I am finishing up now is in memory of my brother, who was one of the great fly fishermen of his time and who was murdered when he was 32. . . . I should have a first draft ready to go to the typist in another month."

In November, Norman delivered a revised version of "A River Runs Through It" to Allen Fitchen at the University of Chicago Press. In recounting how the "little blue book" came to be, Fitchen later told me he stayed up all night reading and rereading the title story and finding it "a work of genius, fiction or not, by one of the university's 'living legends,' crying out for publication." He hatched a plan to send the complete book to an established East Coast publishing house, hoping it would be rejected. Then he would just have to convince the press's governing board to make an exception to the fiction rule and publish Norman's book. He figured that two members of the board, Norman's friends and colleagues Wayne Booth and Ned Rosenheim, could sway the other members.

In the fall quarter, I was taking an independent study in Victorian poetry with Norman and another English faculty member. On our walks, Norman talked about Tennyson, Arnold, and Browning as though they were old friends, about meter and poetic feet, and about his book. His parents had been members of a chapter of the Browning Society when he was a kid. They would get together, talk, and have refreshments and would then read Browning's poetry out loud. Norman had me scanning poems and learning to understand sounds—labial, dental, and velar—and the role of poetic feet so I could better appreciate the poets and the poems and read them aloud.

I felt inadequate, fearing I couldn't learn enough about the technical aspects of poetry to convey what I felt in reading it. He was busy working on his stories in the mornings. Two or three afternoons each week, I climbed to the top floor of Gates-Blake Hall to talk with Norman in his small office. Ned Rosenheim's office was next door, and sometimes he would pop in and offer a comment or two. Norman and I would then walk back toward my dorm on University Avenue, passing the snow-covered clay courts of the Quadrangle Club, where he had played tennis. Toward the end of November, Norman invited a few of my friends and me to his apartment for dinner, a pot roast that must have been delicious because I mentioned it in a letter to my mother. I usually did that only for restaurant food.

At the end of fall quarter, I gave Norman a fifteen-page paper on Robert Browning's "Saul," feeling that it wasn't particularly good or bad, just adequate at best. Norman had other thoughts. In a four-page, handwritten critique, he said it was "just so-so" and was a performance that "lacks distinction." He went on to enumerate the problems in the paper, listing a few ways I could have made it better. One basic thing that would have made the paper better was for me to have chosen a different poet—Browning was his favorite. I think Norman viewed my subpar paper almost as a personal insult, but in those days, I didn't like Browning very much. Norman ended his comments with an acknowledgment that he was being hard on me. He was doing so, he said, because he felt responsible for me. "I am determined you will perform with distinction," he wrote. That critique brought me up short. I remembered what Ned Rosenheim had told me: "To be loved by Norman was to have expectations set on you." I'm sure at eighteen that I was ashamed of myself but unable to appreciate Norman's criticisms. In rereading his comments now, I realize his suggestions were good ones, easily accomplished with effort. From then on, I spent hours writing the papers assigned to me in every course, trying to say something interesting and doing so in a "stylish" way and with distinction.

My independent study and my fly-casting sessions gave me some insight into what kind of teacher Norman had been for the generations of students who revered, and feared, him. With the casting, he had told me the objective and how to reach it, making little adjustments when he felt I needed them, until I accomplished what we both wanted. In evaluating my paper on a Browning poem, Norman didn't belittle me for not knowing something, but he didn't let me off scot-free either. He thought I was smart enough to find out about St. Cecilia's Day, which would have helped me write a better paper, and he wondered why I hadn't known—since I, like him, had been reared going to church and Sunday school—that David the Psalms singer was one of the few figures from the Old Testament who had recognized Christ as the son of God. Why indeed? Had my Baptist teachers failed me? Or was I just lazy? Lazy had no place in the Big Leagues.

Even though he had given a typed, presumably final, copy of "A River Runs Through It" to Allen Fitchen, Norman continued making changes because what he had given Allen was the first draft. In January, Norman finished his revisions. "The story means more to me personally than anything I have written," he wrote to Bud and Janet Moore. "That does not mean, I know, that it is necessarily good. A thing can be so personal that it destroys itself, but I have tried to transcend my personal grief." Of course, he had done just that. Norman gave Allen Fitchen the finished version of all three stories. On January 13, Morris Philipson, the press's director, sent the manuscript of *A River Runs Through It and Other Stories* to a former colleague at Alfred A. Knopf, where it eventually landed on the desk of editor Angus Cameron. In mid-February, Norman sent a copy of the title story to Bud and Janet Moore, telling them: "I spent a year and a half (nearly) writing it. Beyond that, I don't think I'll say anything more about it. It should say itself, and so, among other things, it should say that it is about things that I love."

*   *   *

I saw less of Norman in February and March than in previous months because I had fallen in love with a history major from Evanston who was smart, funny, and kind. We met in a history class. I think Norman approved of him but warned him that, with me, he was dealing with a complicated woman. My history student pointed out that the way Norman described women—as strong and powerful—reminded him of how people talk about horses. I didn't share that thought with Norman. In addition to the history course, I was taking French literature and astronomy and a course on modern British poetry. I felt I lived in Regenstein Library. After I finished working in the stacks, I would study and write—and, occasionally, would bump into Norman there.

According to Fitchen, Knopf editor Angus Cameron called Norman in mid-March to tell him how much he liked the stories and that he would try and make a case for publishing them. But fortunately, or unfortunately, Knopf officials didn't think the stories were right for the publishing house. Unbeknownst to Fitchen and Philipson, Norman sent the complete manuscript to Kenneth Pierce, a former student and friend who was a writer in New York, and Pierce passed it along to a reader for Little, Brown & Company. The reader kept the manuscript all summer, which frosted Norman. Norman liked to say that East Coast publishers had rejected his manuscript, saying "these stories have trees in them," but I'm not sure that happened. It makes a good story, though, and is repeated almost every time someone tells the tale of the book's road to publication.

Years later, as Norman was working on a manuscript that posthumously became *Young Men and Fire*, an editor from Knopf wrote to him, asking if Norman would consider letting him look at the manuscript. Norman corresponded with the editor before realizing he worked for Knopf. In a letter from 1981, Norman bemoaned that he had missed the chance to write a fuck-you response, which could have been "the prose masterpiece for all rejected authors," and said he couldn't understand how such a thing had happened. He told the editor he didn't understand how he could even ask if Norman would consider going with Alfred A. Knopf, "unless you don't know my race of people." He ended by saying that if Knopf were the only publishing house in the world and he were the "sole surviving author, that would mark the end of the world of books."

In 1975, rejection from Alfred A. Knopf, an august, well-regarded East Coast publishing house, was all Fitchen needed to nudge the University of Chicago Press's governing board forward. Norman's close friends and colleagues—Wayne Booth, Ned Rosenheim, and Gwin Kolb—each wrote a letter supporting the book's publication.

"The story is about the accommodation of loss—and rarely, in my experience, have I encountered the unsayable said so well," Booth wrote.

Rosenheim chimed in: "It is hard to assign these stories to a literary species; they are too beautifully shaped to be called memoirs, too movingly personal to be called histories, too respectful of the truth to be called 'yarns.' . . . It is hard for me to see how any moderately worldly reader could fail to be enchanted by this writing."

Kolb said that "Maclean has attempted something new under the sun—short stories that are both compelling aesthetic forms and impeccable historical documents."

The governing board of the press voted on April 9, 1975, to publish *A River Runs Through It and Other Stories*. "I couldn't have been more elated, couldn't have been more excited at the prospect of working with such a rare author toward publication of what I was absolutely convinced would become a literary classic," Fitchen wrote. We now know Fitchen was correct in his assessment of *A River Runs Through It and Other Stories*. It has indeed become a literary classic. As the wheels of publication began rolling, Norman showed the contract to Stuart Tave, then the head of the English department, who told me he skimmed it and encouraged Norman to go ahead and sign.

Norman told him, "But I'm signing away the film rights."

Tave laughed. "Don't worry, just sign it."

Years later, after the movie version of "A River Runs Through It" was released and the copyright had returned to Norman, Tave said with a laugh, "Can you believe I said that?"

Allen Fitchen told me Norman's manuscript was so clean that he had to add only a comma or two. But that isn't true. By poring over Norman's original manuscripts and notes, George Jensen and Heidi Skurat learned that Fitchen had to "standardize" punctuation, capitalization, and hyphenation. Wherever Allen changed something, Norman wrote "stet," and the text reverted to Norman's preference. For example, Norman capitalized the names of fish, and Allen let that slide—even though the *Chicago Manual of Style* disagreed. He also prevailed in having *Through* capitalized in the story and book titles. Compared with other manuscripts, though, Norman's was remarkably free of problems. There were no questions left hanging, no necessary restructuring, no gaps. It was all there, Allen told me. Nick Rudall said *A River Runs Through It and Other Stories* is so satisfying because it contains three recognizable forms: a tragedy (the title story), an epic ("USFS 1919"), and a comedy ("Logging and Pimping"). What more could one want?

"I have already partly accomplished two things that I wanted to do by writing these stories," he told Robert Utley. "I thought it would be important for me in old age to look back on my life to see moments when it took on the beauty of art. I also thought it would be important for me in old age to find out how I had felt about life—and to be doubly sure how I felt about it now. This is a long way from saying that I thought I would find I was a writer."

Norman's friends and former colleagues were amazed that a book, by Norman, was forthcoming. Not because they didn't think he could write—he had been writing memorable letters and zinging reports for years. Not because he couldn't tell a compelling story—he had been telling engrossing stories for decades. What gobsmacked everyone who knew Norman well, said Gwin Kolb, was that Norman had agreed to have something published. That he considered what he had written as meeting his impossibly high standards. And that Norman had written not only stories about early-twentieth-century Montana but also a story that conveys the brief life and violent death of a talented, complicated, and doomed younger brother. Everyone in the English department knew Paul had been murdered in 1938 south of the Midway, Ned Rosenheim told me, even though no one ever talked about it with Norman.

As anyone knows who has looked at his writing output, Norman didn't spend his time turning out scholarly articles, as did most faculty members in the University of Chicago English department. When I was in college, I had no idea of the process for getting tenure in a prestigious university—I thought everyone was there because they were "very good," the highest praise I heard given at Chicago. Of course, that's not true now, and it wasn't true decades ago. Criticism was ethereal, Norman often said, here today and then not relevant tomorrow because tastes change. He may have believed that, or it may have been sour grapes. Years of enduring brutal assessments of his writing from his hypercritical father didn't leave much room for confidence. After receiving tenure in 1940, Norman published two scholarly articles, "From Action to Image: Theories of the Lyric in the Eighteenth Century" and "Episode, Scene, Speech, and Word: The Madness of Lear," both of which were included in the book *Critics and Criticism, Ancient and Modern*. He also gave numerous presentations. This was the decade that marked the beginning of big changes for Norman, involving both his career and his family. He could do scholarship, but he chose to do other things.

In the 1950s, Norman the English literature teacher and Norman the effective administrator joined forces and began putting into place an idea he had kicked around for years. He wanted to create a multidisciplinary program in the humanities, one leading to a master's degree for graduate students. In the spirit of the University of Chicago, the Committee on General Studies in the Humanities would join other multidisciplinary programs on campus that had been offering students individualized courses of study since the 1930s. Having become a full professor, Norman would hand pick the faculty, vet each student, help design the courses, and approve the academic plans. He would be the committee's administrator, promoter, celebrant, and one of its teachers. Under his leadership, the program would increase from fourteen initial students to more than sixty, each admitted with sterling credentials, and it would come to include undergraduate as well as graduate students. He and Jessie would invite those students into their home for potlucks and parties, celebrating their successes and following their futures. Students remembered the Macleans as warm and welcoming.

But while things were coming together for Norman professionally, they were shattering at home. In 1950, the same year she went to work in the university's medical school, Jessie was diagnosed with emphysema. She was forty-five and, like Norman, had been smoking since she was a teenager. Students told stories about Norman chain-smoking in class; one remembered his lighting a cigarette while listening intently to a student and then tossing his lighter out an open window. Years of smoking had given Norman a heart problem, he told me, and in his sixties, he quit cigarettes cold turkey. "But for years, I would dream about smoking, and the smoke would come out of my ears and then form wreaths around my head," he told me. "My doctor told me, 'Norman, if you had never smoked, you would live forever.'"

Friends of the Macleans remembered never seeing Jessie without a cigarette. Lung transplants were decades away, and a diagnosis of emphysema was a slow death sentence. "It wasn't a bring-dinner-over kind of disease," said Jean Maclean Snyder. "It was a gradual thing that you could almost forget about." And though Norman told me he begged her to do so, Jessie didn't quit smoking, even as her disease progressed.

Norman said that when she was using oxygen, she would wear a mask for a while, then take it off and smoke a cigarette. The emphysema fatigued her, he said, but she kept working—she was a career woman—as long as she could. The scope and duties of her medical school job increased until she was not only doing secretarial and bookkeeping tasks but also publishing the alumni bulletin and scheduling scientific meetings, dinners, and alumni events around the country. Along the way, she became the effective housemother for incoming medical students.

Helping Norman cope with these challenges and changes, and greenlighting his Committee on General Studies in the Humanities, was Larry Kimpton. Chancellor Robert M. Hutchins brought Kimpton back to campus from Stanford in 1950 to become a vice president in charge of fundraising, something at which Kimpton excelled. At the end of the year, Hutchins revealed he was leaving the university to join the Ford Foundation, much to Kimpton's dismay, since he had returned to Chicago to work for Hutchins, whom he greatly admired. The board of trustees announced in April 1951 that Kimpton would become the new university chancellor. I imagine Norman was thrilled.

"Larry had to come in looking like a damn Rotarian following this celestial creature," said Ned Rosenheim. "He was the most underrated president in the history of the university."

When he assumed the helm of the University of Chicago, Chancellor Kimpton found an institution with disaffected alumni, few substantial donors, and underpaid faculty, sitting in a neighborhood with a neglected housing stock. The Hutchins College system was "suspect," according to university records. Perceived as dangerous and depressed, the university had difficulty attracting both students and faculty. Kimpton knew he needed to change perceptions as well as realities, and he set about revising the university's academic structure and finding the required money to make physical improvements. It's a testament to Norman's loyalty that he continued to support Kimpton after he jettisoned the Hutchins College, which Norman loved.

In early 1952, Kimpton launched the Boy Scout campaign to raise $325,000—about $3.1 million in today's money. That spring, Norman recalled, there was a mass meeting in cavernous Mandel Hall, led by Chancellor Kimpton and attorney Julian Levi—a Hyde Park native, university graduate, and older brother of Edward Levi, who was then the dean of the law school. Julian Levi was known as "a tough-minded, virtuoso political character, with superb negotiating skills and a reputation for both fearlessness and utter ruthlessness that was worthy of the best Chicago ward political traditions." The meeting brought together university faculty, neighborhood residents, and local bankers. There had been talk about moving the university to Colorado. "At the end of this open meeting we all stood and chanted rhythmically: 'We're here to stay, We're here to stay.' After the chant died down, we elected a committee to organize the South East Chicago Commission." The commission and city officials plowed under historic buildings that in hindsight could have been renovated and rehabilitated. They displaced people, many of them African Americans, from neighborhoods where they had lived for decades. Across the country, urban renewal efforts had similar mixed results. Kimpton had to sell his plans and their results.

"Norman wrote most of Kimpton's speeches," said Richard Stern, a Chicago faculty member, "and the ones he didn't write, he edited."

Kimpton admired Norman's sensitive intelligence. From 1933 until 1955, NBC Radio broadcasted the *University of Chicago Round Table*, assembling scholars from different fields to discuss topics of the day. In March 1952, Norman, Kimpton, and Richard McKeon appeared on the show, talking about "The Humanities and Higher Education." The conversation focused on the question of why study the humanities, and in the Chicago tradition of going granular, the question was divided into what are the humanities and what do they include?

Norman said, "I am glad that you make humanities consist of more than just certain achievements of human beings but also a way of looking at any great achievements of human beings in order to appreciate the human qualities behind them." Later in the program, he used Shakespeare to reveal some of his beliefs:

> I take naturally as my example the case of when one comes to the death of Hamlet. What you feel at that moment, it seems to me, is intrinsic in its value. Hamlet says, "The rest is silence," and his good friend Horatio says, "Good night, sweet prince; and flights of angels sing thee to thy rest!" Now I say that what you say to yourself at that moment is not "This play is going to make me a better man—or a better citizen or help me to adjust my neurosis, or make me a better writer." Some of all of these things may turn out to be true—and I hope some of them will—but I say that, when you read *Hamlet*, that moment in itself is sufficient reason for being.

In the fall quarter of 1952, Norman and other faculty members welcomed fourteen graduate students into the Committee on General Studies in the Humanities, one of the first innovative, individualized, interdisciplinary university programs for humanities in the country. The committee offered a three-year master's degree. The first two years were the junior and senior year of college, plus one year of graduate study, and were geared toward University of Chicago students. To me, the arrangement echoes the academic structure of the Hutchins College. Norman wanted the master's candidates to have both "breadth of view and specialization" and said the broad view had to include history and one of the major humanistic fields.

To get into the program, students had to have at least a B+ average. There were six required courses, listed as Humanities 201, 202, and so on, that introduced students to the advanced study of art, history, language, literature, music, and philosophy. They presented "to the students in a concrete form some of the important methods of investigating the major fields in humanities and at the same time to acquaint them with the diversity of subject-matter in each of the fields," Norman wrote. For literature—the area Norman was associated with—this meant the problems of discovering what an author wrote, understanding and evaluating what he or she wrote, and placing his or her work in different historical contexts to add dimension to that work. Students were also required to write a capstone paper on problems they found during their investigations, "which must always involve relations between two humanistic fields." Arriving in 1955, professional writer Richard Stern was put in charge of both the graduate students and, later, the undergraduate students as they worked on their papers. Stern, who died in 2013 at age eighty-three, wrote twenty books of fiction and nonfiction and is remembered as "the best American author of whom you have never heard."

The number of students admitted into the program was capped at between sixty and seventy—"the number we could entertain at one time in my home," Norman wrote. They crowded into the Maclean apartment on Drexel Avenue, said Gwin Kolb, who lived with his family nearby. "Norman and Jessie liked to invite us over for drinks," Kolb said, "because they had better bourbon."

In a letter to Norman dated May 2, 1952, his mother, Clara, now seventy-nine, wondered about the "finality with which you settled no coming to Montana." Perhaps Jessie's illness or Norman's work with the Committee on General Studies had led to such a declaration. Clara offered Norman one thousand dollars for the purchase of a car, presumably so he could continue to make the trip west. She also said she would be taking flowers to the Missoula cemetery on Decoration Day "and silently prayerfully turn my face to the skies and will feel you present." A few weeks before her eightieth birthday, she died in a Missoula hospital.

With money from Clara's estate, Norman and Jessie bought a large home in Madison Park, a leafy area between Dorchester and Woodlawn, sandwiched between Hyde Park Boulevard and Fiftieth Street. With five bedrooms, three bathrooms, and even a maid's room, it was easily large enough to accommodate crowds. Students recall spending happy evenings at quarterly parties with the Macleans, enjoying animated conversations and arguments, ample alcohol, and food with other students and faculty members.

Another reason the number of admitted students was limited was because the committee was built "on close personal relations, close personal relations among our own students, and among our students and our faculty," Norman wrote. The committee was "a place where a student can try the world on for size and see what of it fits him best, or, if he already knows, a place where he can take one last big look around," Norman wrote. "In the end, though, I think one of our greatest functions is to give students an opportunity to discover themselves."

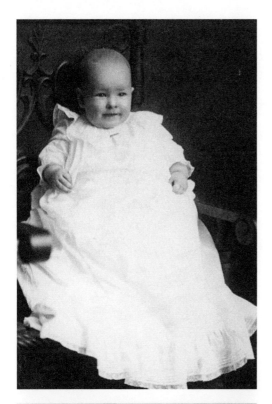

Seen here at nine months old, Norman resembles his mother, Clara, and her Davidson relatives.

This studio portrait shows the Reverend John Norman Maclean in his late thirties or early forties. With his alert expression and round glasses, he looked like the scholar he was.

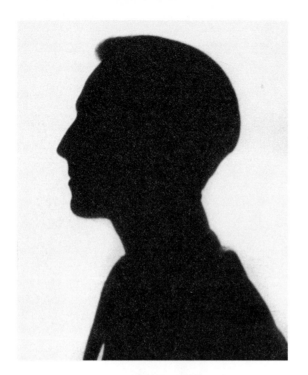

Norman took a lot of silhouettes, shining a light, set up behind the subject, through a bedsheet, a technique he likely read about in *Popular Photography*. In the early 1930s, he created a lot of silhouettes of himself and his friends.

A flapper in the 1920s, Jessie Burns Maclean's outgoing personality is on display in this photo, in the jaunty tilt of her hat and her mischievous smile. She is dressed in men's clothes in imitation, perhaps, of Marlene Dietrich, whom Norman adored. Norman took this stylish photo in 1933.

In this 1933 shot, Norman is copying the style of elegant photographs, showing us Jessie relaxing on a couch. It's unbalanced, but it works *because* it's
unbalanced. Our eyes go straight to Jessie, which is what he wanted.

Here the Reverend Maclean, dressed to go fishing in Seeley Lake, is tying a
fly to the leader on his fly rod.

Tapped to run the Humanities program in the Hutchins College in the 1930s, historian Ferdinand Schevill hired Norman as an instructor and set him on his life's course as a college teacher. Invited to Schevill's summer home on Lake Michigan, Norman met many members of Chicago's literary community, all of whom were friends with Schevill.

Paul Maclean in 1936, wearing his street clothes as he waded into the Blackfoot River to fish. Norman greatly admired his brother as a fly fisherman, believing he was the best of his generation.

Cigarette in hand, Paul Maclean looks intense and defiant. His handsome face drew women to him as honey draws flies. This photograph was in taken in 1936 or 1937.

Lawrence A. Kimpton landed at the University of Chicago in 1943, becoming the dean of students in the university and the administrator for the Chicago Metallurgy Lab. He and Norman bonded over a love of Charlie Russell, drinking, and telling stories.

Jessie and Norman loved Moogan, an Irish setter that accompanied them on walks and trips. Jean Maclean Snyder remembers Moogan from when she was little, when she would lay her head on the dog's tummy. This photo dates from 1945.

University of Chicago student Leslie Travis shows Norman making a point during a 1970 class on lyric poetry. Many students said they developed a lifelong love of poetry after taking Norman's class. Photo courtesy of Leslie Travis.

(*top*) In the early 1970s, forester John B. Roberts Jr. took this photo of Seeley Lake and the Swan Range from Double Arrow Lookout. Built in 1933 by the Civilian Conservation Corps, Double Arrow was one of many lookouts scattered across western Montana. A seasonal employee would staff each lookout, radioing into the district office any suspicious smokes that could blossom into forest fires. Today the lookout is rented to those wanting to stay a night or two.

(*left*) University of Chicago college graduate Leslie Borns was walking around Jackson Park with Norman in 1982 when she took this photo of Norman looking at the lagoon. No matter the weather, Norman took a walk most afternoons, usually around Hyde Park, the university's South Side neighborhood.

9

Searching for a Story

WHEN NORMAN BEGAN his career at Chicago, it clearly wasn't a "publish or perish" world. Teddy Lynn, a beloved teacher in the English department, didn't even have a PhD. Norman wrote little for a decade, though he did take a lot of photographs, of colleagues, family members, and friends in Chicago. Shooting pictures was a way to delay writing his dissertation, which took ten years to complete. On the day of convocation, when he was to receive his hood, he received a letter from Dudley Meek, a friend and publishing executive with Harcourt, Brace and Company. He promised to treat Norman "with the respect due one who has come up unscathed from the torture chambers of Crane and Company." At an upcoming meeting, Meek told Norman he would "see whether a PhD-vocabulary has replaced your very artistic profanity. If I don't hear a profane phrase turned with telling effect, I'll believe that society has lost a true artist."

In the 1940s, Norman was exhausted by administrative and teaching duties as well as from helping to care for his two small children. Standards and expectations changed after World War II. His teaching load was immense—three classes each quarter, usually Shakespeare, Wordsworth, and nineteenth-century poetry. Although he attended several defenses, Norman never directly supervised a doctoral dissertation, though he did offer advice to many graduate students. In the 1960s and 1970s, doctoral candidates in the English department at Chicago had to pass the 75 Book Exam before continuing on to a PhD. The books were drawn from every genre and period—plays, prose, and poetry, from Aeschylus to Tennyson to Orwell—and any departmental faculty member could drop in during any student's oral exam and ask any question. It was an incredibly fraught experience for graduate students. Norman was known as a fair, and supportive, attendant who wanted students to succeed, but he still managed to scare the bejesus out of some of them.

PhD candidate Robert Cantwell, who later taught at UNC at Chapel Hill, recalled that during his exam in the 1960s, when Norman entered the room, "my aqueous brain was suddenly and swiftly evacuated." Norman tossed Cantwell a softball question, "To what does Dr. Johnson appeal beyond criticism?" Cantwell said that even though most English undergraduates at Chicago knew the answer by heart, he was so discombobulated by Norman's presence that he couldn't recall that "there is always an appeal open from criticism to nature," much less anything else. "I don't remember how I got through the exam, which transpired as in a dream, but somehow I passed it."

Terry Myers, who earned his MA in 1968 and became a professor at William and Mary, said that during his exam, he "ran into problems" with Professor Elder Olson, "who had a disconcerting way of asking questions and then cutting the responses off if he thought the candidate could answer the question" or if he thought the candidate couldn't. Thrown off by Olson's methods, Myers felt he was "on the ropes" and "about to go down for the count" until Norman intervened, wrestling away the interrogation and then asking questions "that let me formulate what I wanted to say without the pressure of having the rug pulled out from under me each time I started. I've always been grateful to him for rescuing me."

Throughout his long career at Chicago, Norman invested his time and talents primarily in teaching college students. The letters, notes, and recommendations he sent to and for undergraduates are voluminous—literally hundreds of documents. That's what he was writing, letters for students and letters to friends and colleagues, letters to awards committees, letters to prospective graduate students, letters to employers and more letters. But he wasn't writing scholarly papers. From the 1950s onward, said Gwin Kolb, whose area of expertise was the eighteenth century, "there was the feeling among some people that Norman wasn't a scholar because he never published a scholarly book." But as his output in the 1950s shows, Norman could "do scholarship," Kolb told me. "He was very solid."

Published in 1952, *Critics and Criticism, Ancient and Modern*, featured chapters by Ronald S. Crane and his neo-Aristotelian acolytes. That group included Norman. His first chapter in *Critics and Criticism* is "From Action to Image: Theories of the Lyric in the Eighteenth Century." It's rigorous while reflecting Norman's sly humor: "Few of the late-eighteenth-century writers who deluged the printing facilities with lyric stanzas and sonnets left much in the way of critical opinion, and this is unfortunate. Not that great critical systems abounded then which perished for want of a publisher." A footnote in the essay indicates that Norman's chapter on the eighteenth-century theories of the lyric is part of a larger project he's planning that "will follow the long discussion about lyric poetry from the time when it first became audible to the present" and will relate criticism to philosophy and poetry. Unfortunately for scholars who focus on the lyric, Norman never completed this larger study. Did he think he wasn't up to the task? Or did he simply lose interest? He seems to have been an author in search of the right story.

His second book chapter, "Episode, Scene, Speech, and Word: The Madness of Lear," reads like a poem itself—in places, it scans. As in his other chapter, Norman is funny as well as insightful. Consider: "We must recognize, however, that a certain number of critics read *King Lear* in such a way that Gloucester's lines are taken as a condensation of Gloucester's and Lear's and Shakespeare's ultimate 'philosophy,' although this seems to me to be an interpretation of another book, possibly one written by Hardy." Gloucester famously claims, "As flies to wanton boys are we to th' gods; / They kill us for their sport." As Mary Ellis Gibson, the Arthur Jeremiah Roberts Professor and Chair of English, Colby College, a scholar of nineteenth-century literature, told me in a 2015 interview, Norman here is skewering existential critics without naming them—he reads the play's ending as about tragic love, not existential angst. Norman goes on to note, "Scholars are still in search of the exact meaning of certain speeches in each of Shakespeare's great tragedies—and we should like to assume that those who saw these plays for the first time did not have perfect understanding of all of the lines—but so great was Shakespeare's power to conceive of action from which thought and feeling can be readily inferred that all of us know Lear, Hamlet, and Macbeth more intimately than we know many men whose remarks we understand perfectly." To Gibson, Norman here sounds like someone who was tired of faculty meetings and administrative claptrap. He defends mystery—and intimacy.

"I still admire the usefulness and the critical acumen of the essay—after all these years," Gibson wrote to me. "But I admire the essay's structure and its poetry even more. Norman makes a strong, if implicit, argument that only a fool would prefer the Folio version of his favorite line, rather than the Quarto version (there are two equally authoritative versions of Lear which differ in important respects, including this line). The single line Norman parses, 'Hast thou give all to thy two daughters? And art thou come to this?' he reads brilliantly. From the Quarto, as the more beautifully done. He reads the line all the way down to the scansion."

This essay still holds water more than seventy years after it was published. Clearly, Norman *could* do scholarship. Teachers at Dartmouth and Chicago had approved of his writing. David Lambuth, who wrote *The Golden Book on Writing*, thought Norman wrote so well that he hired him after graduation to teach freshman composition. James Dowd McCallum sent him a note after Norman sent the Lear essay: "The essay marches steadily to your conclusion. It is compact, frequently pithy, and even moving." Norman's dissertation had been solid enough to prompt a letter from Professor Ronald Crane himself a few years later, urging Norman to rework his ideas into a book. "What I want to convey to you now is the very great satisfaction I have had in the clarity of your narrative and in the maturity and wit of your reflections," Crane wrote. "You have the groundwork of a first-rate book. May it be finished soon!" Despite this hearty thumbs up from his major professor, Norman never did transform his dissertation into a book. He didn't share these positive opinions—or at least he didn't act on them.

I believe the years of having his father as a teacher made him his own worst critic. He tells the story in "A River Runs Through It" of having to write daily themes for his father, gradually paring down what he wrote until his father found it satisfactory and then threw it away. Little that Norman wrote was good enough for him—or for anyone else. As he told Richard Stern: "I know my writing has more than its share of blemishes. Words to me are things you take chances with both in what you say and how you say it, and these long shots don't always pay off." And spending days in the stacks as many scholars did just wasn't something he wanted to do. He wanted to spend his summers in Montana, not in the Bodleian or Beinecke library.

Perhaps most importantly, I think Norman was intimidated by Ronald Crane, who was part of the sweeping changes that Chicago president Robert Maynard Hutchins made during his administration in the 1930s. Hutchins divided the university into four branches—physical science, biological science, social science, and humanities, with the college as a separate entity. Richard McKeon, who had arrived from Columbia University to teach philosophy, became the dean of the Humanities Division, and in 1936, Crane became the chair of the English department—he had joined it in the 1920s. Both men advocated jettisoning the traditional way of studying literature and instead applying Aristotelian methods of logic and analysis to texts. His acolytes and he were called the neo-Aristotelians. In place of literary history, students would focus on literary criticism. Younger faculty members, including Norman, embraced Crane's ideas, while some of the older department members did not. The disciples called the chairman "boss."

Crane was a teacher who, according to Elder Olsen, "presented not a mass of facts but a narrative" and an inquiry into the construction of his own narrative. Crane raised questions: What was a fact? When did a fact become evidence? What kinds of history are there? What was a hypothesis? In a seminar, according to Crane, participants pursued questions for which the professor didn't have answers, and they developed insights into foundational ideas underlying scholarship. Crane's ideas about literary criticism had a profound effect on the teaching of English literature on university campuses across the country. I think Norman felt he couldn't meet Crane's expectations, so he decided not to try. Perhaps he found he didn't agree with the boss's ideas but didn't want to challenge him.

"Crane was a serious thinker," said Herman Sinaiko, who served as both the undergraduate advisor and a director of the Committee on General Studies in the Humanities after Norman stepped down. "Norman was a deep thinker. That was part of his problem—he felt he just couldn't measure up."

With Crane in charge, the English department in the 1930s developed a reputation for toughness. There was no way anyone would think that someone as intellectually challenging—and sometimes verbally combative—as Norman, W. Rea Keast, Elder Olsen, or Crane himself was the stereotypical effete English teacher. The department required its college students to pass a week's worth of exams at the end of the senior year. These included six hours of open-book tests and a six-hour test on works randomly selected from two hundred titles. Among them were Aristotle's *Poetics*, Darwin's *Origin of Species*, and Gibbon's *Decline and Fall of the Roman Empire* as well as *Moby-Dick* and *Bleak House*. Students didn't know which titles would be chosen, so as they started their junior year, they began reading like crazy. To prepare for the six-hour writing marathon, they picked courses that would help them interpret the texts. Norman's classes became known as ones that would fit the bill.

At the beginning of every quarter, students would jam into Norman's classroom on the first day, whether or not they were registered, hoping he would let them stay. This didn't happen—the rooms were too small to accommodate a crowd. Like the other Aristotelians, Norman used the Socratic method in his teaching. One student remembered how she would blather a pretentious, banal answer, and Norman would respond: "A safe assumption! A safe assumption!" If a student offered an insightful observation, one that may have contradicted what Norman had said earlier in the class, Norman would agree that the student had said something new, adding, "You're right and I'm wrong."

Because his scholarly output was so paltry, Norman was known as an undergraduate teacher. I know he resented being classified as a mere college teacher, and he worked hard to whittle away the chip on his shoulder. I think he felt the English department's university faculty members didn't value his contributions—although Gwin Kolb and Ned Rosenheim thought otherwise. He cultivated a persona for himself—the persona of Norman Maclean, a lone wolf from the mountains of Montana, where men were men. This Norman Maclean was a plainspoken, truth-telling, profanity-spouting, chain-smoking tough guy, whose deadpan delivery could silence departmental meetings and whose stare could quiet a room of chattering students. Those who didn't know Norman well were afraid of him. He was a campus legend a few years after he arrived on campus in 1928. Even though Norman had retired in the early 1970s, his reputation persisted. In 1974, when I was a first-year student at Chicago, some older residents in my dormitory couldn't believe I was friends with him. They watched as he strode into Pierce Tower to leave notes in my mailbox, and they whispered about him to each other.

What did they really know about him or his background? All they knew was you didn't want to tangle with Mr. Maclean.

10

Student and Teacher

NORMAN CAME FROM Missoula to attend graduate school at the University of Chicago in 1928, leaving behind Jessie Burns, whom he would marry in 1931. In the mid-1920s, after teaching composition at Dartmouth for two years and returning to Montana, Norman juggled working in the woods for the US Forest Service and for the Anaconda Company, in lumberjack camps along the Blackfoot River. For a while, he worked on a Guggenheim smelter in East Helena as well.

The work in the woods was dangerous and exhausting. There were no chain saws—loggers cut trees with two-man saws and axes—and there was a real possibility of being maimed or killed by falling trees or branches. Norman was also trying to write. His parents had moved to Helena, where his father presided over the Presbyterian Church in the state of Montana. On a double date with friends in Helena one freezing December day in 1927, Norman met Jessie. With her bobbed hair and shortened hemlines, she was a typical young woman of the 1920s. After the initial date, they saw each other the following June, when she invited him to meet her family. He was smitten.

The oldest of seven children, Jessie was from a Scotch-Irish family that ran a general store in Wolf Creek, a little town north of Helena. She had twin sisters and four brothers, and they all worked in the store. Her parents had a second house in Helena. Jessie was a lively, well-liked, attractive young woman—Norman described her as tall, thin, with red hair—good with numbers, and very social, attending Montana State (later the University of Montana) after high school and pledging a sorority in Missoula. She looked like a 1920s flapper. After finishing her second year of college, she returned to Helena and found a job in the state capitol as the assistant to the state accountant. Norman liked to say he fell in love with her after she drove them in her Studebaker over a high railroad trestle and through a Great Northern train tunnel, completely calm, while he feared for his life. She was confident, empathetic, and intuitive, completely different from the Calvinist Macleans. By September 1928, Jessie's work as an assistant was going well. Norman's brother, Paul, was entering his last year at Dartmouth, and Norman left Montana—and Jessie—to begin a graduate assistantship in the University of Chicago's Department of English.

I think Norman had dreamed of becoming a writer, not a teacher, beginning in high school, when he won an essay contest. In college, his poems appeared in the *Bema* literary magazine and his sarcastic humor in the *Jack-O-Lantern*. Those dreams went up in smoke, literally, when he was teaching at Dartmouth. In Hanover, Paul and he had lived together in a large apartment building on West Wheelock Street. Norman had stored in his top desk drawer some poems and a novel he had been working on for more than a year. One cold February evening, a fire began in the cellar of the apartment building and raced toward the upper floors, where it consumed most of the Macleans' belongings, including the drawer containing Norman's writing. The fire didn't touch the other three drawers. A story in the *Daily Missoulian* said Norman and Paul "barely escaped with their lives." I can't imagine how Norman must have felt. There were no other copies—he had written the entire book and the poems by hand.

"Unlike Thomas Carlyle, I don't think [Mac] ever rewrote it," Theodor Geisel remembered. He may have not known that Mrs. David Lambuth had invited Norman to work on a second draft in the study of their house. If he did rewrite his novel, did he complete it? Did he submit it somewhere for publication? Who knows what happened to the rewritten version, if there were one? He never spoke about it—as far as I know, *A River Runs Through It and Other Stories* was his first long work of fiction. At least it was the only one to be published.

Instead of becoming a writer, Norman had decided that a career as a college professor of English literature offered a way to bridge the two parts of his life: he could teach a subject he loved for nine months of the year and spend three months in Montana, fishing, hiking, and visiting family and friends. He had applied to the University of Chicago because it was relatively close to Montana and because "it was the one institution of higher learning that was thought to exist west of the Appalachians by the populace east of the Appalachians," he told me. Once again, I had to wonder: why did a lifelong hater of New York care about what the eastern populace thought?

*   *   *

In the late nineteenth and early twentieth centuries, the city of Chicago was notorious for its Union Stockyards, where animals raised on western ranches and midwestern farms were shipped and slaughtered for the country's eastern markets. Norman told me he arrived in Chicago to find that when the wind blew, you could smell rotting flesh and offal for miles. Chicago was known for its architecture and skyscrapers, the first in the country, and for its gangsters like Al Capone and Bugs Moran, who controlled the flow of alcohol and the operation of bars and speakeasies scattered throughout the city. It was dangerous but also beautiful, with parks designed by Frederick Law Olmsted, with stately homes and huge, fanciful department stores, with a renowned symphony and an art museum filled with the best collection of Impressionist paintings outside France. Laced with buses, freight trains, and elevated lines, it was a city on the move.

On the South Side, the University of Chicago had opened its doors ten years before Norman was born, funded by the American Baptist Education Fund and millionaire and Baptist John D. Rockefeller. Norman liked to say that the university and he grew up together, both shedding their early association with organized religion. Retail giant Marshall Field donated land for the new school, and architect Henry Ives Cobb designed the campus. For Norman, the University of Chicago started off in the Big Leagues, with a faculty of established scholars from around the world in different disciplines, including physicist Albert A. Michelson, the first American to win the Nobel Prize. For several months before Michelson retired, in 1929, every weekday at noon Norman would make his way to the Quadrangle Club, perch on a stool, and watch the Nobel Prize winner deftly hit billiard balls around the table. A similar scenario wouldn't have happened at Dartmouth, Norman said: a boy from a small, western town mixing socially with a world-renowned physicist who was the first to measure the speed of light.

Homesick for Montana, Norman thought about leaving Chicago, but he didn't. He wasn't one to walk away from a challenge. The university had a democratic spirit that meshed with Norman's western sensibilities. No one wore robes in class. Women were enrolled as students and employed as faculty. Everyone was "mister" or "miss," regardless of his or her level of education. No doubt there were some pretentious professors, but Norman managed to avoid them. At Chicago, the faculty's prevailing attitude was that if you were good enough to get in, you were good enough to join their community of scholars. Your financial status didn't matter. Unlike at Dartmouth, no one at Chicago demanded he wear a tuxedo. As a paid graduate assistant in the English department, Norman divided his time preparing for his own seminars, teaching English composition, and correcting essays and papers from first-year undergraduate students. Jessie wrote to him regularly from Montana. He earned eighteen hundred dollars for teaching nine classes during the academic year.

Norman recounted his graduate assistant days in an interview, noting that the word *assistant* "gives no idea of how little money and how much servility went with it." Many of the first-year students in his composition classes were from the rural Midwest, so he would go home on Friday afternoon, drink "a couple of shots of Prohibition gin," go to bed, and read ninety one thousand–word essays on "How to Fill a Silo." Then he would have to start preparing for his own graduate classes.

In the summer of 1929, Jessie traveled to Chicago by train to live with Norman. The society pages in the *Helena Independent* said she was on vacation, though she didn't return until the following October. Did their families know they were living together? In Chicago, she found a job waiting tables at a neighborhood restaurant, her daughter told me, and she and Norman ate most of their meals there, free of charge. She registered for a French class at the university and also began looking for a better job. That November, a month after the stock market crashed, a procession in the newly completed Rockefeller Chapel welcomed from Yale the university's new president, thirty-year-old Robert Maynard Hutchins. Like Norman, he was the son of a Presbyterian minister. The "boy president" would try to reorder higher education in America and would forever change academic life at the University of Chicago. In addition to organizing the departments into four divisions, Hutchins made the college its own unit. The Hutchins College admitted qualified high school juniors, who would spend their first two years on general, liberal education, leaving specialization for the last two years, when they moved into academic departments and earned a bachelor's degree. Some students were finished with college at twenty.

While Hutchins was busy putting his plans into place, Norman was traveling the world. At the end of March in 1930, he sailed for Europe with the families of Gustavus F. Swift, part of the Swift meatpacking empire, and A. Watson Amour, another meatpacking millionaire. Norman was to tutor the Swift children. According to his son-in-law, Joel Snyder, Norman was offered a steamer trunk, but he declined the offer, saying the trunk was larger than the room he rented in Chicago. As an old man, Norman told me that waking up and seeing the sun rising on the Adriatic Sea, the same sea that had drawn Shelley and Byron, was a sight he never forgot. While abroad, the Chicagoans visited a monastery in the French Alps. Norman noticed that only one monk, the man escorting visitors, was allowed to speak. The cells housing the monks were cold, the beds stone, and the views from their narrow windows beautiful. "You can't help wondering what manner of men with what overwhelming disappointments would withdraw from the world to a life of silence by day and to a stone slab by night," Norman wrote decades later.

He was at the Grande Chartreuse, a Carthusian monastery world famous for creating a chartreuse-colored cordial made from a secret concoction of various flowers. I'm sure Norman was aware that Matthew Arnold had visited the monastery with his bride and that the visit had inspired an 1853 poem, "Stanzas from the Grande Chartreuse." Given his fondness for Victorian poetry, Norman would no doubt have been familiar with Arnold's poem. Norman wrote he had never seen anything like the cordial, and, he believed, neither had Jessie. He bought a bottle, and they kept it for years, not drinking it. The green liquid finally evaporated, leaving behind only glimmering gold flakes.

In July, the Swift family and their tutor returned to the United States. Norman traveled to Montana in August to visit his parents in Helena and his brother, Paul, who was working for a newspaper in Great Falls. Jessie came home to Wolf Creek from Chicago in early September. When she and Norman returned to the University of Chicago campus, their lives changed immediately for the better. To head the Humanities Division, Hutchins had picked historian Ferdinand Schevill, whom Norman described as "warm-hearted . . . to whom nothing human was outside his range of interest." He was one of the few remaining original members of the Chicago faculty. Schevill's responsibility was to construct for the college a yearlong basic course in the humanities, to staff it, and to manage its operation. According to Schevill's colleague, history professor Arthur Scott, the course was designed to generate "straight and independent habits of thinking" and foster in students a "more critical, rational, tolerant, and broad-minded attitude."

The course had ninety fifty-minute lectures over three quarters, with a weekly discussion session for twenty-five students. The students talked about an assigned original document or documents. Schevill, Scott, or other experts in the humanities would give the lectures. According to longtime Chicago college dean John Boyer, the lectures followed a chronological trajectory, combining narrative social and political history with studies of novels and works of art.

To lead the discussion sessions, Schevill hired Jimmie Cate, a history graduate student; Eugene Anderson, a history student; and Cate's pal Norman Maclean. Norman would start his new job in the fall quarter of 1931, a few days after Jessie and he married in Helena at her parents' home. The Reverend officiated at the ceremony, and Norman's brother, Paul, and Jessie's sister Marjory served as witnesses.

Norman's new position meant he earned more than slave wages, and Jessie returned to her secretarial job for Waldemar Koch, head of the department of physiological chemistry. It gave her access to grain alcohol, a useful ingredient during the last years of Prohibition. "And so followed at least ten years of the happiest and most exciting years of our lives, his and yours, I am sure, as well as mine," Norman wrote to Frances Cate after her husband, Jimmy, died. "Remember, Frances, all the excitement of those days of the new Hutchins College, and the wonderful, warm times we had when our staff was invited to Barnswallow. How long ago this was and how lovely."

Barnswallow was Schevill's vacation home in Michigan City, Indiana, a resort town on Lake Michigan accessible by train, frequented by Chicagoans. They called the train the "Yellow Peril." Norman liked to tell a story about meeting Sherwood Anderson and Carl Sandburg, both of whom were friends with Schevill, who knew other members of the Chicago literary scene as well. Norman soon learned that Anderson hated Sandburg, especially the moaning way he read his poetry, "and thought he was full of crap," Norman said in an interview. After one of Anderson's outbursts about Sandburg, Schevill admonished Anderson, saying Sandburg didn't reciprocate Anderson's animosity.

One spring weekend, Norman and Jessie rode the train to Michigan City to be Schevill's guests. Anderson was already there, hoping to beat Schevill in a long-standing game of croquet the two had been playing for years. Norman and the two friends went to visit Sandburg, who was renting a lake cottage with his family. When they arrived, Sandburg was talking on and on about Emerson, "the first really great true American." Anderson interrupted him in mid-sentence to say, "Emerson was the first great Rotarian." And that was the end of the evening. Norman told me he once saw the two writers tussling on the train and broke up the fight before either did any damage.

11

A Choice Soul

NORMAN REMAINED GRATEFUL to the university his whole life for keeping him employed throughout the Depression—the sight of bread lines in the Loop and scores of people riding freight trains in and out of the city were reminders of how others were suffering. His first year as an instructor, Norman earned an award for his outstanding teaching. He was a memorable, and in some cases life-changing, teacher. Dean of the College Chauncey Boucher described Maclean's work in the humanities general course as the product of a "choice soul and a teaching genius. . . . His hold upon students is most remarkable." More than a half-century after leaving the university, alumni who had taken courses or been in lectures with Norman in the 1930s onward remembered him vividly, as a wiry, energetic man, pacing and smoking in the front of the class. He seemed to mumble and talk out of one side of his mouth, they recalled. Early in his career, he developed a reputation for toughness and kindness.

Norman also became known among his colleagues and friends for his artistic photographic portraits. In the early 1930s, Norman had taken up photography in a serious and sustained way, using a Leica II with a

50 mm, f/3.5 Leitz Elmar lens. It must have been a gift from a university donor because Norman couldn't have afforded such an expensive camera on his meager salary. He put the camera to good use, experimenting with style, setting, and lighting. Taking photos was one way to stay busy and to avoid working on his thesis, family members say.

The class of 1937 adopted him as an honorary member, and he told them he felt closer to them than to anyone from his own college class. They had started, together, in 1934, when things in the country were dire, and finished four years later, when, thanks to FDR, things were looking up. Norman took his humanities classes to visit the Art Institute of Chicago, one former student said, where "we concentrated on the French Impressionists. I remember that in our discussions afterward he pointed out their use of light and their revolutionary painting techniques. His enthusiasm was contagious." Another student described him as intense "and so into his subject that his enthusiasm was catching. Quick of speech, lighthearted in quipping and joking, even sarcasm overlaid with tolerance and good will. Boredom out of the question."

He kidded with the wunderkinder in the Hutchins College, telling them, "You guys think you're so sophisticated, but compared to Egyptian youth in the days of the Pharaohs, you're like monkeys climbing in the trees." One student remembered how kind he was to her after her mother was killed in a car accident: she wondered if she had really earned the A she received in the course. Another said Norman would back up to the blackboard, throw his tie over his shoulder, and cross his eyes, just to get the class's attention. A Catholic student was startled to hear Norman announce one morning that Christians should be called "Paulists" instead of Christians and that the Catholic Church had the sanest teachings on sexuality—this from a Presbyterian minister's son with no experience of nuns railing against sins of the flesh. What could he have been thinking? In a letter to Clara Maclean, Jessie described Norman giving a 1935 lecture on *The Song of Roland* in Mandel Hall, a cavernous auditorium with horrible acoustics:

He came on the platform grinning and they [the students] gave him a big hand. He looked beautiful far away down in front over the heads of hundreds of students. . . . He started out by saying: "I am talking today about a lean, hard poem. I am talking about a fighting poem"—you know the way he would say it, making the words lean and hard and fine and liking to talk about the fighting. It is a fine lecture. He had the kids with him from the minute he stepped on the stage. . . . When it was over, they gathered in groups and talked about him and about the lecture and the ones who knew him were proud and the ones whom he didn't know wished that they did and determined to hear more of him. I went on to work with his voice ringing in my ears and my heart singing with pride.

No doubt Clara was also proud of her elder son.

*   *   *

What was the family like that had produced such a person as Norman? And what was the Montana he tried to capture in his stories? When his parents moved from California to Montana in 1897, the state was only eight years old, and it had the feel of the frontier. There were cattle and wheat farms, but by and large, it had an extraction economy: natural resources such as gold, silver, copper, and timber were mined, refined, cut, packaged, and shipped out of state. A little over twenty years earlier, the Battle of the Little Bighorn—in what was to become southeastern Montana—had spelled the end of the free Sioux Nation.

Born in 1862, before the Little Bighorn, John Norman Maclean grew up on the frigid slopes of Beaver Mountain, in Antigonish County in Nova Scotia, one of ten children, seven girls and three boys. The family had its roots in the Scottish island of Coll, where MacLeans (with a capital L) had been lairds for more than four hundred years. John Norman's grandfather and his father were both carpenters, and he learned how to handle tools from his father. He attended Dalhousie College in Halifax, where he wrote for a monthly humor magazine—his articles and poems usually focused on fishing. John Norman finished his undergraduate degree at the University of Manitoba in Winnipeg, having gone west to ease his respiratory problems. He stayed in Winnipeg to attend seminary and earned an MA in theology. Though John Norman had headed inland to Manitoba, most of his sisters, and his brother Neil, stayed on the coast, migrating to Boston, along with their mother, where they opened a laundry. They were all proud of John Norman and his career as a minister because, unlike the other men in the family, he made his living with his head, not his hands.

Working as a schoolteacher in 1889 and 1890 at Mowbray School in southern Manitoba, Clara Davidson met John Norman one summer when they both were evangelizing for the Presbyterian Church in the province. She had started teaching when she finished high school, but she also took classes at the University in Manitoba, though university records show she never received a diploma. After earning degrees in Canada, John Norman traveled even farther west to attend San Francisco Theological Seminary in San Anselmo, California. After his ordination in 1893, he could accept assignments from the Presbyterian Church in the United States. He and Clara were married on August 1 of that year in Manitoba. The Reverend then took his bride back to California, where, for the next four years, he became the full-time minister north of San Francisco, in Vacaville, a congregation he had served while in seminary. After Vacaville, they spent five years in Bozeman, where they were naturalized as American citizens in 1900 and where the Reverend took over the oldest Presbyterian church in the state. There was great fishing in the area, and I'm sure the Reverend was on the Gallatin, Madison, and Yellowstone Rivers as often as possible.

In 1902, the Reverend and Clara were called to a church in Clarinda, Iowa, a bustling little city close to the Nebraska border, where Norman was born on December 23 of that year and Paul on November 5, three years later. The Macleans became beloved members of the Clarinda community, and they stayed almost eight years before returning to Montana.

Like many small midwestern towns, Clarinda was laid out in a grid centered on a wide-lawn courthouse. Chestnuts and Dutch elms shaded the town's streets. The nearby Nodaway River meandered southward through wide cornfields that stretched to the horizon. Summer brought blazing heat. Winter transformed the scene into a white landscape, interrupted here and there by a distant silo. The 1900 census of Clarinda had tallied 3,276 residents, most of whom would have known the new preacher and his charming wife.

It was a prosperous community, with businesses supplying the needs of surrounding farms or processing agricultural products for market. The town had two schools, a Carnegie Library, and a mental health asylum. Hawley's Opera House attracted vocalists and touring companies. And there were church suppers, amateur theater performances, picnics, and community dances. Clarinda was a safe, sheltered place, with fourteen churches, mostly Presbyterian and Methodist. There were no police officers, just two night watchmen, and the jail was usually empty. Each August, Clarinda hosted a Chautauqua assembly at its fairgrounds, featuring two weeks of concerts, speeches, lectures, and talks from authors, explorers, and political leaders.

No doubt, Clara found Clarinda's proper pleasures gratifying. And what may have delighted her most was that like the rest of Iowa, Clarinda was dry—no liquor license had been issued there since 1882. Druggists couldn't sell alcohol even with a doctor's prescription. Clara was a lifelong teetotaler and a member of the Woman's Christian Temperance Union, which promoted abstinence and preached against the evils of alcohol. Even when Norman was an adult, neither he nor Jessie ever drank liquor in front of his mother—though they were both glad enough to toss a few back when outside the maternal orbit.

Not long after their arrival in Iowa, a story in the *Clarinda Herald* described a welcoming reception at which the Reverend's parishioners "invoked his work and help," but his wry response was that he never did any work "he could get someone else to do." He also said he wouldn't undertake any civic reforms, and he expressed the opinion that it paid to attend to one's own business. As a new US citizen, perhaps he thought he should just keep his head down and focus on his flock. The following Sunday, he took the pulpit at First Presbyterian and delivered a sermon on one of his favorite New Testament passages, the miraculous draft of fishes. In the story, after a night of poor fishing, the soon-to-be disciples throw their nets off the right side of the boat, as Jesus directs, and haul in a copious catch of fish. An accomplished and avid fly fisherman, the Reverend attached special value to the Bible's piscatorial passages, as Norman later told me.

The Macleans had been in Clarinda a few years when a friend and fellow Presbyterian minister told the Reverend about a pastoral position at First Presbyterian of Missoula. John Norman must have missed the outdoor life. No decent fishing in Iowa. No alcohol in his tea. A 1907 news notice stated, "Mr. Maclean formerly lived in Bozeman and spends his summer vacations there regularly." During one of these trips, he had vacationed in Yellowstone National Park with another Presbyterian minister and had enjoyed it immensely. And with his fondness for fly-fishing, he surely longed for the rivers and trout streams in Montana.

In an interview, Clarinda resident Phyllis Fulk remembered how her father would fish the Nodaway in the 1920s and '30s and bring home "only catfish that tasted like mud." Any reader of "A River Runs Through It" would find it hard to imagine the Reverend bringing home catfish. Missoula would be a better place for teaching boys to fish—and to fish without bait. Although man's chief end may be to glorify God and to enjoy Him forever, the Reverend seems to have been a man who could enjoy Him most while practicing the "art that is performed on a four-count rhythm between ten and two o'clock." He surely rejoiced when called to fill the empty pulpit in Missoula.

On January 28, the Reverend told the stunned Clarinda congregation that the family was heading to Montana. The family's departure in February 1909 was marked by a crowded farewell gathering at a church member's home, during which Clara received gifts from the church's Young People's Society and from the women of the church. There were speeches, tears, thanks, and acknowledgment of Clara's guiding influence. The men of the church gifted the Reverend one hundred dollars—generous in 1909, when a Presbyterian minister's salary averaged less than a thousand dollars a year—to help cover the costs of their lengthy upcoming trip. A few days after the tearful gathering, the Macleans were gone, traveling first to Massachusetts to visit the Reverend's family before heading on to Montana.

* * *

In Montana in the early part of the twentieth century, the Amalgamated Copper Company, later the Anaconda Mining Company, was expanding its grip on the state's economy. It owned copper mines in Butte, the smelter in nearby Anaconda, the forests, the sawmills that cut the trees, and the timber that fed the furnaces, giving the company sway over the jobs and lives of those who worked in the mines and woods. It owned newspapers and legislators across the state, and its influence extended to faculty appointments in the university in Missoula.

The Maclean family didn't know a lot about Missoula when they deboarded from a Northern Pacific train on a snowy February day in 1909. South of the train station was Higgins Avenue, with shops and banks, cafés and saloons, and a large department store, the Missoula Mercantile, which sold fashionable clothes and furnishings. The Higgins Avenue Bridge, rebuilt after a flood the year before, linked the north and south parts of the city. Members of First Presbyterian, who had called Reverend Maclean to his new pastoral position, welcomed the family—John Norman, Clara, and their sons, Norman, six, and Paul, three. They ushered them into a horse-drawn carriage and carted them to the manse on Stevens Street, a few blocks from the church at Stevens and Pine Streets.

From their home, the Macleans could hear the whistle of the Northern Pacific trains, carrying to market produce and lumber from the five mountain valleys that emptied into Missoula. The city library was within an easy walk. The growing state university was nearby, across the Clark Fork River. The Maclean family would learn that although Missoula was settling down into a regional center for commerce, education, and culture, it still had vestiges of a wide-open western town, with ample opportunities for vice and sin. At the far end of West Front Street, prostitutes worked out of redbrick cribs. Honky-tonks took the wages of drunken lumberjacks, ranch hands, and miners. Gambling was illegal, but bribes kept the dice rolling, and many saloons never closed. Some proprietors made a show of dropping the building's key down the toilet on the opening day. Historian Lenora Koelbel claims that in the early twentieth century, a lumberjack walking back to camp from Missoula might stagger off the road, get lost, freeze to death, or be eaten by wolves.

Two developments shortly after their arrival brought home to the Macleans just how different western Montana was from Iowa. Missoula was to become the setting for a free speech struggle that October involving Elizabeth Gurley Flynn of the Industrial Workers of the World. Local miners stood up against mine owners to gain the right to openly organize a union. The second, more memorable, event occurred in the summer of 1910: the biggest forest fire of the twentieth century. After April of that year, no rain had fallen in eastern Washington, northern Idaho, or western Montana. Throughout May, June, July, and half of August, the forests dried and baked. Cinders thrown from the coal-powered Chicago, Milwaukee & Puget Sound Railway trains ignited little fires along the tracks in Montana and Idaho. The company hired spotters to handle these fires, but they couldn't keep up. Dry lightning, careless loggers, arsonists, and homesteaders created other fires.

By mid-August, an estimated three thousand small fires were burning from British Columbia to Montana. On August 20 a cold front out of eastern Washington with hurricane-force winds crossed the Snake River and slammed into the region, blowing the smaller fires into one giant conflagration that created its own weather system. It leaped across lakes and rivers as it swept over Idaho and western Montana, burning three million acres, killing eighty-five people, gobbling up towns, and spewing airborne ash so thick and black that day became night. The smoke was seen in New York, and ships as far as five hundred miles off the Atlantic coast couldn't navigate by the stars. This catastrophe shaped fire policy for years to come, convincing local, regional, and federal officials of the need for a national system of forest management. Only five years old, the US Forest Service established its first regional headquarters in Missoula.

Even as they settled into the community, the focus of the Maclean family remained First Presbyterian Church. Although Reverend Maclean wasn't their first choice, the congregation was grateful to have him as its minister. "He is considered one of the brightest of the younger ministers of the Presbyterian Church and the Missoula congregation is considering itself fortunate in being able to bring him from the east," read a story in the *Weekly Missoulian*. In Clarinda, he had left a "greatly attached people" and a town that valued "highly his moral and intellectual qualities." A story in the *Clarinda Herald* about his resignation a few months earlier said Reverend Maclean "is no sensation monger" nor "the kind of tradesman who has all the best goods in the front window."

At forty-six, he was unpretentious, sincere, sympathetic, and "patient with the processes of truth," the story said. Standing almost six feet tall, Reverend Maclean was handsome, slim, and looked the scholar, his wire-rimmed glasses shielding bright-blue eyes. His thick mustache was a Scottish red, his hair strawberry blond. He spoke with a slight Canadian accent, rhyming *about* with *snoot* and *again* with *brain*, but he never affected the burr then popular among Scottish Presbyterian ministers. One churchgoer remembered being at a gathering where the Reverend and other Scotsmen were telling stories—the longer they talked, the more their dialects emerged, making them almost unintelligible.

In Missoula, a studied reserve replaced the lively sense of humor and wittiness that had characterized Reverend Maclean in college in Nova Scotia, where he had been known for his quick quips and his funny toasts. When you're considered one of the smartest men in town, you comport yourself as if you are one of the smartest men in town, which means adopting a serious air. And when your father is considered among the smartest men in town, you try hard to measure up to him—in some ways. Pastoral pressures to set a moral example for the congregation also accounted for the Reverend's aloof manner.

"I always felt that my father had lived a somewhat unnatural and unhappy life because he could not swear," Norman said. "Just as Chesapeakes are coded for retrieving, Scotchmen are coded for profanity."

To his Iowa parishioners, the Reverend Maclean had been "a man's man," an outdoorsman often seen out on his own, hunting and fishing the fields and waters of the surrounding countryside. Montana offered many more opportunities for him to indulge his outdoor passions— years later, he and a despondent Clara moved from Helena to Poplar, supposedly for pastoral reasons but really so he could fish the Missouri River. He may have been the only sibling in his family not to make his living with his hands, but the Reverend was a skilled carpenter as well as a crack shot and a good fly fisherman.

In his late fifties, he had handled most of the construction of the family's log cabin on the west side of Seeley Lake, helped first by Norman, then Paul, and even Clara. While Norman peeled most of the bark from lodgepole pine logs, the Reverend notched each one with a hammer and chisel and treated them with linseed oil before joining them together. Sawn from the lake's shores, the notched logs formed a box on top of a foundation of local stone. Paul and the Reverend cut out the doors and windows and did the framing, and with some help from Clara, managed to put on the roof before snow fell.

The *Daily Missoulian* noted that Clara Maclean was said to be "a great helper in her husband's church work and shares with him in the devotion and appreciation of their people." When interviewed in 1999, Missoula residents Dorcus Northey and Helen Helms fondly remembered Clara, who had been their Sunday school teacher. Clara was "bouncy and pretty," they said, "peppy and fun." Clara was "gregarious and well-loved," Mrs. Helms said, and "so lively that her husband was embarrassed by some of her antics," a sentiment echoed by others who remembered them. She was ten years younger and ten inches shorter than the Reverend. A longtime member of First Presbyterian of Missoula, Mrs. Northey, said the Reverend's reserved, sometimes dour, character—"He could be a bit of a Scot"—stood in sharp contrast to his wife's ebullience. At the Seeley Lake cabin, Clara "was one of those chipper ladies who was always pleasant, usually baking a pie or cookies," said Missoula native C. W. Leaphart, who grew up attending First Presbyterian and spent weeks in Seeley Lake in the summers.

The Reverend's formality extended to his family—he didn't want to kiss anyone goodbye on a train platform. Though affectionate with friends and church members—many recalled him hugging different people—he was strict and even cold with his family, never telling his sons he loved them, Norman remembered. The Reverend was also perhaps somewhat vain. In 1910, a friend and fellow Presbyterian minister had recommended to his Iowa alma mater that the Reverend receive an honorary doctoral degree. In June 1910, Parsons College in Fairfield conferred on John Norman an honorary Doctor of Divinity degree. Thereafter, his congregation and the wider community knew him as Dr. Maclean, and newspapers referred to him as "the Rev. Dr. J. N. Maclean, DD." In public, Clara, too, called him Dr. Maclean, though there's no record he ever did any academic work to obtain his new title. Norman said his mother "ran the church" while his father worked on his sermons. She taught both Norman and Paul their letters and numbers. Together, Clara and her husband would build the Missoula church into a center of community life for its many families and, later, for college students at the university.

Although as an adult he considered himself an agnostic, Norman was molded by the family's involvement in church. In addition to the daily readings and prayers, there were Sunday school, two church services, and Christian Endeavor on Sunday evenings as well as a Wednesday night prayer service and supper. When he left home, Norman rejected formal religion and never belonged to a church, but he remained grateful to First Presbyterian for helping make him who he was. Sunday after Sunday, along with two other boys, Harry Urton and Joe Dunham—who also landed in Chicago—Norman served as an usher, seating worshippers, passing the collection plates, and taking the plates to the front for his father to bless. The boys took up the collection "so many years and were prayed over so many times that we never had to look at each other as we carried the plates to the front of the church where we arrived at the same step and bowed at the same moment," Norman said. "We felt bound to each other, and tied together through our shoulders . . . the church of Missoula is forever a part of me. It is something inside of me where I stand bowed and above me my father bends over and prays and to my sides are friends tied to me through my shoulders into my heart and behind me in a pew is my mother very proud of me and her minister and in her lap my young brother lies asleep."

For Norman and Paul, Missoula offered many of the same pastimes as had Clarinda—baseball and football games, swimming, trips to the public library. In both towns there would have been duck hunting and boat rides on the river. But in Missoula, the current of the Clark Fork was swift, and nature was always close at hand. A boy could hike out across the ancient bed of Lake Missoula, see bands of Flathead Indians who had come to camp, and dig camas roots. Bears sometimes wandered into town. In Clarinda, silos and church steeples had been the tallest things for miles around, but in Missoula, mountains dominated the landscape, rising in every direction. An hour's steep hike from his house could take Norman to the top of Mount Sentinel, beyond which lay the forests of the Sapphire Range, peak upon peak, marching southeast to a distant horizon. On Sunday afternoons, his father took Norman and his brother on long walks into the surrounding countryside, up Rattlesnake Creek or out along the Milwaukee Railroad tracks to Spring Gulch. The Reverend had taught Norman to shoot at an early age, and he spent many afternoons exploring the woods on his own, shotgun or rifle in hand.

Missoula also featured raucous pastimes the boys would never have encountered in Clarinda. Animal fights drew big crowds—cockfights, dogfights, and, most popular, fights between badger and bulldog. Each year, instead of Clarinda's educational Chautauqua assembly, there was the pandemonium of the Missoula Stampede, a huge rodeo that attracted every uncouth cowhand for a hundred miles. And perhaps most significantly, there was downtown Missoula, with its saloons and bordellos, just a short walk from the manse. For a ten-year-old boy, it would have been difficult to avoid direct contact with—or at least, firsthand accounts of—the crude side of Missoula, its lewd whores, saloons, and drunken, randy loggers. There were certain Missoula streets respectable women studiously avoided. A drunk might stand on a downtown street corner with a prostitute on his arm, spew obscenities within earshot of children, and never pay the sorts of penalties a small-town Iowan would have faced. There would be no tsk-tsking tongues, no ostracizing.

As a halfback on the high school football team during his senior year, Norman carried the ball across the goal line to win the game against Butte. His writing abilities landed him on the staff of both the school newspaper and the high school yearbook. He also won a gold medal for placing first in an essay contest by the National Society of Colonial Daughters. His high school yearbook said Norman kept his English teacher, Mabel Rich, "'continuously amused' by arguing with her," adding that given his imminent departure for college, he had "graciously offered to teach some daring young junior the Art of Contradicting Your English Teacher Tactfully."

It has been the fate of almost all preachers' sons to be tested and tormented by their peers, and the situation wasn't any different for Norman and his brother. After they moved to Missoula, the two boys learned to fight, and they did so often throughout their lives there. Though he was younger than the Maclean boys, C. W. Leaphart knew "both of those boys could fight like the devil. In those days, all ministers' sons had to be able to do that because someone was always after them. Those guys could fight with no fear."

There was a division in town between north and south, marked by the Clark Fork River, and Paul and Norman would cross the Higgins Street Bridge ready to swing. "Some guy would try to beat the hell out of my brother and me, just to see what we would do," Norman told me. "Most of them tried only once."

The two brothers would loiter downtown with their friends, telling tales. "There was no radio in those days, so you had to make your own entertainment," Norman said. "We did this by telling stories." Whoever had his story voted best had his evening paid for by the losers. In numerous interviews, Norman said that winning a fight on Saturday night allowed Paul and him to stay in bed Sunday morning; losing meant they had to get up for church. The Reverend knew something about fighting—his father and uncles were known in Antigonish, Nova Scotia, as "the fighting Macleans."

"My parents had us late in life, and we were very precious to them," Norman said. His father was forty when he was born, his mother thirty. "In many ways, they were very lenient." His mother wanted him to be a flower girl, he said, and his father a tough guy, so he became "a tough flower girl," whose temperament and physical appearance were like his mother's. Often he felt closer to her. A little taller, a lot broader than Norman, with chestnut hair and a square face, Paul resembled the Reverend. Norman was handsome, but girls in Missoula thought Paul was "movie star handsome."

As we know from "A River Runs Through It," for the first four years of his life in Missoula, Norman spent half of every weekday reading, writing, and reciting in the manse on Pine Street. After breakfast, Reverend Maclean would first read aloud to the assembled family from the King James Bible or from poets, usually Robert Browning or William Wordsworth. Norman later said his father's reading aloud "was very good for me because in doing that, he would bring out the rhythms of the Bible. That reading instilled in me this great love of rhythm in language." When the Reverend had finished, the family would kneel and pray. The lessons would then begin. While Paul played or read with his mother, Norman studied at a table in his bedroom, while his father worked on sermons in his study across the hall. He would write an essay and hand it to his father, who would read it and tell him to make it shorter and shorter, until his father would throw it away. As an adult, Norman wrote and spoke often about his stern father and the four years of this training. In referring to the writing of "A River Runs Through It," Norman wrote, "It would be more gracious as well as accurate if I said my father in certain basic ways wrote every page of this book when I was between six and ten and a half."

I have long wondered why the Reverend thought it would be better to keep Norman at home and to teach him himself, since there's no indication the Reverend knew anything about teaching children. Clara had been a teacher before she married, and she taught her sons their numbers and letters. Norman wrote that the Reverend "had heard of another Scot, James Mill, who had achieved some spectacular effects by keeping his son, John Stuart Mill, at home by teaching him himself." Maybe he felt that Norman's accomplishments would reflect on his own brilliance. There's no reason to think Reverend Maclean ever physically disciplined Norman or Paul. His harshness was manifested by a lack of emotion and an insistence that his son learn his lessons completely and by frequent, honest, often negative, assessments. Had Norman started public school at six instead of ten, perhaps he would have received a better foundation in mathematics—a deficit that later hampered him. Perhaps early socialization with other children would have made him less judgmental and eased the loneliness he carried most of his life. In some ways, being trained to emphasize literary economy was invaluable, but Norman later admitted he had spent many mornings crying in his bedroom as he pared down a two hundred–word composition, only to have it end as a crumpled wad of paper. Acknowledging that "perhaps the training was too tough and constricting," Norman said his father made him justify every word he used in each paper. Many children have had kinder beginnings.

12

Tragedy and Accident

IN JUNE 1975, Norman headed to Seeley Lake. I stayed in Chicago, working in Regenstein Library and trying to write a missing English paper. My brother John called from Montana one day to tell me Dotty Burns, Norman's beloved sister-in-law, had died in Helena "after a brief illness." She and Norman had been allies, Norman told me, because both had married into the large Burns family, and he missed her the rest of his life. In a handwritten log Norman kept, his July 30 entry says the summer was proceeding "numbly." He realized that having Kenny and Dotty in the cabin—cleaning, buying groceries, fixing meals—had enabled him to write four to six mornings a week. He told himself he now had three options: hire a cleaning woman, marry "or put up with" a woman, or give up his Montana cabin. Norman didn't want to spend his time doing housework—in Chicago, a paid housekeeper kept his condominium tidy. He wanted publication to move faster; he had approved the final copy of "Logging and Pimping" only in the beginning of July and had just received the final copy of "USFS 1919" from the press. He talked with his friend Bert Sullivan, the Seeley Lake postmistress, about his dilemma. She recommended he hire a local woman as a housekeeper, and that woman worked out well.

The log says Norman "hadn't the faintest idea" of what project he should try next, but a talk with Bud Moore the week before convinced him to return to writing about Mann Gulch "after I had almost given up." Mann Gulch was the 1949 US Forest Service catastrophe in which thirteen forest firefighters, twelve of them Smokejumpers, were killed by a roaring fire north of Helena. The Smokejumpers are the Forest Service's elite corps who parachute to fires. Three crew members survived virtually unhurt, including the foreman Wagner Dodge. Norman and Kenny Burns had visited the site in 1949, while the slopes were black and smoking, and Norman was haunted by it. Returning to writing about Mann Gulch would both gratify and frustrate Norman for years to come, and yet he was drawn to the challenge of making art from a tragic catastrophe. As he told Bud and Janet Moore, he had made an appointment to talk with Patricia Morris Dodge Wilson, the widow of Wagner Dodge. She had grown up in his father's church, and they had known each other a long time. He was looking forward to speaking with her about her late husband, who had died of cancer six years after the Mann Gulch fire.

A log entry from September 4 lists the information Norman felt he needed in order to write the book. Much of what he wanted could never be known—since most of the young firefighters had died—such as what was said and thought when crew members decided not to follow the foreman's orders and how the foreman's then-undiagnosed cancer had influenced his decisions during the fire (if it did at all). He also wanted to learn about the character of the firefighters and said, "I have no business trying this story unless I can make people see the fire and the outside and inside of the men." He thought that had Dodge not been exhausted and sick, he, too, would have tried to outrun the fire. He cautioned himself not to "get caught up in any inch-by-inch account of fire—the kind of

Custer battlefield thing—keep to the main stuff and keep it simple." The story had something in common with the Little Bighorn—the young and elite facing a foe they couldn't defeat and dying a good death.

Already, he saw the story in larger terms, that of a "romantic" notion of "youth" versus "authority." Writing a complicated, factual story involves assembling as much information as possible before you start structuring the story—if you focus only on the structure, you may miss crucial details that prove you wrong or don't fit the final structure. The information dictates the structure—or as Louis Sullivan said, "Form follows function." But Norman was right in many ways. Details matter. And, too, Norman wasn't reporting a story; he was telling one, creating it out of ashes. "A storyteller," he wrote, "unlike a historian, must follow compassion wherever it leads him. He must be able to accompany his characters, even into smoke and fire, and bear witness to what they thought and felt even when they themselves no longer knew."

In October, university friends Nick Rudall, Kenneth Northcott, and John Cawelti headed with Norman to Jasper-Pulaski Woods, south of Michigan City, Indiana, to watch sandhill cranes come through on their way south. The expedition had become a tradition for them. While the men were waiting for the birds, their discussion turned to writing, then to Mann Gulch and Norman's problems with the manuscript. Nick Rudall told me that Norman seemed determined to structure the story as a tragedy, and he was grappling with balancing his academic and his literary senses.

"There was a kind of anguish for him," Rudall said. "He wanted the fire to have more of a plot, but it was just an event. It was hard, if not impossible, to make a tragedy out of an accident."

Norman's least favorite Shakespeare play was *Romeo and Juliet*, Rudall said, because there's no sense of a tragedy unfolding; there's just loss. In that play, Rudall saw parallels to what Norman was writing about in Montana—young lives lost through a series of mishaps and mistiming.

But accidents and nature don't produce a full-blown tragedy, at least not in the R. S. Crane sense of tragedy. Moreover, what Norman was unearthing with Mann Gulch was history, and he couldn't square history with tragic convention. And yet Norman spent years trying to make the pieces of the story fit the form he had chosen, just as he had with events surrounding George Armstrong Custer and the Battle of the Little Bighorn. Many things are tragic; few are tragedies. John Cawelti says Norman was trying to reconcile history with imagination. In the end, I believe, imagination and compassion won.

*　*　*

The 1960s and early 1970s saw Norman struggling—to write his book about Custer, to continue teaching, to shepherd the Committee on General Studies, to deal with various health problems, and to accept Jessie's steady decline. He told me she never quit smoking even when hospitalized. As we know now, quitting tobacco is almost as difficult as quitting heroin, but it must have frustrated, alarmed, and angered Norman to watch his wife ignoring his pleas and slowly dying.

In 1960, Norman had another one-quarter spring sabbatical—though he still had to meet his administrative duties—to work on his Custer book. He told Robert Utley in a letter that he hadn't written "a line since last September" and "as you well ought to know by now, writing is largely a matter of courage, or not knowing any better." Later that summer, Norman and Jessie made the drive to Montana. But after 1960, Jessie no longer accompanied him to Seeley Lake—she stayed in Hyde Park and continued working for the medical school's alumni society. She wasn't up to the rigorous lifestyle of the lake. In Chicago, those who knew her professionally loved her. "She was very nice to work for, she appreciated everything you did," said Hyde Park resident Ruth Bowen, who edited notes and interviews for Jessie in the early 1960s. "She was a good editor, and she knew everyone. The

Medical Alumni Bulletin was a good little magazine, and she was very proud of having created it."

In early March 1963, Jessie lost Marcia Kimpton, one of her closest friends. When her husband, Larry, left the university in 1961 to work as a director with Standard Oil of Indiana, Marcia and he had moved from Hyde Park to the near North Side of Chicago. One evening, while Larry was in another room of their house, Marcia was smoking in bed and talking on the phone when ash from her cigarette dropped onto her synthetic nightgown, which burst into flames. Her screams brought Larry running, and he rushed her to the hospital. The fire had burned 60 to 75 percent of her body, and she died in Billings Hospital on March 7. She was forty-eight. Then, in late May 1964, Muriel McKeon, Jessie's other close friend, died of cancer. People remember Jessie sitting with Muriel nightly in Billings Hospital after work.

Visits to Little Bighorn and subsequent research weren't yielding the results Norman wanted, and in 1962, he confessed to Robert Utley that he seemed "to be defeated by the defeat." He went on to say, "I am trying to deal with defeat as an ultimate common magnetic power that has drawn so many people to this rather small encounter in military history." Then, too, Norman was walloped by chronic health problems, including dysentery and kidney infections. He often landed in Billings Hospital for weeks at a time during the early 1960s. He told Utley in a July 1963 letter that he tried not to be depressed about a lack of progress on the Custer book but that "two of my last three summers have been obliterated by sickness."

Norman nevertheless managed a few weeks in Montana, where he continued to compile his annual chairman's letter that recapped the accomplishments of students and faculty members who were part of the Committee on General Studies in the Humanities. "Every summer I like to take a little time off from fishing to look back at the Committee and to tell you what the view is like from here, and usually the view is better than the fishing. This year is certainly no exception. I suppose one can't expect the fishing to go on being what it was once, but the Committee is never a disappointment and year after year goes right on making prize catches."

Jessie also was periodically hospitalized as her emphysema continued to advance, but she was determined to continue working at least until 1964, when Jean would finish college at the University of Chicago. "It was a horrible disease, but she didn't want anyone feeling sorry for her," said Ruth Bowen. Joel Snyder remembers telling Norman, who was then a patient in Woodlawn Hospital, that he and Jean would marry after her graduation. That year found Norman in the hospital four different times, making it "the year of the Black Plague for me," he told Utley. In a letter from January 1965 to a prospective student, Norman wrote that he had spent half of 1964 in the hospital. "If I could," he said, "I would never think of 1964 again. The Egyptians, as I remember, used to refer to the unutterably bad and unutterably good as 'One'; as far as I am concerned, 1964 was the year One."

Norman told university administrators in November 1965 that he intended to resign his committee chairmanship the following spring. I'm sure his chronic sicknesses and Jessie's decline had prompted his decision. When it came to celebrating the students on the committee, they worked as a team.

"It is a good time to resign and I think too much of the Committee—and myself—to want to resign just any time," Norman wrote. He had seen others being forced to resign various positions and didn't want to be in such a group. "The old chairman is finally torn loose from his moorings and his successor has to spend the next few years swimming under water looking for the ropes that held the rig together." He planned to spend the last two years before his retirement at age sixty-five teaching "with a little freshness again and to have some choice about what I do with the rest of my life."

Friends and fellow faculty members on the committee wrote tributes to Norman. Popular culture teacher John Cawelti recalled a story about serving with him on a college policy committee. The group was trying to "straighten out the General Education curriculum by pruning this and hacking that," finally deciding to pare the number of required courses from ten to eight. Moments before a final vote, Norman asked a few questions such as why did the committee want to revise the curriculum? And what were its goals?

"Suddenly all of us realized that the emperor had no clothes; that we had been engaged in meaningless tinkering with numbers, hours, and courses; and that none of us had any real conception of what this had to do with education," Cawelti wrote. "That speech was the most consummate piece of political timing I have ever directly encountered and it brought alive in my mind all the legends I had heard of Norman's political skill in the academic infighting of the past. Norman's speech was also the expression of a man who was tough enough to demand that a policy committee think about policy before it set out to play politics."

Historian William McNeill, a faculty member of the Committee on General Studies and a member of Beta Theta Pi when Norman was involved, recalled running into Norman on campus shortly after the 1963 publication of McNeill's *The Rise of the West*. Norman had read the book while he was hospitalized, McNeill said in a letter, "and you praised my work, not with condescension or surprise, as some of my other teachers had done, but with sympathetic wonder and reverence at seeing another stage of the unfolding of a man who had been growing up with the circle of your friendship for so long. . . . Who else has your ability to care and watch and admire growth in everyone who comes within his ken?"

Tributes from former students paint a picture of a teacher who talked with, not at, students, who cared about them as people, and who expected—and got—the best from them. "And, of certainly greater importance, through your kindness and inexhaustible understanding, which surpasses every expectation I have had of goodness in a human being, you've shown me how one person can truly help another. In every good project or relationship I attempt there will be something of Norman Maclean" one student wrote.

Another student wrote, "So, Mr. Maclean, besides the academic boost you gave me, there was an introduction to a balanced life of cooperation and joy which I shall cherish always. And if you don't think I'm grateful for the conversations we've had in your office, on the street, in your home, you've got another thought coming."

In the summer of 1966, Norman went alone to Montana, where he attended the fifty-year celebration of the building of First Presbyterian's sanctuary during his father's tenure there. "Everyone who spoke had his own style and was good, and everyone said wonderful things about my father and mother," Norman wrote to Jessie. "They built a church so simple and beautiful that, without almost any alterations in half a century, it is modern still. . . . Of course, I couldn't help but be saddened by old memories and old friends, but essentially it was a joyous occasion to me. All my family seemed immediate and alive and building."

The next month, he thanked Jessie for adding staff to her medical school office, "but I notice that you have said nothing about any new move to find your successor. Jessie, Jessie, you are tired in your heart of the job, but don't be so tired of it that you won't work to get rid of it. We shall all be in better health when you no longer have to breathe the unchanged air of that office anymore." He missed Jessie, and he hoped she would come to Montana with him in 1967, "even for a short time." Even so, it had been cold and wet during the summer of 1966, and he was glad she wasn't in Seeley Lake. "But in a more normal year—well, I won't urge you, although it is the only place in the world where my troubled soul feels at peace."

I have to wonder, why, after not traveling to Montana for six years, would Jessie suddenly decide to go? She clearly was someone not to be bossed around, and she was very ill. Norman was dreaming. He was also deluding himself, thinking that if Jessie kept walking and taking an interest in her surroundings, her "body and spirit will revive," even though she had told him that every breath made her aware that she was dying. Or maybe urging her to keep moving was the only thing he knew to do.

Norman also visited the Little Bighorn Battlefield, where he stayed at the Sage Motel near the battlefield with a Crow Indian and a Park Service employee, according to Norman's son-in-law. No one could sleep, so they drank a bottle of whiskey and then drove to the battlefield before sunrise. They crouched in the tall grass as the Crow began chanting "Hey-hey-hey," "and as the field turned amber, the Indian started calling out the names of the dead," Joel wrote. Each name brought out a bunny who stared at them with twitching nose and then departed. Norman told Joel it was the only real mystical event of his life. John Cawelti said Norman told him he wanted to write a book about the Sage Motel, about the Little Bighorn–obsessed people who stayed there and where each one's particular obsession led him or her—but that project never materialized.

By the late summer of 1966, Norman knew he wouldn't be spending any more time on his Custer project. "I don't think . . . that I'll ever take up Custer again—at least seriously," he told Robert Utley. "He was one more life than I could live, and he didn't tie up with any of my others." He had written at least four chapters, with plans for others, but that was all he would write about Custer. His failure to finish a project he had struggled with for so long must have been disappointing, if not humiliating.

13

The Crux of It All

IN 1966, after sixteen years of service to the university's medical school, Jessie Maclean received the Gold Key Award for Distinguished Service by the Medical Alumni Association, the first time the recipient wasn't a graduate of the medical school, a physician, or a biologist. "There was more to Jessie's contribution to the school than all of this work. There were things beyond the efficiency, and even beyond the style, the grace and the tact which she brought to her work," wrote Sidney Schulman, a medical school faculty member. "Jessie knew what was to be said. She said less than she knew, but she said enough, and she said it with humor, with literary allusions, and with simplicity." She remained on the job several more months before the exhaustion of illness prevented her from working any longer.

In August 1968, while violence erupted in Chicago around the Democratic National Convention, Norman was in Montana, reading, writing letters and notes, and fishing. That fall he was in and out of the hospital with intestinal problems but trying to maintain his teaching schedule. Jessie was also hospitalized—it was the beginning of the end for her. Undergraduate math major Howard Masur remembers taking a Shakespeare course with Norman during fall quarter, and though Norman missed a lot of classes, the ones he did make were memorable. Norman spent days on the first few lines of *Hamlet* because, Howard learned, that's the whole crux of the play: identity.

BARNARDO Who's there?
FRANCISCO Nay, answer me. Stand and unfold yourself.
BARNARDO Long live the King!

It was Norman's favorite Shakespeare play. The discussion never went further than the first scene. "I'm sure I got a C on my paper, but Professor Maclean's class really increased my appreciation for Shakespeare and made me want to take other humanities classes."

During a hospital visit with Jean and Joel Snyder in early November, Jessie—an unreconstructed Franklin Roosevelt Democrat—told them she didn't want to live in a country that had elected Richard Nixon as president. With Jessie deteriorating in Billings Hospital, Norman, like-wise, was hospitalized in late November as his health got worse. On December 7, Jessie died of esophageal cancer in the hospital where she had worked for so many years. She was sixty-three. Within an hour of Jessie's death, two of Norman's longtime friends—Edward Levi, who was the university's new president, and former president Larry Kimp-ton—went to Norman's hospital room to tell him Jessie had died, "to comfort me and honor her," Norman later said. When English department faculty member Ned Rosenheim told me about that day, he choked up and wiped his eyes. "She had been sick for so many years that we had all come to think (her doctors included) that her courage transcended medical reality," Norman wrote.

Norman remained in the hospital "a good while afterward," Jean Snyder recalled. When he emerged, Norman's many friends and his family checked on him as often as they could without offending his dignity, said Gwin Kolb. He recovered enough to teach during summer quarter—he wasn't heading to Montana. Two of those in his summer seminar on Victorian poetry were David Levi and Larry Nadel. Levi was a Harvard undergraduate who was home for the summer—his parents were Ed and Kate Levi—and Nadel was a University of Chicago English major who worked at the Quadrangle Club, where he often spotted Norman eating dinner by himself. Nadel also took a Shakespeare course with Norman. Both remember that Norman looked wan and drawn, that he smoked Lucky Strikes during class, and that he was a brilliant teacher. They remembered the emotional way he read Tennyson, "looking up at the class after each quatrain," Nadel said. "He was able to convey his awe and love of poetry. I still love Tennyson because of Norman."

Nadel said he wasn't aware that Norman's wife had recently died, but he thought Norman was withdrawn, melancholy, a little shy, "and tightly strung. He used a lot of baseball analogies—he told us Shakespeare had a fastball, he had a changeup, all the pitches. He also told us, 'While you're worrying about your B+, at the same age Keats had already written 'On First Looking into Chapman's Homer.'"

When he took Norman's course, David Levi had finished his first year at Harvard University, where campus life was chaotic, disrupted by protests against the Vietnam War. His father, who later served as US attorney general, hadn't wanted any of the Levi children to attend Chicago while he was the president. As Norman's class progressed, David told his parents there wasn't anyone like Norman at Harvard and that he had gone to the wrong school. He had known who Norman was—a friend of his parents—when he was a child. During that summer, Norman and he sometimes took walks, during which Levi told Norman he was thinking of studying history. "I remember him saying, 'Good for you, stick it to the old man, don't go to law school,' as if my father would have objected. My father didn't care what I studied," Levi said. He laughed. "I love that 'stick it to the old man.'" As things turned out, Levi did go to law school; for years, he served as the dean of Duke University's law school.

Student Howard Masur told his girlfriend, now his spouse, Elise Frank, a psychology major, about how wonderful Norman's Shakespeare class had been. In the fall of 1969, during her fourth year of college, she followed his recommendation and took Shakespeare with Norman. She remembers him as "very wry," with a strange way of speaking out of the side of his mouth, as though he had had a stroke. He followed his typical method of reducing the play to an act, then a scene, and finally a few words, Elise said. The word for *Much Ado about Nothing* was *syncopate*, referring to the dance between Beatrice and Benedict. During the quarter, Elise said, she dropped in on a Shakespeare class Howard was taking, taught by a different teacher, "in a large classroom, where they were speculating about whether Hamlet was in love with his mother and whether he wanted to sleep with her. That never would have happened in Norman's class; he was interested in the words, not in speculation."

For most of 1970, Gwin and Ruth Kolb were in London, where Gwin, a scholar of Samuel Johnson and eighteenth-century British literature, was doing research. The Kolbs stayed in Chelsea. Sometime in early 1970, Norman collapsed and was hospitalized in Chicago, suffering an emotional and psychological collapse, his son-in-law told me. He spent four of the first six months in the hospital. Late in the spring, Norman went to England for a visit, intending to stay two or three weeks, and settled into a bed-and-breakfast close to the Kolbs' rooms. Also in England were Jehanne Behar Williamson, the widow of Norman's colleague George Williamson, and Wayne and Phyllis Booth. Norman had hoped to develop a relationship with Jehanne, but that didn't materialize. He also planned to travel to the Lake District to see Wordsworth's home and then go on to Scotland. But those plans went awry. Ruth Kolb told me Norman was "very unhappy, and he stood too close to the tracks when we rode the subway," so she would take his arm and pull him back. The three friends visited Hampstead Heath and saw the house where Keats had lived, and they ate lunch in a pub, Gwin remembered.

And then, the next day, Norman didn't show up when he was expected. They searched for him for hours before alerting officials at Scotland Yard, who found Norman confused and wandering around London. Gwin told me he called Joel Snyder and told him: "Norman just can't manage. He can't manage." The Kolbs talked with Wayne and Phyllis Booth, and the couples decided Norman should fly home to Chicago immediately. Gwin and Ruth were alarmed by Norman's behavior and felt they couldn't help him, but Ruth helped the only way she felt that she could. She told me she went to Norman's bed-and-breakfast, and while he sat in a chair, she packed his suitcase. She laid Norman's sleeveless undershirts on the bed and folded each one into a small packet as he stared out of a window, silent. When the plane landed at O'Hare, Jean and Joel Snyder took Norman straight to the psychiatric ward of Billings Hospital. He was suffering from depression—and possibly from undiagnosed atrial fibrillation.

A few months later, Norman was released from the hospital. His daughter didn't want him to live alone in the large Madison Park house. English department administrator Catherine Hamm found a suitable graduate student to live with Norman—Michael Curley, whose major professor was Gwin Kolb. Curley, a medievalist, was writing his dissertation. Norman and he would eat lunch together, Curley told me, and then he would walk the mile or so to campus and head for Regenstein Library. He usually grabbed dinner somewhere close to campus, he said. When he would return from the library after nine or ten in the evening, Norman would ask him, "Hi, Sport, want a drink?" and even though Curley wasn't a regular drinker, they would each have a whiskey.

One evening, Curley and a female friend were walking along Lake Michigan north of Fiftieth Street when they were approached by a group of teenagers. They began talking trash to the woman, and when Curley objected, one teenager bashed Curley on the head with a sharp rock. He started bleeding. A lot. Alarmed by the copious amounts of blood, the teenagers fled, and Curley made his way to Billings Hospital, where he got several stitches. He returned to Madison Park after midnight, wearing "a tweed jacket full of blood," he told me.

When Norman answered a knock at the front door and saw Curley, he said, "Jesus Christ, Curley, what happened to you?" Norman sat him down and gave him a drink. To console him, Norman said he was going to tell him a story, something he had never told another person. And then, Curley told me, "he told it straight," the story of his brother, Paul, venturing into the wrong neighborhood after dark and getting killed.

"You're someone who had a close shave," Norman said. Paul had walked streets he shouldn't have, and things ended badly for him, so Curley needed to learn where he could and couldn't go safely in Hyde Park. The way Norman told the story of Paul's death wasn't the way he told the story in "A River Runs Through It," which has Paul dying in Montana. Curley realized there was "Norman as Norman, and Norman as The Writer. He came out of an oral tradition in which he could tell a story a lot of different ways. When you write it down, there's just one version. He could have told the story of Paul eight or ten different ways."

Curley told me that while he lived with Norman in Madison Park, Norman was in several minor car wrecks. Twice, he had blacked out—was it because of a then-undetected heart ailment? Or because he was drinking too much? Or a combination of both? Once Curley found Norman in "bad condition" at home and called Joel Snyder, and Norman ended up in the hospital. Norman was subsequently diagnosed with arrythmia, in which the heart beats irregularly and the brain sometimes doesn't get sufficient oxygen. If your heart slows, you can barely stand. If it speeds up, you feel sick. Alcohol exacerbates the problems. When Curley went to see Norman in the hospital, Norman told him he had been put on medication for his heart, adding, "By the way, I've been drinking too much."

That fall, student Brian Alm was taking a graduate course with Norman on Wordsworth. He said Norman came into the classroom, sat behind a desk, and began talking; "You know, sometimes a thing happens in your life that takes all the joy and color and music out of the world, and you are gray in spirit and oblivious to the world around you. And then one day you tune back into the music of nature, and the gray fades, life returns. Now, I thought, I want to teach Wordsworth just one more time. So let's get started." Alm later realized Norman was talking about Jessie.

Norman told the class what a good teacher was: "A good teacher is a tough guy who cares very deeply about something that is hard to understand." For Alm, that definition captured Norman perfectly—"a tough guy who cared very deeply about the things he taught, read and wrote, and he took up the toughest things he could. Wordsworth didn't seem so tough going in, but he turned out to be: Maclean showed why he was so hard to understand and then took us on to understanding."

Months later, in early 1971, Michael Curley called Joel, who arrived to find Norman flat on his face in his house. Joel thought Norman had had a stroke, so he took him to Michael Reese Hospital for treatment and left him lying in bed. When he returned to the hospital, Joel learned Norman hadn't had a stroke and wasn't in his room. He had been taken to Michael Reese's psychological ward. To reach Norman, Joel was buzzed in through several sets of doors. He found Norman alone in his room at the window, gazing at icy Lake Michigan. Norman said hello to Joel and then started describing what he was seeing in lush and lovely terms—only he wasn't talking about the lake; he was sketching a picture of Macalester College in Minneapolis. When Joel told him what he had said, Norman turned to him, amazed. "No kidding," he said. A few seconds later, he added: "I'm sick of this shit. This is going to change."

The following day, "Norman was different," Joel told me. "He was going to have a life. It was the affirmation of something I've never seen before." Norman sold his Madison Park house and downsized into a two-bedroom condominium close to campus. "Within three months, Norman was writing, getting dressed, coming over," Joel said. "He just changed his life."

14

The Work Never Ends

THROUGHOUT THE FALL of 1975, whenever Norman would visit Allen Fitchen in the University of Chicago Press offices, he often would stop and chat with Virginia Heiserman, who was working in the publicity department. It was hard to miss Virginia—she was stunning. Norman had seen her at English departmental functions with her husband, Arthur, over the years. In early December 1975, Arthur Heiserman died of cancer, "and Norman could see I was unhappy and exhausted," Virginia recalled in a 1999 interview with me. She took time off after her husband's death, which meant she wouldn't be heading the promotional campaign of *A River Runs Through it and Other Stories*.

A log entry on January 25, 1976, says Norman had returned to Hyde Park after spending a week fishing in Florida with Larry and Mary Kimpton, and he was ready to get down to "some steady and systematic work on the Mann Gulch Fire." His working title was "Burning Bright: The Life Story of a Tragedy." Even as *A River Runs Through It and Other Stories* moved toward its spring publication, Norman wanted to start establishing a routine of "reading, planning and thinking" about Mann Gulch so he could have "two months of a start on a first draft" completed in Chicago before heading to Montana. He planned to do research in Montana for two months after arriving in Seeley Lake and then to begin writing, returning to Chicago with a completed first draft. He wondered if he could finish Mann Gulch by fall 1977 and then move on to a third book. We know now he struggled with the book for almost ten years before setting it aside.

Mann Gulch, he wrote, was something "that I deeply have to write, but it leaves out a lot of me, and I should like toward the end to write something in which I can more fully express myself. The motto from here on has to be: 'Do not tarry.'" He had sections of the book laid out, with questions he needed to answer as he proceeded, but as Robert Burns said long ago, "The best laid schemes o' Mice an' Men / Gan aft agley," and that certainly was true in Norman's case. The publication and success of *A River Runs Through It and Other Stories* and his subsequent dealings with people in the movie industry both disrupted his plans for writing and researching his second book, slowing his progress for months, if not years. I think *Young Men and Fire* is a wonderful book, and I know that once Norman got involved, he felt he had to continue. But I wish he had decided to tell a different, less demanding story. I don't think he was prepared to learn how the federal government had mishandled its investigation into Mann Gulch, changing the timeline of events and the testimony of survivors and conspiring to prevent the parents and the public from knowing what had happened. The knowledge alarmed, depressed, and angered Norman. "These questions haunt me and alter my basic feelings about the story and for the time being cripple my progress with it," he wrote. He told himself he had to keep going, to make sure the young firefighters weren't forgotten.

As *A River Runs Through It and Other Stories* went into production in early 1976, its promotion began. Weeks before the book's April release, the first review ran in *Publishers Weekly*. It called *A River Runs Through*

It and Other Stories "a stunning debut by MacLean [*sic*] who shows he can fish hearts as well as the Big Blackfoot." Red Smith, a syndicated sports columnist, quoted the story's entire first paragraph in the *New York Times*. Norman was thrilled at the book's positive reception. In a February 26 letter about the *Publishers Weekly* piece, he asked Ken Pierce, a former student, "How could I have asked for a finer or more literary review?"

According to his log, Norman wrote an essay, "Black Ghost," now anchoring *Young Men and Fire*, on the same day. It describes his learning about Mann Gulch within a few days of the disaster and his fighting a forest fire on Fish Creek in the Bitterroots when he was a teenager. He sent a letter and a copy of the *Publishers Weekly* review to Bud and Janet Moore, telling them: "It's not a good time for me, I admit, I'm almost completely enveloped by my own stories. I'm trying to get some work done on a regular basis on my new story, as well as render some help in the delivery of *A River Runs Through It*." Norman then asked Bud to send him information on firefighting and smokejumpers so he can "know the young guys better." It's too bad he couldn't let himself take a few weeks off to congratulate himself and to realize it was indeed a very good time for him.

In Melbourne Beach, Florida, recovering from various health problems, Larry Kimpton read his early copy of *A River Runs Through It* and wrote Norman afterward, saying he was "savoring every word. I think the style is unique. The future will call it the Maclean style. It owes something to Charlie Russell but it is mostly you." He said he thought Norman's brother had been killed in Chicago, not Montana, so it seems Norman may have talked with Kimpton about Paul. Kimpton said the book had parts that were funny, lyrical, and beautiful, that he had never heard Norman talk about his father, and that he had "never appreciated what an art form [fishing] could become. It's a great book, Norman, and I'm looking forward to the next one. It can't be better but it could be as good."

In early March, Norman got more advance copies of *A River Runs Through It and Other Stories* and sent them to family and friends. More adulation followed. A review by fly-fishing writer and Hunter College professor Nick Lyons in the spring issue of *Fly Fisherman* said the book would become a classic and launched a friendship between the two men. Ken Pierce reviewed the book for the *Village Voice*, noting that Norman was probably the only person who could use *beautiful* and *pig fucker* in the same sentence. Norman was incensed, saying he would never say such a thing, until his daughter, Jean, told him what Ken had written was true. "But it looks so much worse in print," Norman sighed. A few weeks later, the *Spokesman-Review* from Spokane, Washington, and the *Pittsburgh Press* also featured positive reviews. Stories were popping up in publications across the country like smokes after a giant forest fire. Norman was understandably thrilled, Virginia Heiserman told me: "Because he knew he had written a great book. He had very high standards and believed the absolute truth of what he wrote."

In early April, there was a reception for Norman's book at a crowded Ida Noyes Hall at the University of Chicago. Norman talked a bit about the book, read some passages, and signed copies for the long line of people waiting to speak with and congratulate him. But even as he celebrated the publication of his first book, Norman continued working on his second. In mid-April, he headed to Washington, DC, to peruse US Forest Service files on Mann Gulch in the headquarters of the Department of Agriculture. He was also continuing to nudge Bud Moore into writing his own story about the Lochsa, the area in the Bitterroot Mountains where Bud had grown up. Norman had told me and others that he wanted to write more stories about his formative years in Montana, about early life at the University of Chicago, and about Montana women—but none of these had the dramatic urgency of unearthing the stories of young men who had died trying to outrun a monster forest fire.

During the spring of 1976, Virginia Heiserman and Norman grew closer, taking walks and eating meals together. Before becoming intimate with Norman, Virginia asked Joel Snyder what his father-in-law was like, and Joel responded, "He is as advertised." Virginia told me Norman asked her to visit him in Seeley Lake in the summer, cautioning her, "Darling, I don't know what that'll do for your reputation, but I know what it will do for me." Norman's notoriety continued to build. On June 8, radio journalist and author Studs Terkel brought Norman on his syndicated show, *Art of Conversation*, which ran for forty-five years on Chicago's WFMT. The two talked for almost an hour in a wide-ranging interview that touched on the themes and characters in *A River Runs Through It and Other Stories*, Norman's Montana family, Scottish clans, history, and the craft of writing. Maybe Norman and Studs had talked before, maybe not, but during their conversation, Norman was relaxed and revealing. Other radio stations across the country carried the interview, and book sales rose. Norman said he knew as a kid he had to work harder to compete against his brother because Paul was "kind of a genius who was perfect" in the art of fly-fishing.

By July, I was working on a Forest Service fire crew close to Idaho, in St. Regis, Montana, a tiny town with many bars and few restaurants. Norman wrote to me about Mrs. Heiserman's visit, saying they were going to a rodeo in Helena and asking if I knew her. I had passed her once on campus, in Regenstein Library, and remembered how beautiful she was. He also told me not to let the Forest Service bastards grind me down and to "write a poem." I was spending my evenings in the Forest Service compound trying to do pull-ups and run the fitness course. I didn't have any mental energy for writing poems. Heiserman later recalled details about the trip—that she and Norman went fishing, visited with his "cronies," including Bud and Janet Moore, ate at different Seeley Lake restaurants, and even spent a few days with Norman's brother-in-law Kenny Burns before and after the rodeo in Helena. She said Norman sat on the lakeshore near the cabin, watching her while she swam in Seeley Lake. He didn't swim. After she had returned to Chicago, Virginia told him she wished there was a phone in his Seeley Lake cabin so she could talk with him. She signed the letter, "Love, Virginia." She never returned to Seeley Lake.

"He was in love with me," Heiserman told me, "and I loved him, but I was afraid of his being older than I was [by twenty-eight years]." "He told me, 'Darling, I love you too much to marry you.'" Reading their correspondence, I think Virginia wasn't very forthcoming in telling Norman her true feelings. Perhaps she didn't know them herself. For almost two years, she professed to love and miss him, but there were months-long lapses in their correspondence that must have made him nuts before finally driving him away.

In Montana that summer, Norman continued working on the Mann Gulch story. Almost every other day, he traveled from Seeley Lake to Missoula to talk with Forest Service officials about Mann Gulch, about smokejumping, firefighting, and fire research. He met and bonded with Laird Robinson, a former smokejumper foreman in charge of the Smoke-jumper Visitor Center, who knew little about Mann Gulch when they met but who learned much, much more. Laird would become Norman's research partner, his "alter ego," Norman called him, for the Mann Gulch project, checking Norman's manuscript for inaccuracies, accompanying him to Mann Gulch, finding documents to examine and people to interview.

Back in his Seeley Lake cabin, Norman would write up the interviews he had conducted the day before. "I get a good deal of pleasure spending hours talking to some of the big shots in the Forest Service. On the whole, they are pretty impressive guys, and I am secretly pleased to think I would have been something like this if I had lived my other life," he wrote Allen Fitchen. His other life was the one he had fled as a young man. After retiring from the university, Norman would talk sometimes about how he had *almost* joined the US Forest Service, though when he was young, he was trying as hard as possible to get out of Montana.

One of his habits illustrates Norman's tenderness and loyalty. At least three or four times each summer, he would pick wildflowers in the

Mission Mountains and take them to the City Cemetery in Missoula. There he would lay them on the graves of his parents and his brother, on the grave of Frank Roberts, and on the grave of Ben Stowe, a childhood friend who had been a barber in the Florence Hotel. Frank Roberts was the father of Norman's lifelong friend, outdoor writer David Roberts. Norman said he remembered Roberts's mother and father almost as well as he remembered his own parents.

In July, he wrote to Mann Gulch survivor Robert Sallee in Portland to tell him about his project and to ask for an interview. I can't imagine how such an out-of-the-blue letter affected Sallee—his son said he had never talked about the fire until Norman contacted him, and Sallee himself said that after the 1949 fire, he shut down emotionally for the rest of his life. Despite that, Norman flew to Portland to talk with Sallee about the fire and Sallee's sprint to survival. In late August, Norman traveled by truck to the top of Meriwether Peak, "where I could see and study the whole of Mann Gulch, but I wouldn't take the chance of going from there to the bottom of Mann Gulch."

In September, Norman sent his daughter Jean two thousand dollars from his book royalties to help cover the cost of her law school tuition. He lamented how much time it had taken him to write *A River Runs Through It and Other Stories* and said his hourly fee reminded him of his first job. In Missoula, at age twelve, he had ridden his bike to weed vegetables for Sliman Nasser, an Armenian truck gardener who chewed garlic all day and who paid him ten cents an hour for ten hours a day. "Well, working for Sliman was something like working for Morris Philipson, except that Morris smells better," he wrote. "Bless you, my dear," he closed the letter, "and I wish it had been a better book so that it could have been a bigger gift. But I could not have wished for a better daughter. May the Lord's sun shine upon you."

The little blue book, as Norman liked to call it, continued to accumulate positive reviews, and he started fielding requests for interviews and appearances. He told David Roberts he was "enraged" that outdoor magazines hadn't reviewed the book. Roberts responded that he considered most of them "crappy" and told Norman to reread Nick Lyons's review rather than worry. Norman tried to balance his work on Mann Gulch while tending to *A River Runs Through It*, but that balancing act proved difficult. In early November, he wrote to Walter Rumsey, the second living Mann Gulch survivor, and told him about his interest in the fire, hoping for answers to some questions. He was having a hard time settling down to work. Sales of *A River Runs Through It and Other Stories* were increasing every week, a story about him had appeared in *People* magazine, and he had signed a three-year option with Paramount to make a movie of the title story. The university community—Chicago colleagues, staff, and students—had known and appreciated Norman for years, but now he had been catapulted onto a national stage.

Christmas sales of the little blue book were brisk. Norman felt Virginia Heiserman's personal feelings interfered with her position as the book's publicity director. He told her that he believed—and as it turns out, he was right—his book's popularity was continuing to grow, organically, by word of mouth, one person insisting a friend buy it, another giving it as a birthday present, and that person passing it along to another. He was getting more invitations to speak at conferences and meetings and more interviews. *Chicago Magazine* was planning to do a long piece on him, he said. But he wanted advice from Virginia and from Allen Fitchen on how to proceed with his book. He told Virginia he didn't think *A River Runs Through It and Other Stories* was dead, "although any life it lives from now on must come out of whatever vitality it itself possesses and not out of flyers from the Press." He wanted to see "what the fish were biting on" and then deferred to her as the publicity expert, suggesting they meet and talk about how to proceed. "I put too much of myself into [my book] for it to have such a brief mortality," he wrote.

He closed with the admission that the main reason he sent the review was to have an excuse to break another of their long silences. In late January, Norman had been "hung up with a scriptwriter from Paramount, morning, afternoon and night—which is a lot of Hollywood for a boy who grew up on the west side of Seeley Lake before there was a road over there." Early February found Norman heading to Florida for a week with Larry and Mary Kimpton—Larry's declining health worried Norman almost as much as it worried both Larry and Mary, an economist whom Larry had married after Eleanor's death. In Florida, Norman told me, Kimpton and he went deep-sea fishing, ate seafood as often as possible, shared memories, and told stories, the way one does with old friends.

Whether he was watching sparrows outside his living room window, pointing out squirrel tracks in the snow, or transplanting alpine wildflowers to his garden in Seeley Lake, Norman's lifelong love of wild things never left him. In the early spring of 1977, Chicago faculty members and friends Nick Rudall, director of the Court Theatre; Kenneth Northcott, a German scholar and an actor; and John Cawelti, a popular culture expert, all traveled with Norman once again to Jasper-Pulaski Woods, south of Michigan City, to watch sandhill cranes on their migratory journey north.

The birds would stay four to six weeks before heading to Canada. The woods were a quiet, lonely place, and in the spring, there would still be patches of snow on the ground, Rudall told me. They'd see waterfowl and deer and walk on a dike, along the wetlands, watching turtles sunning themselves and hearing the honk of Canada geese, while hundreds of cranes were flying overhead to land and feed in the cornfields. Moving closer, they would watch the birds perform their mating dance, which involved throwing twigs and leaping. It was magical. Usually, they headed to Jasper-Pulaski Woods on a Saturday, after lunch, and walked for two hours or more, ending the day with the Reverend's favorite outdoor drink, a thermos of hot tea and half a small jar of whiskey. In the dusk, an owl once flew over their heads, and Norman explained how an owl's downy feathers enabled it to fly silently.

When the talk turned to writing, as it often did, Norman seemed tormented that the fire didn't have more of a plot, Rudall said. "The story was more about the compression and the comprehension of time, but the critic in him was stopping him from writing." The four friends met often at Norman's condo for a nightcap and conversation.

In late March 1977, Norman traveled to Montana to speak at the Institute of the Rockies in Billings, on "Energy and Montana Memory." He talked initially about his lifelong struggle to connect the two parts of himself—his years in the woods and in the classroom, teaching beautiful literature. If it can be said that people carry themes with them, then Norman's was "Who the hell am I, anyway?" It was one of the first things he talked about with me, the idea that only young people question their identity. "The problem of self-identity is not just a problem for the young," he wrote. "It is a problem all the time. Perhaps *the* problem. It should haunt old age, and when it no longer does, it should tell you that you are dead."

He told the Billings audience, "So when I went about writing my first book, as you will see, I went back to my memory of Montana for my energy and to my years of teaching literature for the power lines to conduct it," thereby joining the two parts of himself into a whole. In "USFS 1919," the protagonist sees "life changing from a series of happenings to something approaching an art form." Jewish girls from New York had written to tell Norman they had experienced the same thing, that "they had seen themselves for the first time become parts of a story. To me, one test, and just one test, of whether you have told a Montana story well is whether some New York Jewish girls think it happened to them." He wanted regional writers in Montana to aim for a wider audience.

Norman also returned to Washington, DC, to further examine Forest Service records, maps, and photographs about Mann Gulch, and he gave talks about writing and his book at both the University of North Carolina and Duke University, where he had friends. His April schedule left little time for writing. Norman was in Chapel Hill, North Carolina, with his former student Bill Harmon, chairman of the English department, when the winners of the Pulitzer Prizes were announced. The fiction committee "enthusiastically" recommended giving the prize to *A River*

Runs Through It and Other Stories. The larger panel declined to award a prize for fiction, saying 1976 was a "thin year" for fiction—only the tenth time in the prize's sixty-one-year history that it had done so. Herman Kogan, who had been the book editor for the *Chicago Sun-Times* and head of the fiction committee, said, "For me, as a reader and a critic, it [Norman's book] had meaning far beyond what he was talking about."

A reporter who was writing about the Pulitzers called Norman for comment. Norman said he wasn't happy about the situation but that he didn't have time to get "sore": "I've got to conserve my energy. I'm 74 now and I hope to have time in life to write two or three other books." But of course, he did get "sore" and stayed that way at the bastards in New York who had robbed his little blue book of the award it deserved. Later he realized his not getting the prize probably generated more publicity than winning it would have.

Summer came, and Norman returned to Montana in June to continue his research and writing on Mann Gulch. I was once again part of a US Forest Service fire crew in St. Regis. But this summer, I had been assigned to Superior, the county seat, where I shared a trailer with my firefighting partner and handled little fires in the eastern part of the district. When I managed to get into Missoula on my days off, my boyfriend and I met Norman for dinner once or twice. He was up to his eyeballs with Mann Gulch research and writing, but he delighted in hearing me talk about fighting fire for the Forest Service. I showed Norman I carried a card with me stating the "Ten Standard Fire Fighting Orders," which were devised in the wake of two US Forest Service firefighting disasters. The order I took to heart was to obey the crew boss, something the Smoke-jumpers didn't do when facing the fire in Mann Gulch.

* * *

On that hot August afternoon near the Missouri River, crew boss Wagner "Wag" Dodge set fire to a patch of land before the roaring conflagration engulfed him. As Norman said, "He burned a hole in the fire." In a split second, Dodge reasoned that, deprived of fuel, the fire would pass over the burned area. He called to the crew to join him, but no one did—a situation Norman wanted to better understand. Perhaps the crew members didn't know or trust Wag Dodge. Perhaps they believed they were better off running from the fire. Perhaps they heard someone say, "I'm getting the hell out of here." Norman learned that most of the crew hadn't worked with Dodge before. Whatever prompted them to reject Dodge's backfire, they surely didn't understand why he was doing what he did. Lying face down in ashes, Dodge stood up a few minutes later, alive; thirteen young men did not. As we know, Walter Rumsey and Robert Sallee survived by slipping through a crevice in a ridge and crossing into a rockslide. Others weren't so lucky. Their charred bodies were scattered on the hillside.

15

Loose Ends and Long Friendships

A LETTER FROM Virginia Heiserman in late August fractured Norman's relationship with the University of Chicago Press and its director, Morris Philipson. Philipson had told Virginia that she needed to reduce her duties at the press and her hours and to decide, going forward, what she wanted to do and what others should do, working on a part-time basis. Norman was more than a little steamed, believing his friendship with Mrs. Heiserman had prompted Philipson's pronouncement. His distress grew into fury not only at Philipson, whom he called "a prick with ears," but also at friends in the English department whom he believed didn't try to help Virginia. He nurtured his indignation into a grudge. A few weeks later, the situation would give him a chance to ride in with the cavalry and rescue her. Virginia Heiserman later left the press and moved to New York, where she found another job and eventually married a University of Chicago alumnus.

Norman was still making the fifty-two-mile trip from Seeley Lake to Missoula regularly to research the Mann Gulch story. Laird Robinson and he climbed the steep slopes above the Missouri River in Mann Gulch one hot August day. Decades earlier, fire scientist Harry Gisborne had made the same climb into Mann Gulch, weeks after the fire, to look for clues about how the fire had behaved. He had had a heart attack and died, literally, on the trail.

"It is hard to believe that there was much about Harry Gisborne's life and character that did not reveal itself in Mann Gulch on the day of his death, and my guess is that most of us would hope, probably vainly, that we could be almost as completely alive in death as he was," Norman later said. Suffering from heart disease, Norman occasionally told friends he would be happy if he himself died while hiking in Mann Gulch or fly-fishing on the Swan or Blackfoot River. He was always hoping for what he called "a good death," dying, as he said, "with his boots on." But as we will see, that didn't happen.

Month after month in 1977, nothing was happening on the movie script other than a meeting, some letters, and a few phone calls. Norman's dealings with officials from Paramount amounted to "too much swishing in the kitchen for the fewness of the foods." "A year of squabbling among lawyers has almost destroyed my interest in having a film made of the story," he wrote. "I say to myself, 'For Christ's sake, if it's this bad just trying to get started, what will it be like if it really gets underway?'" He found his dealings with Paramount to be so humiliating that "for a long time I thought I should write a story reproducing the degradation to which Paramount subjects an author."

In September, Norman mounted his horse and charged the University of Chicago Press, intent on skewering Morris Philipson. He wrote Fitchen "with great reluctance since the director of the Press performed his humiliations and amputations on Mrs. Heiserman, who, like yourself, committed the crime of being a friend of mine and being very helpful in making a book of mine successful. This could be a message to you, too, and it is difficult to read it other than as a message to me to be sure to terminate my relations with the press and resign." As it often does, love blinded Norman to reality. I don't believe Philipson was trying to hurt Virginia but to help her.

A story Norman had written about his family's duck hunting dogs, which I knew as "Almost Duck Dogs," was retitled "Retrievers Good and Bad" and was running in the October issue of *Esquire*. A talk he had given in Chicago months earlier was going to appear in *Chicago Magazine*. "Allen, I've sold everything I've written or talked since I retired," Norman wrote to Fitchen. Teachers were using the little blue book in English courses, and the title story had been included in an anthology. He told Fitchen the Mann Gulch book was not much longer than it had been before he left for Montana, "but it is much better. I think when it is finished it will be close to what I want my second book to be. I wish I did not have to work so hard to make it so."

On October 31, Larry Kimpton died in Melbourne Beach. He had turned sixty-seven a couple of weeks earlier. His friends told me he had developed a staph infection in his ribs after open-heart surgery, one that antibiotics couldn't eradicate. Rather than suffer and die by degrees, he killed himself. Norman and he had been close friends since Kimpton arrived on campus in 1943. I can't imagine losing a friend with whom you had shared so much for so long, one who loved not only you but also your entire family. During a memorial service two months later in Rockefeller Chapel, Norman was one of several friends and former colleagues who talked about Kimpton, his life, and his many accomplishments. Part of Norman's eulogy mentioned Kimpton's writing style, and I think it applies to Norman's as well: "It is a simple style made in America for work, but he was able to achieve in writing what most of us only hope to: to put pieces of ourselves together into one piece, in his case, his simplicity and his complexity, his warmth and his toughness, even a little of his poetry and a lot of his humor."

January 1978 was very harsh in Chicago, with mountains of snow and temperatures far below freezing. The bitter Chicago weather, Kimpton's memorial service in January, and problems with his Mann Gulch research made for a blue February for Norman. He couldn't get over the Forest Service trying to whitewash and shelve the story of Mann Gulch or that what he was finding wasn't what he expected or wanted. "I try to work every morning, but with a numb head and heart," he told the Moores. "My research on the fire hasn't come out the way I expected it to or wanted it to. No wonder statements about it were marked 'confidential' and you had to use the power of your office to get me what should have been the more ordinary kinds of evidence. I keep working but I'm numb, too." Bud had used his many contacts in the Forest Service to help Norman access the materials he needed.

The Chicago winter continued cold and snowy, but as was his habit, Norman managed to take a walk every day, usually in Jackson or Washington Park. He believed that if you could keep moving, taking walks and being outside, you could stay healthy. On those walks, he told the Moores, he had seen no prints in the snow, not from another person, not a dog, not even from a squirrel, and the unmarred landscape was beautiful. He continued working on Mann Gulch into the spring, struggling to create complete portraits of those long dead and understand where and why they died. His further dealings with Paramount continued to exasperate him, and a script he received in May was "so distended now that a lot of steam has escaped but that isn't all."

In early May, Norman asked to be released from the agreement in the option clause of his contract with the University of Chicago Press. He wanted to take his next book elsewhere and not allow the press to have the right of first refusal. A May 8 letter from Morris Philipson said he regretted "that you see me as the culprit and that what I have done for you and your book is not listed among your memories of what you are grateful for, or take pleasure in—because it was I who tried to get Alfred A. Knopf, Inc. to publish the book, and after they had rejected it, it was I who authorized Allen Fitchen to prepare the docket in which all publications are proposed to the faculty board." Over the next two years, the ties between Norman and the press were further loosened. Allen Fitchen chided Norman for implying Virginia Heiserman was the only press employee who cared about and promoted *A River Runs Through It and Other Stories*, then listed what others had done and continued to do to promote the book. Ultimately, the press granted "all rights related to broadcast, performance, and dramatization" of his book to Norman and his heirs. Norman thanked Philipson for the letter, saying, "I probably won't utilize practically any of the rights you have assigned to me—at my age, what I am shortest of is time, and my experience with an earlier movie option tells me another would be a waste of still more time, so my gratitude for your letter is primarily because it makes me feel better about the Press and things in general, and I think it is important for a retired member of the faculty of the University of Chicago to try to feel good about both."

Even as he smoothed over his relationship with the press, Norman continued to chip away at his Mann Gulch project. The spring weather lifted Norman's spirits. A letter at the end of May to Robert Sallee and Walter Rumsey seems almost optimistic. "By the end of the summer," Norman wrote, "if God tosses me a break, I'll be finished with the first draft of Mann Gulch. If I don't, God may well finish me." He wanted the two survivors to accompany Laird Robinson and him back to Mann Gulch because "there are still questions on that hill that make it a minor Custer Battlefield, and I am sure those questions—the major ones anyway—can be answered by the four of us, or three of us, if we can get together for an afternoon on the north side of Mann Gulch." As we know from *Young Men and Fire*, on July 1, 1978, Norman and Laird, along with Sallee and Rumsey, went by boat and foot to Rescue Gulch and from there to Mann Gulch, a site the two survivors had long left behind.

Almost thirty years after they had raced to safety, Sallee and Rumsey spent hours that hot July day determining where their crew boss had set his backfire and where his fire had burned. They looked for landmarks to figure out where they had found their badly burned crew member Joe Sylvia. And most important to Norman, they said they had found where they had crossed to safety through a crevice. Days later, both Norman and his assistant, Laird, felt that the survivors' memories didn't add up. They believed Sallee and Rumsey had identified the wrong crevice. "Maybe when you die almost before you live there is a mechanism in you that makes you reduce your memories of death so most of life will not be based on death," Norman later wrote.

* * *

Though she had relocated to New York, Virginia Heiserman continued writing to Norman. With Virginia fresh on his mind, Norman wrote a blistering letter to his longtime friend Wayne Booth, telling him: "I try to keep steady and do not allow myself to fall in the easy criticism that you are a chicken-shit in a crisis. The truth is, I no longer know what you are, because I also know when Virginia was in a crisis you did absolutely nothing." Norman told Wayne that he intended to "sever all future ties with the University of Chicago Press as long as Morris Philipson is the director."

"He was furious about Virginia," Wayne Booth told me. "I believe Morris didn't want to lose her, just give her some breathing room, but Norman believed Morris had behaved immorally. Norman's reaction comes from Scottish tribal warfare. You're either in the tribe or out of it. When somebody violated his code, they had been disloyal to the clan."

Aggression seems to have been hereditary with the Maclean clan. On one occasion, Norman's grandfather and his four brothers were quarreling with local farm families in Nova Scotia who were also members of the area Presbyterian church. The Macleans caught an owl, set it on fire, and released it during worship. The frightened creature touched off fires in the rafters, vacating the sanctuary and almost burning the building to the ground.

In early October, Norman closed up his Seeley Lake cabin and returned to Chicago. A month later, he knew his relationship with Virginia Heiserman was over. The long lapses in communication hurt him, and he wrote and told her it was time to "put an end to the whole proceedings" after it took her three months to acknowledge a letter from him. The bitter feelings Norman had felt for Wayne Booth wore off weeks after he returned to Chicago, and the two friends reconciled, eventually. Norman resumed taking walks with Wayne and his wife, Phyllis Booth. They would drop in on him, unannounced, when he was living on Woodlawn Avenue, and go for a brief walk or invite him to dinner. "We never felt he was keeping us away," Phyllis said.

Early in 1979, Norman contracted shingles, a very painful reappearance of the chicken pox virus that inflames the ends of nerves in different parts of the body. His case started at the top of his head and ran to his throat and, for a while, affected his eyesight. "When you have [shingles] in your head, they give you a chance to learn that there are a lot of nerve ends in your head," Norman wrote. While Norman was recovering, William "Bill" Kittridge, a University of Montana creative writing teacher, invited Norman to participate in a four-day conference on the University of Montana campus called "Who Owns the West?" Grateful for a ticket to Missoula, Norman said yes, as long as he didn't have to spend all four days at the conference—he had research to do at the Smokejumper Base and the Fire Lab. Kittridge eventually agreed.

There was nothing for Norman to do but write, though he had "almost no desire to. I wish I had never got mixed up in this Mann Gulch thing. Some parts of it I don't even like—I don't like the role played by the Forest Service and the Board of Review." The Forest Service had tried to dismiss the catastrophe, and the board had changed the testimony of survivors Sallee and Rumsey. Norman told Bud and Janet he wasn't "taking any more shit" from the Forest Service about the sewage treatment plant near his Seeley Lake cabin. A letter a few days later continued his theme of being stymied by his own writing: "Given the time you [Bud] have been writing on [the story of the Lochsa], you might as well as have been writing on the Mississippi. As for me, I might as well have been writing on the 1910 fires not just Mann Gulch."

For the past few months of 1979, the contract dealings with Paramount had seemed to go further into nowhere—the idea of the company creating sequels and novelizations and owning the characters in Norman's stories just wouldn't fly. By March, the contract had been canceled. "It enrages me to think of the time, money and pride we sacrificed in dealing with them," Norman wrote to Estelle Steinspring, the manager of contracts and rights for the University of Chicago Press. It cost him two thousand dollars to get out of the contract. "Sometimes I think I will write a story based on our humiliations in dealing with Paramount, but that would be wasting more time, wouldn't it?"

In the first part of the year, he had received a request from novelist Richard Ford for permission to include the story "A River Runs Through It" in an anthology of fishing stories that Raymond Carver and he were assembling. Ford mentioned that he, like Norman, was a fly fisherman who "cannot think about fishing in Montana now without imagining it through the prism of your book." Norman loved it when another writer, especially a fly-fishing writer, revered his book—it was as if he were being welcomed into a club he had longed to join. Norman wanted his story in Ford's anthology, he told Estelle Steinspring, because "if *A River* has any power to be remembered, it [will] be remembered by fishermen." Little did he know his book would be revered as well by people whose acquaintance with fish was limited to fish sticks.

By May, Norman had an answer for Ford. The story "A River Runs Through It" could not appear in whatever book Ford and Carver were planning. University of Chicago Press officials felt that having the story appear in an anthology would affect sales of their newly published paperback edition. Ford didn't give up easily. His wife, Kristina, and he even visited Norman in Chicago in late spring on their way to Montana. Norman and he later exchanged friendly letters, but the project never materialized.

The second half of 1979, Norman was twice in Missoula to participate in conferences—Kittredge's conference on "Who Owns the West?" and one on firefighting in the 1980s. At the firefighting conference, Norman read a section of his Mann Gulch manuscript about fire researcher Harry T. Gisborne, who had visited Mann Gulch on November 9, 1949, a few months after the fire. Accompanying Gisborne was Robert Jansen, the US Forest Service district ranger. Gisborne realized at day's end that his initial theories of how the fire had behaved were wrong, and he was looking forward to coming up with something new and accurate. As dark was falling in the mountains, Gisborne had a heart attack and died. "For a scientist, this is a good way to live and die, maybe the ideal way for any of us—excitedly finding we were wrong and excitedly waiting for tomorrow to come so we can start over, get our new dope together, and find a Hypothesis Number One all over again. And being basically on the right tracks when we were wrong," Norman wrote in *Young Men and Fire*. He could have been writing about himself.

The trip to Missoula gave Norman time to visit Janet and Bud Moore at their cabin in the Swan Valley. Afterward, he wrote to Bud and Janet: "It was worth the trip out to see you—and to see the forest floor covered with the yellow snow of tamarack needles. You two are so warm-hearted and good you make me elevated and probably better than I really am." In December, he wrote them a Christmas note, saying, "I'd like it, Bud, if this coming year we recovered from our delayed infantile paralysis and finished up the Lochsa and Mann Gulch."

Christmas wishes seldom come true, and for Norman, they didn't.

16

No Time to Tarry

DURING THE LAST decade of his life, Norman was almost as busy as he had been during the demanding 1940s. He was being pulled in different directions by people and projects. He logged thousands of miles and hundreds of hours in researching and conducting interviews for his Mann Gulch project and in writing, and rewriting and rewriting, his manuscript. And complaining about his project to his friends and families. He was also fielding interviews about *A River Runs Through It and Other Stories*. Norman handled the demands well, aware of "time's winged chariot hurrying near," remembering that neither of his parents had reached eighty.

In a letter to a friend whose husband had just died, he talked about the time after the funeral, after the public adoration and grieving has ended "and you are suddenly everything and hardly capable of being [alone] so soon. You not only don't know what you are going to do but what you were, and you are not even sure that, in review, how well you knew who has just died or just how well you helped to bring out that was best in him . . . what faced me most starkly when I became alone after Jessie died was the realization that I had not known her very well when she was alive."

Norman had little time for such reflection. There were different editions of the little blue book to check, including one featuring beautiful photographs by Joel Snyder that required a narrative, *On the Edge of Swirls*. People wanted to discuss *A River Runs Through It and Other Stories* with Norman, to learn how he wrote it, why he wrote it, and when he wrote it, wanting to celebrate the book and its author. Others aspired to help make the title story into a film by providing advice and scripts. As exciting as it sounded to have the story on a movie screen, Norman demanded ironclad assurances that no one would vilify, debase, or demean his family members. Only Robert Redford offered such assurances, and he did so in writing.

Norman wanted to turn his full attention to his second book, to focus on the events of August 5, 1949, at Mann Gulch. Hence, for the first six months of 1980, Norman "lived inside a small world bounded on all sides by strict discipline" in his Chicago condominium and finished a "very crude first draft" of all but the last chapter of his Mann Gulch manuscript. He knew he would be returning to his Seeley Lake cabin, and he dreaded doing so, but he had to be in Montana to do his research. Norman's Seeley Lake cabin had been built on land his family had leased from the federal government. About one hundred yards from his cabin, Forest Service engineers had constructed a sewage treatment facility that created a stench that had become so powerful and pervasive that he couldn't sit on his screen porch without the odor choking him. At times, the smell fouled the lake as well. After enduring the noxious fumes for a few years, Norman told Bud Moore, "I'm enraged, and don't think I'll take this shit and like it." Adding insult to injury, the Forest Service kept raising the cost of Norman's annual permit. His outrage was probably as overwhelming as the smell.

From his Hyde Park home, Norman fired off a barrage of letters at a flock of Forest Service professionals across Montana, from a lowly district ranger to the supervising regional forester, hoping to wing at least one. Living close to the sewage treatment plant in the hot summer months had created for Norman "a mixture of nausea, rage and heartache." How hard it must have been to sit, much less write, in such a fetid atmosphere. Different officials assured him the problem would be solved, but still, it persisted. In the 1960s and '70s, Norman had talked about giving up his Seeley Lake cabin because it had become too much for him to deal with. In the 1980s, Norman told friends he intended to leave Montana and the Forest Service behind, because "of the sustained smell of their shit, but it is the smell of their incompetence that's even more sickening." The stinky facility was open seven long years. During that time, as much as he loved Montana, Norman came to distrust and dislike the Forest Service bureaucrats and to grieve what they were doing to his home state. At times, he told friends he would take on the agency just as consumer advocate Ralph Nader had taken on General Motors.

In May 1980, Norman flew to Bozeman to receive an honorary doctorate from Montana State University, an award that delighted him. "I admit, it is a good feeling to be well thought of in the country one loves and thinks he knows," he wrote. It was the first of many honors he would receive during the 1980s in Montana. Other awards included an honorary doctorate from the University of Montana; the H. G. Merriam Award for Contributions to Montana Literature; the Montana Governor's Award for the Arts in Literature; and his most valued prize, the Dan and Helen Bailey Award, given to someone who embodied the values of two legends in the fly-fishing world. In 1938, Dan Bailey had opened a shop selling fishing flies in Livingston, Montana. The shop grew until it became the premier mail-order fly-fishing company in the country, and Dan and Helen Bailey became well known voices for protecting rivers and wilderness.

In accepting the award and a box of Bailey flies, Norman said: "If a man or woman lives after death only in the memory of those who were close to him then he will not have a very long or extensive afterlife. One's friends are limited and mortal. But people like me who did not know the Baileys but admired them greatly and number in the hundreds of thousands are bigger and more durable than reality and make legends that will continue to remain long after us."

His alma mater, Dartmouth College, also awarded Norman a doctorate, which softened his feelings toward the school—especially when a fellow graduate sent him a class memento, his Sphinx cup, and a story about him appeared in the alumni magazine. He was invited to give talks at conferences and festivals, including Stanford University's Distinguished Professor Lecture and a lecture at Lewis and Clark State College. Writers from the *Wall Street Journal*, the *Los Angeles Times*, and other national publications came calling. Radio personalities interviewed him on national broadcasts. The attention was gratifying as well as exhausting, but Norman had a hard time saying no. Being a member of the community of writers was demanding.

Two months after the award ceremony in Bozeman, Norman was fishing by himself on the Swan River, near Bud Moore's cabin, when something happened to make him realize he wasn't immortal. He woke up in the river. Exactly what occurred isn't certain. Did Norman slip and hit his head? Did he have a small stroke? Suffer a heart attack? No one knows. What is clear is Bud found him lying on some rocks out in the river, dazed and disoriented. It must have shaken Norman and made him question whether he should fish alone any longer. Weeks later, writer Pete Dexter visited Norman in Seeley Lake to profile him for *Esquire* magazine, and Norman talked with him about the accident. He planned to keep doing what he had been doing, what he had always done, regardless.

Norman was fast approaching seventy-nine, the age at which both his parents had died. But he had a book to finish. Whenever he wanted an excuse to turn down yet another invitation, he would say, to anyone within earshot, "I don't have that much time in life." The "episode" on the Swan River made him double down to use productively the time he had left. Whatever had happened on the Swan, he wasn't quitting on his second book, and he wasn't going to stop returning to Montana. But he did alert Bud Moore whenever he was fishing on the Swan near his cabin.

In the early 1980s, Norman struggled to know exactly what had transpired at Mann Gulch to kill so many firefighters. Why had they not run into the burned area with Wag Dodge? Why did only two young men survive? Had the fire just been impossible to outrun? He wanted to understand the mechanics of fire behavior. He thought that information was key for writing a true and accurate account so the dead would be remembered and honored. He found rewriting the story "confusing." Norman made multiple trips to the Fire Lab, where he talked with fire behavior experts and looked at mathematical models they had created. One fire behaviorist, Richard Rothermel, said Norman's eyes would glaze over when he tried to explain how the fire had "blown up" and caught the young men. Rothermel eventually wrote a paper about Mann Gulch called "The Race That Couldn't Be Won."

Because the mathematical modeling confounded him, Norman just couldn't let it go. He admitted his math training had been sparse. Dorothy Pesch, who did typing for Norman, remembered his rewriting that particular part over and over and trying to draw diagrams that made sense "because he wanted everyone to understand it." "He was fascinated with it," she told me. But I don't think he ever understood Richard Rothermel's computer-generated models of fire behavior.

When they had visited Mann Gulch with Norman and Laird Robinson in 1978, fire survivors Walter Rumsey and Robert Sallee had relied on their memories and landmarks to re-create what they, and other crew members, had done. Laird Robinson and Norman had used historic information, a tape measure, and photographs to create a minute-by-minute account of what happened at Mann Gulch. Their version of events didn't square with what Sallee remembered, and Sallee believed Norman's account in *Young Men and Fire* wasn't accurate. Norman chalked up the differences to "the problem of what men who have escaped death remember about the incident and [I] have long suspected, for other reasons, that what they remember most accurately occurred along the periphery of the incident after they had escaped danger and what they most lack certainty in relocating is where life and death was a matter of seconds."

According to Mark Matthews's book *A Good Day to Fight Fire*, Sallee resented Norman saying that he and Rumsey couldn't remember what they had done during the fire. Sallee said he never forgot the location of the crevice in the rocks through which he and Rumsey had passed to safety. How could he? Had Sallee agreed with the alternate version of events Norman offered, he thinks Norman would have finished the book instead of setting it aside. Norman wrote sections of the Mann Gulch manuscript at different times. If one part of the story conveyed what he wanted it to, he was pleased and set that section aside. When he looked back on everything he had written, he was amazed at his output. He also realized how much he had to revise and to discard to keep the narrative flowing. It was as if the information had gotten away from him.

"I have worked way too long on [my forest fire story] already, and I won't be able to live with myself if I don't finish it by the end of this coming winter," he told Nick Lyons in October. "Never again will I try to write a story that is historically accurate in every detail. It is clear to me that the universe in its truculence doesn't permit itself to be that well known. At my age, [I] should have know[n] that, but at my age I no longer have the choice of turning back."

In 1981, after rewriting and reworking the manuscript for months, he wrote a detailed analysis, chapter by chapter, listing possible changes, noting what was missing, and cheering when he felt a chapter was complete. Norman talked to himself in these notes, saying he needed to cut pieces of this chapter and beef up that one, congratulating himself when a chapter worked and castigating himself when it didn't. He was afraid of repeating himself. On one page, he said: "I don't know what I was doing when I wrote these 70 pages. It must have taken me several months to write 70 pages, so it must have been a long, long time that I didn't know what I was doing. . . . The hell of it is I can't see how it can be much shortened—10 or 15 pages at the most." There are repetitions in the book, but rather than detracting from the narrative as he feared they would, I think they enhance the story. Norman added more details that force us to look closer at the events of August 5, 1949, to see the fire and feel the terror of the young men running for their lives.

Typing these many versions of the manuscript was Dorothy Pesch, a secretary in the University of Chicago's Office of General Studies in the Humanities. She had heard from others that Norman could "be a mean SOB, but I found him grateful. He had no trouble relating to women as equals, and he appreciated the work I did for him." She learned to read his handwriting—not always an easy task—and she also relied on a cassette tape on which Norman recorded himself reading what he had written. When she started typing for him, she told me, "the book seemed about finished, except for the fact that he constantly rewrote it. He paid me a dollar a page, but I felt that I should be paying him, because I loved it. The writing was just so wonderful. And hearing him read it was better than reading it myself."

Pesch and Norman became friends. They went out to dinner in neighborhood restaurants and took walks in Jackson Park and in the forest preserves. When she moved to a new apartment, Norman helped her transport her belongings and get settled. She typed two letters Norman wrote to actor William Hurt, who expressed an interest in making a movie of "A River Runs Through It." (His first attempt to fish with Norman was delayed when Hurt arrived without a fishing license.) In one letter, Norman remembered a pleasant day that Hurt, George Croonenberghs, and he had spent fishing on the Blackfoot River. He then launched into his objections to a proposed contract. By 1985, Norman was finished with Hurt, who had acted in an unresponsive and somewhat reckless way, leaving Norman not angry but feeling "bitched, buggered and bewildered." Making a movie with him "was a nice fantasy while it lasted but now the vision has passed." He would continue creating a script with University of Montana faculty member Bill Kittredge, whom he knew from the "Who Owns the West?" conference, and Kittredge's partner, film producer Annick Smith.

In Chicago, in the spring of 1983, Norman started taking afternoon walks around Hyde Park with Jean Block, an expert on the neighborhood's architecture and the author of books about the university's Gothic buildings. He had known who she was for years; he even knew her daughter's nickname. What he hadn't known was how much he would enjoy her company. One afternoon, the two walked into the courtyard of Burton-Judson, a Gothic-styled residence hall on Sixtieth Street. Dean of Students Chuck O'Connell had asked undergraduates to monitor visitors that came inside easily accessible residence halls like Burton-Judson. A student stopped them and asked if they needed help. Norman "bristled and chewed the kid out, like he was upholding Jean's honor," O'Connell told me. "And then he blasted me, told me to get the hell out of Hyde Park when I retired because his presence had been challenged." O'Connell assured Norman that the student had been right to question him, and eventually, Norman calmed down and even agreed. He and O'Connell repaired their relationship. Norman began seeing Jean Block on a regular basis and went to a Memorial Day picnic in 1983 with her and her extended family. "The only thing to be feared, as far as I can see, from the 4-generation, 4-dimensional family is the certainty of dying from overeating," Norman wrote.

That Christmas, slammed by all the demands on him and struggling to rewrite his Mann Gulch manuscript, Norman sent out a holiday letter to friends. He answered questions about Mann Gulch by saying: "Right now, I am in the state of revision in which I am proving the claim of many experienced writers, 'The second book is the hardest.' The true story of the Mann Gulch fire has been hard to find—often it has been the fox that went the other way. As a result, in its present form parts of my story of the Mann Gulch fire are as well written as I can write them and other parts wander around and are not." He believed it would take him another year to finish his second book.

Norman saw Jean Block often. Aside from taking walks, they enjoyed going to concerts together, her daughter Elizabeth Block told me. Norman wrote her a long, sassy letter from Montana the following summer, telling her in detail about the yellow Buick Skylark his next-door neighbor in Seeley Lake, a used car dealer, had ready for him. Norman's daughter, Jean Snyder, had worried for years about her father driving the sixteen hundred miles between Chicago and Seeley Lake by himself. She finally asked him to stop. When he insisted he would continue doing so, she told him not to bother coming to her house any longer. He realized she was serious, so he bought a car to drive in Montana, telling people—including me—that it had belonged to a prostitute from Stevensville.

Norman told Jean Block he might have the car brought to Chicago. "I will drive you all around in it . . . and that yellow-and-white color combination should go well with your complexion and social status," he wrote. He also detailed going to fish on the Swan River, falling into some downed trees, and embedding a fishhook deep into his hand. Luckily, Bud and Janet Moore were in their cabin, and they removed the barbed hook and bandaged Norman's injured hand. He ended the letter with this: "I was very touched by your placing my note to you next to my citation and both in your bedroom drawer under your jeans. In fact, I was so impressed with your idea that I am liable to steal it. When I return this autumn, I am thinking of hiding myself in your bedroom drawer under your jeans but will pop out any time of the night at the slightest sign of encouragement. It should go without saying that I love you very much."

But by the next June, their relationship was ending. Norman asked if he could see her before he left for Montana at the end of the month. Who knows if he got to do that? Norman asked Jean Block to marry him, said Elizabeth Block, but Jean knew if she married him, he would expect her to spend several months in Montana, and she didn't want to do that. She preferred spending time in Elkhorn, Wisconsin, with her extended family, who gathered at a summer house, one equipped with a bathroom and hot water. She also objected to Norman's frequent use of Anglo-Saxon words. *Fuck* was particularly off-putting.

"My mother wasn't prissy, but she was a lady, and Norman's language bothered her," Elizabeth Block told me. "It was just who he was. He was rough-hewn."

Other relationships in the mid-1980s worked out better, at least for a while. In 1981, the actor and director Robert Redford had taken a trip to Montana. His friend, writer Tom McGuane, and he began discussing western writers and authenticity, and McGuane insisted Redford read *A River Runs Through It and Other Stories*, telling him Norman "was the real thing." Redford immediately wanted to bring the title story "to the screen," even though "what I had heard about Maclean was that he was not easy to approach." The two men met at Redford's Sundance Institute, where Norman had traveled with Bill Kittridge and Annick Smith—the three had formed a partnership in 1985—to explore making a movie. Redford found Norman to be "polite, courteous but wary, and surprisingly innocent." Since he had published books and was well versed in creative writing, Kittridge was to write the script, and Norman was to approve it. By August 1986, with Kittridge writing away, Redford was "pleased to hear the progress on 'A River Runs Through It.'" He told Norman he would spend time with him after he finished directing *The Milagro Bean Field* and after Norman sent him a revised script.

Norman continued getting requests for interviews. He was usually generous with his time, especially if the interviewer was a young person—in most cases, that is. A young Chicago writer wanted to profile Norman for a middle school magazine, published by a company in the northern Chicago suburbs. Her editor, she told Norman, had censored the interview. Norman was irate: "It often does not seem possible to me that here in the United State of America the words 'hell' and 'booze' (two of the oldest American words) should be removed from my stories of the woods in the west in order for them to be thought safe to be read by people reading in order to learn how to write the American language. And by an editor by the dubious name of [name omitted], a clay pigeon seething with righteousness who should be released in a trap shoot where all sport loving Americans can get a clean shot at him. I guarantee you I will pour lead into him as long as I live." The interview never ran.

The Christmas letter Norman sent in 1986 said Robert Redford was coming to Chicago in January 1987 to go over the script with him, line by line. Early that month, Redford wrote Norman a letter detailing some of the problems he found in Kittridge's script. He realized any film of "A River Runs Through It" needed to shift its focus to Norman because "the voice is Norman's and Norman is a character. But the light is on Paul. So we must feel Norman in a very special way." Later remarks in the letter reveal Redford thought that Kittredge's script "has tried hard to be reverent to your wishes and the letter of the book. But it does not work yet as a film." He planned to come to Chicago three times in six weeks to talk with Norman about the project. Redford wasn't sure the story could be made into a film: "It is a maddeningly elusive piece, dancing away from the reader like the boxer Norman had once been, coming in fast to whack you between the eyes with the beauty of its language, or in the solar plexus with the depth of its emotion."

True to his word, Redford did come, and he and Norman went over the script together. Norman felt that both Kittridge and Smith needed to be fairly compensated for whatever work they had done to advance the movie, but he didn't want to work with them any longer. At the end of January, Norman battled his way through bad weather and sketchy flight connections to Helena to accept the Governor's Arts Award for Literature. Montana had determined his character, for better or worse, he said, and Helena was the place he had met and married Jessie. His acceptance speech seems a little melancholic to me. Perhaps I'm wrong. Norman conveyed much of his emotion through his voice, and I didn't hear this talk. He does say that "awards like this, coming in old age, also come with pain," as he remembered the family he loved who are no longer with him. "Part of the pain of this evening is that they are not present to be able to see me at least partly justify the sacrifices they made so that I could realize whatever was good within me."

Redford returned to Chicago in early February and met with Norman, who kept notes of their meetings and calls. "Although I know little about movies, I know enough about literature to recognize a gifted literary man at work," Norman wrote. "Redford is very impressive." Redford read the working script in detail, and he told Norman that Bill Kittridge "has almost no experience with movies and doesn't see how close to the story the script can come." After spending a few hours talking about ideas for a movie version of the story, Norman began to regret ever having formed a partnership with Annick Smith and Bill Kittridge, saying, "The two of them are far less gifted than in my Romantic old age I thought they were." Redford returned to Hyde Park in late February and in March 1987, and after talking about the movie with Norman, ate dinner with him and Jean and Joel Snyder and their older son, Jacob, at a Japanese restaurant. During dinner, Joel and Redford talked baseball, Norman wrote.

That spring, Norman received an honorary doctorate from Dartmouth, but instead of attending the reception held in his honor, he spent most of his time lying in bed in his hotel room. A few days after he returned from Hanover, Norman was diagnosed with prostate cancer. The medication he took reduced his nighttime bathroom visits to two or three instead of five or six, and because he was sleeping better, he felt more upbeat. In early May, he traveled to Lewiston, Idaho, where he delivered a lecture at Lewis and Clark State College, "at the confluence of two of the mightiest tributaries of the mighty Columbia—the Clearwater and the Snake Rivers. I was deeply moved. Nearly 70 years ago I worked in the Forest Service at the headwaters of those rivers."

Time's winged chariot was drawing near for Norman, who felt he had no time to waste. In a May 19 letter to Robert Redford, Norman said that while he had enjoyed meeting and working with him, "no matter what is ahead of me, I cannot afford to let the next eight months pass with as few tangible results as the last eight months." He told Redford that no one had yet invested a lot of money in the effort to make a movie of "A River Runs Through It," just a lot of time, which "is the one thing I'm liable to run short of."

One early morning in late May, Norman lost his balance and fell as he was heading to the bathroom, and he hit his head against the wall. He lay there several hours before finally crawling four yards to the phone in the living room and calling his son-in-law. Joel Snyder remembers Norman saying: "I fell on the floor. I've been here a few hours. Don't come right over or you'll scare me." His daughter and son-in-law didn't know it then, but that accident marked "the beginning of the end for him," Snyder said. After Norman had recovered somewhat, when someone would say something to him, he could read the person's face. He'd give a formulaic response that would satisfy the speaker.

"He was so alert and on top of it, he seemed like himself, but there were times when he wasn't there," Snyder told me. "His habits sustained him." One habit he couldn't continue was writing. He had to put aside his unfinished Mann Gulch manuscript.

An August 4 letter from Robert Redford assured Norman that he was serious about making a movie with him. A week later, Norman wrote back, telling him "the most beautiful letter I ever read was one from you pledging that a movie of 'A River Runs Through It' will be completed by you and your able staff. Almost from the moment I came to know you well I felt the story was yours as much as mine." In the same envelope was a letter saying Norman's children and his son-in-law were giving Redford permission to proceed with the movie, unimpeded.

Redford wrote in early November to tell Norman, "I know you are slowly working your way up to the surface, for which I am glad." He said he planned to rely on Joel Snyder for updates on Norman's recuperation, and he promised to send a final proposal and lock up the deal "so you can get some money." He was true to his word, and the money allowed Norman to have round-the-clock care during the last years of his life. In January 1988, Norman sent a late Christmas letter to friends and family members, telling them about his accident, saying: "Wobbly as this prose is, there were weeks when there was only a dark cave with no light anywhere, just not anywhere—a tunnel with no end. So this early prose, no matter how wobbly, is a sign I'm getting better." He said the love and care he had received from his daughter and son-in-law had helped him recover.

A few weeks later, Norman replied to Redford, saying, "Thank you for your remembrance and devotion, and in turn this is the first complete sentence (if it is one) that I have written since my near fatal accident when for a long time I seemed to have left the world in darkness for good."

At Norman's urging, Jean and Joel Snyder brought Redford to Norman's Woodlawn Avenue home for a visit. When Norman suggested they go out for lunch, Redford said meeting in a public place wasn't a good idea, given that everyone would recognize him as a movie star. Nonetheless, Joel Snyder told me, they walked a few blocks from Norman's condominium to the Medici, a beloved Hyde Park coffee shop and restaurant. As Redford looked around at the people ignoring him, Norman said: "Listen, pal, this isn't Rodeo Drive. This is Hyde Park." They had an uneventful meal, with no one bothering them, "and Norman was so proud of Hyde Park," Joel said. That was one of Norman's last outings.

Screenwriter Richard Friedenberg wanted to visit Norman in 1988 to talk about his family and his early years in Montana, believing that research could help "recreate the book's magic without having the benefit of the book's methods." He believed stories from Norman's early life "could add dimension and substance to a script." Norman was too frail and ill to meet with him, so Friedenberg turned to Jean and Joel Snyder, who "were full of information, insights, explanation." The Snyders shared documents, letters, and stories from Norman and Jessie's lives with Friedenberg, who also traveled to Montana, talked with Norman's friends there, and perused his high school annual, deciding to set the movie in the 1920s.

While the movie script was taking shape, Norman was ensconced at home. He didn't want most of his friends to see him as he was. But Dorothy Pesch and Jim Chandler, a Wordsworth scholar and a member of the English department, did visit Norman regularly at his home or in the hospital during the last two years of his life. The television was often on, tuned to a baseball or football game, and they would settle in to watch with him. Norman didn't speak much, but when he did, "he had an abstract way of looking at a game," Chandler said. "He saw bodies governed by skill and grace. What the players did well wasn't part of the discourse of the game. He made you see something by description."

Most everyone wants to die suddenly and painlessly, but few people have a "good death," as Norman defined it, by continuing their activities and staying aware of what's happening around them and to them until the end. To me, what constitutes a good death is to know you are loved and will be remembered and missed. Norman had such loving assurance from his children and his two Chicago grandsons, Jacob and Noah Snyder, who visited him regularly and who called him "Moose." They both told me Norman talked to them as equals, even when they were little, asking for their opinions and offering his. Only when he was in English classes at the University of Michigan did Noah Snyder realize his grandfather cast a very long shadow.

Over the last two years of his life, Norman endured a series of relapses and rallies—taking brief walks, landing in the hospital, returning home to round-the-clock care—before breaking a hip in early 1990 and contracting pneumonia, "the old man's friend." Pneumonia was one of several ailments that could have killed Norman. His prostate cancer could have metastasized. His heart could have given out. He still had stories he wanted to write. The cause of death isn't important to me. On August 2, 1990, he died while sitting at the dining room table in his apartment with his son-in-law, preparing to eat breakfast. Afterward, Joel Snyder called Dorothy Pesch, who wrote a notice and circulated it among the English department faculty. His longtime friend Gwin Kolb, who had helped launch Norman's professional writing career, was stunned. Norman had survived so much, I think Gwin believed he might rally.

Norman's children scattered his ashes in the Swan Range. From the Swans, on a clear day, you can see the Mission Mountains and Seeley Lake. I think Norman would have given them an A+.

Forever
Loneliness is not always lonely.
It can go on to ecstasy.
When I am alone in the woods
I am the universe.
What is there
I do not know
Or cannot do?
Do not tell me I cannot live forever.
I already have.

—Norman Maclean, 1977

17

Honors and Unfinished Work

AFTER NORMAN DIED, a memorial service that October filled the cavernous Rockefeller Chapel with his family, friends, former colleagues, and former students. A few years later, a college residence hall at the University of Chicago was named Maclean House in Norman's honor, though it has since been demolished. The Norman Fitzroy and Jessie Burns Maclean Scholarship, which began when Norman retired, continues to support a needy student concentrating in English. There's also the Norman Maclean Faculty Award, which "recognizes emeritus faculty members for their extraordinary contributions to teaching and to the student experience of life on campus." Most of those receiving the award have been active faculty members.

Norman's Mann Gulch manuscript wasn't cremated with him. Jean Maclean Snyder had been reading different versions for years—Norman's papers have numerous files marked "Jean's Copy"—and sometimes making suggestions for her father, which he, as usual, ignored, she told me. She knew the book was probably finished long before Norman's failing health dictated he set aside his many chapters. Norman just couldn't see the book was complete. After he had been working on it a few years, his friend Chuck O'Connell suggested it was done: "'Surely, Norman, you're finished by now, why not quit?' He was furious with me. 'Don't ever say that again to me.' I realized he thought he was keeping those boys alive, all by himself." Writing was keeping Norman alive—he changed his Do Not Resuscitate order months before his death, instructing the medical staff to "pull out all the stops" and telling his doctor he had a book on western women he planned to write.

The spring after Norman died, his children signed a contract with the University of Chicago Press to bring their father's work to fruition. They entrusted the unorganized and unfinished sections to Alan Thomas, then the press's humanities editor. He took the manuscript to Japan, where his wife was doing research, and began working on it there. After returning to Chicago, Thomas took trips to Montana and Mann Gulch and the US Forest Service's Regional Fire Lab in Missoula. He talked with Laird Robinson, fire behaviorist Richard Rothermel, and Bud Moore, double-checking and editing and organizing Norman's work. Norman's friend and colleague Wayne Booth was the arbiter for the manuscript, making decisions about what to keep and what to omit.

The final book was published as *Young Men and Fire* in 1992. It's about more than a fire disaster; it's about an old man coming to terms with making art out of tragedy and dealing with death. "There's a lot of tragedy in the universe that has missing parts and comes to no conclusion, including probably the tragedy that awaits you and me," Norman wrote.

The book received the National Book Critics Circle Award, which would have delighted Norman. He would also be happy that a trail now leads to the crosses in Mann Gulch marking where the thirteen young men died. And that hikers routinely visit, leaving flowers and sometimes notes. The US Forest Service promised to keep watch on each of the crosses, replacing them if need be and laying wreaths to honor the dead young men. Norman would be relieved that the Forest Service today studies the aftermath of big wildfires on the ground instead of in the classroom and spends time training fire fighters on the importance of communication among crew members. Better communication might have saved lives at Mann Gulch.

Also in 1992, Robert Redford released his film version of "A River Runs Through It," focusing not on Paul but shifting the spotlight to Norman and Jessie. The movie won an Oscar for best cinematography and Oscar nominations for both best screenplay based on previously published work and best musical score. I think Norman would have been pleased. Maybe. He was picky and paranoid about how his family would be portrayed, even by a director he liked and admired.

The success of the movie spurred further sales of *A River Runs Through It and Other Stories*. It has sold more than two million copies worldwide and has been translated into more than twenty languages. The book's celebration, and mythologizing, of Montana, the Blackfoot River, and fly-fishing have helped make recreation the biggest driver of the state's economy. Records show the movie produced a 25 percent increase in sales for the fly-fishing industry throughout the mid-1990s. Numerous researchers have plotted the rise in the number of people taking up the sport, the skyrocketing increase in tourism dollars in Montana, and the flood of interest in protecting—and sometimes, unfortunately, exploiting—the state's rivers.

Norman's little blue book "was a national treasure," said native Montanan Judy Blunt. The author of *Breaking Clean*, in 2021 Blunt was the chair of the English department at the University of Montana Missoula. She was also director of the university's creative writing program, the oldest such program in the country.

"It's not a regional story, it's a personal family story that can be interpreted from a lot of different directions," according to Blunt. "It threw a spotlight on Montana as a place where literature might occur." Norman's book also put the University of Montana's creative writing program on the map. The book and the movie, Blunt said, "made us a cool place to be." The program counts two recent Pulitzer Prize winners among its graduates: William Finnegan for autobiography in 2015 and Andrew Sean Greer for fiction in 2018. I think Norman would be happy about helping aspiring writers in his beloved Montana.

With the publication of *A River Runs Through It and Other Stories*, Norman became what he always dreamed of being: a real writer. He also became a little bigheaded. Receiving five hundred positive reviews, all slathering praise on him like butter on a scone, might do that to you. Fan mail came from celebrated people across the country, including accomplished writers such as John McPhee, Geoffrey Norman, and Richard Ford and CBS news journalist Eric Sevareid. I think Norman was entitled to be bigheaded. In the many interviews he endured, he could come across as modest or miffed when the interviewer expressed shock that someone in their seventies could write a book—and such a *good* book. Sometimes Norman would respond graciously, sometimes almost combatively, if he thought the questions were beneath him. In late 1987, for example, a newspaper's book editor asked Norman if there was a connection between the art of writing and the art of fly-fishing. "That's kind of an asinine question, isn't it?" Norman said.

After decades of teaching Shakespeare and nineteenth-century poetry, Norman really did understand what made for good writing. He knew how tragedy unfolded, in literature and in his own life. Without his years at the University of Chicago, Norman might not have been able to untangle his past and his upbringing to write *A River Runs Through It and Other Stories*; without a childhood and summers in Montana, he wouldn't have had the story he wanted to write. Norman saw events, like my sister-in-law's death at twenty-nine, as part of a bigger story, something my family would cope with for years, that would change me, my brother, and others I loved in profound and permanent ways. He could see the extraordinary in the ordinary. I think at the end of his life, he finally figured out who he was: a storyteller who wrote books centered on tragedy and guided by compassion. In completing *A River*

Runs Through It and Other Stories and *Young Men and Fire*, he shows us the two joined parts of his bifurcated life.

What makes his achievement even more remarkable is that Norman overcame self-doubt and depression to write a masterpiece with the title story of "A River Runs Through It." At different periods of his life, the depression was debilitating, landing him in the hospital for weeks at a time. He set aside the humiliation he had felt after abandoning his project on George Armstrong Custer and the Little Bighorn. He also escaped the rigid rules erected by R. S. Crane & Company, who considered plot the foundation of a work of literature. Norman once summed up the plot of "A River Runs Through It" as "they drink, they fish, they drink, and they fish some more," effectively saying there isn't much of a plot, not in the Aristotelian sense. Character—and language—drive the book. He also blew apart Crane's insistence on the importance of genre. As I said earlier, I think Norman created a new genre with his little blue book: a fictional, poetic collection of stories with elements of autobiography, history, memoir, tall tale, and myth. His emotions moved him from one to another.

I believe the story's elegiac tone echoes that in William Wordsworth's "Ode: Intimations of Immortality from Recollections of Early Childhood." Norman liked to say "the Cumberland Cowboy" was strong in him. The poem is considered one of Wordsworth's greatest works. Its eleven stanzas have irregular rhyme, and in it, the poem deals with issues such as aging, the glory of nature, the innocence of childhood, and hope for understanding one's fellow man. In the first four stanzas, the narrator is despondent because, no longer a child, he cannot see the divine in nature as he once could. In the first sonnet, he says:

> It is not now as it hath been of yore;—
> Turn wheresoe'er I may,
> By night or day,
> The things which I have seen I now can see no more.

It continues:

> The sunshine is a glorious birth;
> But yet I know, where'er I go,
> That there hath past away a glory from the earth.
> . . .
> Whither is fled, the visionary gleam?
> Where is it now, the glory and the dream?

At the end of the poem, the narrator finds that "Though nothing can bring back the hour / Of splendour in the grass, of glory in the flower," he will find solace

> . . . in what remains behind;
> In the primal sympathy
> . . .
> In the soothing thoughts that spring
> Out of human suffering
> In the faith that looks through death,
> In years that bring the philosophic mind.

The title story in *A River Runs Through It and Other Stories* has something for everyone. It didn't emerge in one piece—over three years, Norman wrote many, many versions, gradually making it less a fly-fishing manual and instead focusing on poetry and family dynamics and the limitations of love. The family dynamics aspect—Paul as the black sheep—attracts readers who believe it to be a story of helplessness and love in the face of addiction and self-destruction. The fly-fishing instruction and adventures reel in fishermen of all abilities who can tell themselves fly-fishing isn't just an expensive pastime but can also be an art. The poetry part appeals to teachers of composition and would-be writers trying to figure out how Norman managed to write such a beautiful story with language so simple and so complex. Prose stylists, rhetoricians, and composition teachers use Norman's books to teach high school and college students how to write. On the internet are study guides for *A River Runs Through It and Other Stories,* as well as teacher guides, student notes, and lesson plans. The title story has become an American classic, compared with Ernest Hemingway's "Big Two-Hearted River" and Henry David Thoreau's "On the Concord and Merrimack Rivers." Not bad for someone who didn't start writing until his biblical allotment of threescore and ten.

Norman thought of himself as a good fly fisherman but not a great one, reserving that rating for his brother, Paul, and to some degree his father. Norman studied and worked hard to become a good fisherman, following his father's many imperatives and teachings. As with other areas of his life, Paul developed his own rules and skills as a fisherman, leaving both his brother and father in awe of him. He didn't need his father's help to become a great fly fisherman; he had an innate ability. My fly-fishing friends tell me there are wonderful trout streams in Wisconsin, Michigan, and Minnesota, but Norman didn't fish there. His lifelong friend, outdoor writer David Roberts, a native Missoulian, tried several times to persuade Norman to fish with him in the Upper Midwest or to travel in order to fish in Alaska, Canada, or Scotland, to no avail. Norman didn't even bring his fishing gear to Chicago—it was packed away in the Seeley Lake cabin. I never heard him mention it, so I assume he wasn't fly-fishing in New England while he was in college there.

For Norman to fish, he needed to be on the Blackfoot, Clearwater, Clark Fork, or Swan Rivers or one of the many glacial lakes in the Missions and the Swans. Because he wasn't just catching fish, he was casting for memories, and to do that he needed to be in the places where he had made those memories. Even after his parents died, if he returned to the cabin following a late afternoon of fishing, he could imagine he was coming in with a full creel of trout for his mother to exclaim over and to batter and fry on the wood-burning stove—even though he practiced catch-and-release. Today, with lines for electricity and a telephone, the cabin still looks much the same as it did when the Maclean family built it more than a century ago. There's still no indoor bathroom. Some of the furniture hasn't changed. The boxing gloves Norman and Paul used still hang in the screen porch. As an old man, when Norman was casting on the Blackfoot, he could picture Paul and his father as they were during the last time they fished together, content and confident. Fishing in western Montana meant fishing with spirits.

"I was trying to write a kind of tragedy that would occur to many of us," Norman said, "with life's problems and joys and recessions and seemingly permissions and probably with nothing really too serious until almost at the end all the permissions and excesses and incompletions have piled up and tragedy is inevitable and when you look back just before the end or soon after, you see it was inevitable."

ACKNOWLEDGMENTS

At the urging of University of Chicago English professor Gwin Kolb, I started assembling this book in 1991, a few months after Norman died. I talked with and wrote to Norman's colleagues from the university. When possible, I conducted face-to-face interviews. Each person would share stories about Norman—and sometimes Jessie—and then suggest someone else for me to talk with. Norman had a very wide circle of friends and admirers. Later, a notice I placed in the university's alumni magazine produced a torrent of letters from Norman's former students, from every decade, those who had been in his introductory Humanities classes in the 1930s, others who had quaked in their chairs during oral exams for their doctorates in the 1970s. When these alumni remembered their college days, they thought first of "Mr. Maclean," described as a compact, energetic guy—tough, often critical—reading aloud the first scene from *Hamlet* or a poem by Hardy in a voice that brought tears to their eyes. He cared about literature, and he cared about them. I talked and corresponded with as many of these members of the Maclean flock as possible.

Had he not taught at the University of Chicago for so many years, I believe Norman wouldn't have been able to write his masterpiece. Just as he had taught students how to read Shakespeare and Donne, so at last he zeroed in on his own life. But he was always a teacher. As the intense language of *A River Runs Through It and Other Stories* carries us along into the lives of the Maclean family members, we learn about Montana in the early twentieth century and about fly-fishing, firefighting, and working in the woods. He called that time "the end of history," history being when hands and hoofs and hand tools moved the world. We also learn how Norman felt about his work.

I don't know how many times Norman said to me, "I want to know just who the hell I am, darling." The problem of identity was central for him, just as it is for Hamlet. This book is my own attempt to find out something about Norman's life and to place him in the two worlds he straddled. I wanted to offer my portrait of the man whose goal in life was to bring forth the best in himself and others, to try to figure out just who the hell he was. I think that through his writing he met his goal of fitting the pieces of his life together into a whole.

I would have been sunk from the get-go if not for the encouragement and counsel I received from Norman's daughter and son-in-law, Jean and Joel Snyder. They are generous, intelligent, warmhearted people. I talked with them regularly for years. They shared memories and told stories, directed me to people and places, fed and housed me in Hyde Park while I wandered through Norman's papers in the University of Chicago's Special Collections Library. They facilitated my participation in the 2015 Maclean Festival in Seeley Lake, insisting I stay with them in the Maclean cabin. Thanks to Jacob, Dashiell, Noah, Julie, and Josh for letting me intrude on a family gathering, and thanks to Jacob and Noah for talking with me about Moose. Norman's son, John Maclean, a fellow former journalist, now a national authority on firefighting tragedies, practices, and policies, has been kind and helpful, even while writing his own important books, including his memoir *Home Waters*.

The staff at Regenstein Library's Hanna Holborn Gray Special Collection Center has been professional and efficient, as has the research staff at the Athens Clarke County Public Library. And the staff at the University of Montana Library's Mansfield Library and the Missoula County Public Library. Researchers at Dartmouth's Rauner Special Collections Library were generous and helpful. My former sister-in-law, Nancy Dupree, past state genealogist for Alabama, unearthed more about the Maclean and Davidson families and Lois Nash than I thought possible. Missoula resident Jim Habeck, a retired University of Montana botany professor, is *the* authority on the Reverend Dr. J. N. Maclean and First Presbyterian Church in Missoula, and he shared whatever he thought would help me. Folks in Missoula and Seeley Lake shared stories, and so did the late Bud and Janet Moore. Former smokejumper and outdoorsman Martin Onishuk kept pestering me to hurry up and git 'er done.

The members of my Athens writers' group, Sara Baker, Heidi Nilsson, and Kathryn Sears gave each version of the manuscript a close and careful reading before making suggestions. Faraway friends Pam Rice Porter, Nadine Honigberg, and Jan Jarrell offered great ideas. Jan was a Maclean Scholarship winner and knew Norman, so her remarks and editing suggestions were spot-on. Rhetoricians Heidi Skurat and George Jensen, Maclean scholars at the University of Arkansas at Little Rock, know more about the writing and rewriting of the title story in *A River Runs Through It* than anyone else, and they happily shared with me pertinent pieces of their scholarship. University of Chicago friend and former roommate Daryl Koehn, a philosophy professor well acquainted with Aristotle, steered the ship of folly from the rocks of destruction.

Without the constant nudging, cajoling, and cheering from my husband, Gene McCarthy, I would have stopped researching Norman years ago. He uncovered important details about Norman's life and work when I asked for help, and he edited and reorganized entire sections of the book until we were both satisfied. He assured me I had something important to say and insisted I say it. Gratitude and love as well to my patient, supportive, and kind agent Gail Hochman, who knew Norman slightly, who waited years for this book, who calmed me down, cheered me on, and kept me going.

And love to my oldest brother John B. Roberts Jr., known as "John the Beloved" in our family, who took the photo of Seeley Lake from Double Arrow Lookout that graces the first paperback edition of *A River Runs Through It* and who insisted I meet Norman so many years ago, believing we would become good friends. He died as I was finishing this book.

NOTES

CHAPTER 1. MEETING MACLEAN AND CHICAGO

5 **My brother and sister-in-law insisted I call him "Dr. Maclean."** I continued calling Norman "Dr. Maclean" into my twenties, when he finally said, "Goddammit, Rebecca, call me Norman."

11 **"It tries to say directly how I feel about the mountains of Idaho and Montana"** Norman Maclean to Marie Boroff, November 3, 1972.

12 **Norman became, for me, a critic of my poetry** Norman Maclean to Rebecca McCarthy, May 10, 1973.

13 **Norman asked me, "Did you know you had a male poet in the family?"** Norman Maclean to Rebecca McCarthy, November 1972.

13 **"Today is the anniversary of my wife's death"** Norman Maclean to Rebecca McCarthy, December 7, 1972.

14 **"I would rather not teach at all than not to teach well"** Norman Maclean Papers, box 19, folder 9, Hanna Holborn Gray Special Collections Research Center, University of Chicago Library.

14 **"I don't believe for a moment you teach less well."** Maclean Papers, box 10, folder 13.

14 **"Chicago is a rather large place"** Norman Maclean to Rebecca McCarthy, January 4, 1973.

CHAPTER 2. LIGHT AND SHADOW

19 **Norman went to Florida to spend ten days with Larry Kimpton** Norman Maclean to Rebecca McCarthy, February 5, 1973.

19 **he wrote another letter of support** Norman Maclean to Rebecca McCarthy February 5, 1973.

19 **Norman was working on his** USFS **story, corresponding with Bud Moore** Maclean Papers, box 14, folder 29. Personal communication with Maclean scholars George Jensen and Heidi Skurat Harris of the University of Arkansas at Little Rock.

19 **"I'll try to finish my story on the good old** USFS**"** Norman Maclean to Rebecca McCarthy, February 14, 1973.

20 **Norman also won sixth place in the 1923 Witter Bynner poetry contest** *Daily Missoulian*, November 21, 1923.

21 **"Dream a bit with me—"** *Daily Missoulian*, January 21, 1922, quoting the Dartmouth *Bema*.

22 **"You know, I am picking you to be an extra fine woman"** Norman Maclean to Rebecca McCarthy, January 7, 1973.

22 **His wife, Jessie, had undergone radiation for cancer** Norman Maclean to Rebecca McCarthy, April 12, 1973.

23 **"The poets are always talking about the lights and shadows"** Norman Maclean to Rebecca McCarthy, May 11, 1973.

23 **Norman was going to be attending a retirement barbecue** Norman Maclean to Rebecca McCarthy, May 17, 1973.

24 **An English major writing to support Norman told administrators** Maclean Papers, box 6, folder 15.

24 **he also received a one thousand–dollar check "and an ovation"** Norman Maclean to Rebecca McCarthy, June 10, 1973.

24 **a postcard of Seeley Lake arrived from Norman** Norman Maclean to Rebecca McCarthy, June 16, 1973.

25 **I learned that he had written to a friend** Norman Maclean to Bud and Janet Moore, February 1980, Archives and Special Collections, Mansfield Library, University of Montana Missoula.

CHAPTER 3. SEELEY LAKE SUMMER

30 **On the first draft, he criticized his work** Maclean Papers, box 34, folder 1.

31 **My brother, he wrote, was spending his evenings courting women** Norman Maclean to Rebecca McCarthy, September 8, 1973.

32 badgered John D. Rockefeller into funding a university When in Rockefeller Chapel, some alumni sing a version of the Doxology that begins: "Praise John from whom oil blessings flow."

32 Norman spoke about the art of teaching Norman Maclean, "This Quarter I Am Taking McKeon: Some Notes on the Art of Teaching," *University of Chicago Alumni Magazine* 66 (January–February 1974): 8–12.

33 he started immediately writing another iteration Maclean Papers, box 33, folder 13.

33 Norman told him he had finished the first draft of "a long story" Norman Maclean to Bud Moore, February 24, 1974, Archives and Special Collections, Mansfield Library.

34 "This Quarter I Am Taking McKeon" *University of Chicago Alumni Magazine* 66 (January–February 1974).

34 Norman felt writing "is all hard and tortuous" Maclean Papers, box 6, folder 15.

35 "I saw a famous man eating soup. That's what Sandburg might say." Here's the entire Carl Sandburg poem:

I saw a famous man eating soup.
I say he was lifting a fat broth
Into his mouth with a spoon.
His name was in the newspapers that day
Spelled out in tall black headlines
And thousands of people were talking about him.

    When I saw him,
He sat bending his head over a plate
Putting soup in his mouth with a spoon.

CHAPTER 4. WALKING THE CITY THROUGH STORIES

38 Fifty-Fifth Street had been one of Hyde Park's major areas for shopping and entertainment Whet Moser, "Chicago's Urban Renewal Displaced an Astonishing Number of People in the 20th Century," *Chicago*, January 18, 2018, https://www.chicagomag.com/city-life/January-2018 /Chicagos-Urban-Renewal-Displaced-An-Astonishing-Number-of-

People-in-the-20th-Century; "Hyde Park Remembered," *The University and the City: A Centennial View of the University of Chicago*, Hanna Holborn Gray Special Collections Research Center, accessed November 1, 2023, https://www.lib.uchicago.edu/collex/exhibits/university-chicago-centennial-catalogues/university-and-city-centennial-view-university-chicago/university-neighborhood/hyde-park-remembered.

38 **The buildings that had gone up in the late 1950s and early 1960s** In the late 1950s, crews demolished 638 houses, apartments, and businesses, displacing 4,000 families, and built 2,100 new structures in Hyde Park. "South East Chicago Commission: A Long Legacy," https://www.secc-chicago.org/about/legacy.

41 **one of Norman's favorite sculptures, *Fountain of Time*** The sculpture has been restored and renovated many times. "*Fountain of Time*," Wikipedia, last edited on 5 October 2023, https://en.wikipedia.org/wiki/Fountain_of_Time.

42 **there was a sculpture that looked to me like a giant skull** Daniel Diermeier, "Commemorating the 75th Anniversary of the First Sustained Nuclear Reaction," University of Chicago Office of the Provost, September 17, 2017, https://provost.uchicago.edu/announcements/commemorating-75th-anniversary-first-sustained-nuclear-reaction.

42 **the next decade saw Norman juggling family duties in Montana and Chicago** "Commemorating the 75th Anniversary."

43 **what Norman remembered about the war years was being "exhausted all the time"** William Kittredge and Annick Smith, "The Two Worlds of Norman Maclean: Interviews in Montana and Chicago," *Tri-Quarterly* 60 (Summer 1984).

43 **"It was an unreal life on the campus."** Norman Dolnick to Rebecca McCarthy, 1999.

43 **the university began offering preinduction military training to volunteers** Professor A. L. H. Rubin to (university president) Robert Hutchins, November 17, 1941, Presidents' Papers, University of Chicago, 1925–45.

43 **Norman told Chicago student George McElroy that he used the same method** George McElroy to Rebecca McCarthy, September 2000.

44 **He was earning an annual salary of $3,150** University of Chicago,

"Llewellyn John and Harriet Manchester Quantrell Awards for Excellence in Undergraduate Teaching," accessed November 1, 2023, https://www.uchicago.edu/about/accolades/35.

44 "The study of English literature, especially lyric poetry, is the best preparation for the law" *Chicago Tribune*, July 16, 2019.

44 "He taught me to read every word of a poem" Bill Barnhard and Gene Schlickman, *John Paul Stevens: An Independent Life* (Dekalb: Northern Illinois University Press, 2010), 40.

44 The effort to have Chicagoans donate to the university had begun in the early 1900s Ron Chernow, *Titan: The Life of John D. Rockefeller* (New York: Random House, 1998), 497.

44 Celebratory events culminated in September 1941 *Chicago Tribune*, September 21 and 27, 1941.

45 "When they called his name, he stood up" Maclean Papers, box 2, folder 32.

45 Participants talked about new discoveries *Chicago Tribune*, September 21 and 27, 1941.

45 Norman said his own presentation "went very well." Maclean Papers, box 2, folder 32. Norman says Hutchins appeared before his lecture had begun and grumbled: "Where's Maclean? I came for Maclean!"

45 "I feel alive a thousand times more talking before a big crowd" Maclean Papers, box 2, folder 32.

45 Two weeks after the bombing of Pearl Harbor, Norman wrote President Hutchins Norman Maclean to Robert Maynard Hutchins, December 17 and 26, 1941.

45 A letter to Norman late that December from the Reverend John Norman Maclean Maclean Papers, box 2, folder 31.

46 renewed their friendships with old friends and First Presbyterian members Interviews conducted with First Presbyterian Church members in Missoula, 1999.

46 In Ringling, Montana, the conductor stopped the train Maclean Papers, box 6, folder 2.

46 The Reverend E. R. Cameron of First Presbyterian eulogized John Norman *Daily Missoulian*, January 14, 1942.

47 **Both Norman and Jessie adored her.** Reported by numerous Maclean friends and family members.

47 **In a letter two months later to President Hutchins** Norman Maclean to Robert Maynard Hutchins, April 23, 1942.

47 **He applied to be a gunnery officer in naval aviation** Norman Maclean to Robert Maynard Hutchins, June 29, 1942.

47 **He was offered a commission in the naval reserve** Maclean Papers, box 15, folder 13.

47 **Norman, ever the teacher, cowrote with Everett C. Olson** Norman Maclean and Everett C. Olson, *Manual of Instruction in Military Maps and Aerial Photographs* (New York: Harper & Sons, 1943).

48 **he turned them around and around to confuse them** Norman Maclean to Kenneth Pierce, May 6, 1983, Maclean Papers, box 22, folder 18.

48 **"His letter must have been most persuasive"** Gordon McTeague to Rebecca McCarthy, July 22, 1999.

48 **Gans wrote Norman that "his investment paid off"** Herbert Gans to Rebecca McCarthy, August 10, 1999.

48 **a former student, on leave from the US Army, stopped by to see him** George McElroy to Rebecca McCarthy, July 1999.

49 **Norman, he recalled later, "was clearly glad"** Edward Muir to Rebecca McCarthy, August 31, 1999.

49 **"more news from The Light of Nature"** Norman was referring to naturalist John Muir.

49 **"So that's what's wrong with you," Norman shouted** Edward Muir to Rebecca McCarthy, August 31, 1999. Established in 1920 by Horace Spencer Fiske, the annual John Billings Fiske Poetry Prize is open to University of Chicago students.

50 **Colleagues said Norman was "always political"** Gwin Kolb and Ned Rosenheim interviews, summer 1999.

50 **"I heard you say in tones not untouched by manly sorrow"** Norman Maclean to Robert Maynard Hutchins, December 26 and 27, 1944.

51 **"I don't remember that very well"** Kittredge and Smith, "Two Worlds of Norman Maclean."

51 **"There are only a few people who have ever made a hell of a lot of difference to me"** Larry Kimpton to Norman Maclean, December 1947.

51 **Friends mattered to Norman and Jessie** Personal communication with Jean Maclean Snyder; Norman's eulogy for Joe Dunham.

52 **he picked up a copy of *Time* magazine** "Education: Worst Kind of Troublemaker," *Time*, November 21, 1949, https://content.time.com /time/subscriber/article/0,33009,856329-1,00.html.

52 **Norman responded to the story with a six-page letter** Maclean Papers, box 22, folder 3.

52 **"This guy Sterling . . . doesn't know an idea from six bits"** Lawrence Kimpton to Norman Maclean, December 1949, Hanna Holborn Gray Special Collections Research Center, University of Chicago Library.

CHAPTER 5. FINDING MONTANA

59 **"If you didn't kiss the ass of the Anaconda Company, you were a dead duck."** *Billings Gazette*, June 1, 1984, quoting a talk Norman gave to MSU students.

59 **He told me he had been miserable at Dartmouth** When I was thinking about plans after high school, Norman took me in hand and told me, in no uncertain terms, the Ivy League was "full of swells, pricks and bastards who don't know their ass from a hole in the ground. It's not the place for you. And how they treat and demean women. God." He wanted to spare me what he told me he had endured in the Ivy League—social stratification, puzzling traditions, secret groups, the pain of being an outsider because no ancestor had debarked from the "goddamned Mayflower." After warming up with more profanity for a few minutes until he was in high dudgeon, Norman offered suggestions for what the Ivy League could do with body parts and barnyard animals. Although I hadn't thought much about college, Norman's diatribe kept me out of New England altogether for more than a decade.

60 **Dartmouth was long celebrated for the quality of its teaching** Norman Maclean to Noel Perrin, December 4, 1978.

60 **Its buildings bordered a long, open expanse** "Use of the College Green and Campus Grounds," Dartmouth Student Affairs, accessed November 1, 2023, https://student-affairs.dartmouth.edu/policy/use -college-green-and-campus-grounds.

60 **A notation in his high school yearbook** *Bitterroot*, Missoula County High School, June 1920.

60 **Harvard had accepted him** Norman's younger cousin Arthur French, the son of his father's sister, would later attend Harvard and become captain of the winning football team.

60 **it was "the only outdoor college in the country"** Kittredge and Smith, "Two Worlds of Norman Maclean."

61 **Frost "talked straight to you"** Nicholas O'Connell, *At the Field's End: Interviews with 22 Northwest Writers* (Seattle: University of Washington Press, 1987), 228.

62 **Norman boxed with fraternity members and men from the community** Once, when he was with his father's family in Boston, Norman met the revered boxer John L. Sullivan. Thereafter, he sometimes used the phrase "Shake the hand that shook the hand of John L. Sullivan."

62 **It offered jokes and mocking editorials** The jokes in the *Jacko* were fairly gentle:

No, Petrarch, Christian Scientists are not forbidden by their creed to exercise with the medicine ball.

I'll kill the next man who says he hasn't been able to wade through Ludwig Lewisohn's "Up Stream."

News item—"A little girl returning from the movies was run over by an automobile and instantly killed." This is another horrible example of the dangers of children going to the movies.

62 **Another bright spot was his friendship with Theodor Seuss "Ted" Geisel** Theodor Seuss Geisel, *The Beginnings of Dr. Seuss: An Informal Reminiscence: Theodor Seuss Geisel*, edited by Edward Connery Lathem,

together with an introduction by President James Wright, published in commemoration of the one hundredth anniversary of his birth, March 2, 1904–2004 (Hanover, NH: Dartmouth College, [2004]), https://www .dartmouth.edu/library/digital/collections/books/ocm58916242 /ocm58916242.html.

63 **Dartmouth English professor David Lambuth** Though he was correct about Norman writing poetic prose, Lambuth vastly underestimated Norman's talent as a teacher. At the University of Chicago, Norman was the only faculty member to win a prestigious award for Excellence in Undergraduate Teaching three times. After forty-five years at the university, Norman retired as the William Rainey Harper Professor of English. I think he would have given Lambuth an F on his predictions.

63 **He had spent most summers working for the Forest Service** *Daily Missoulian*, September 13, 1924.

63 **Bravig Imbs, one of Norman's contemporaries, offers a glimpse** Wiki-pedia, s.v. "Bravig Imbs," last modified March 26, 2023, https://en .wikipedia.org/wiki/Bravig_Imbs.

63 **Norman makes an appearance in the book** Bravig Imbs, *The Professor's Wife* (New York: Dial Press, 1928), 285, HathiTrust, https://babel .hathitrust.org/cgi/pt?id=mdp.39015031500278&seq=291&q1=Douglas.

64 **He told the story of an "observer" visiting his class** "This Quarter I Am Taking McKeon," *University of Chicago Alumni Magazine* 66 (January–February 1974): 8–12.

CHAPTER 6. WESTERN FRIENDS

71 **he was thinking of giving up his cabin** Norman Maclean to Bud Moore, April 22, 1974, Archives and Special Collections, Mansfield Library.

71 **Norman appeared in the office doorway of Allen Fitchen** Maclean Papers, box 39, folder 8.

72 **"When we non-writers try to start writing in old age"** Norman Maclean to Bud and Janet Moore, May 26, 1974, Archives and Special Collections, Mansfield Library.

73 **chemists and physicists from around the world moved to Chicago**

Richard Rhodes, *The Making of the Atomic Bomb* (New York: Simon & Schuster, 1995).

73 **Some of the young chemists in the lab had taught at Deep Springs College** *Chicago Tribune*, December 22, 1951; and "Lawrence A. Kimpton, 1951–1960," Office of the President, University of Chicago, accessed November 1, 2023, https://president.uchicago.edu/directory /lawrence-kimpton.

74 **"Larry had been brought in"** *University of Chicago Record*, February 28, 1978.

74 **Lawrence Kimpton** Information from Norman to Rebecca McCarthy.

74 **He was called into Kimpton's office** *University of Chicago Record,* February 28, 1978.

75 **Kimpton didn't bond just with Norman** Gwin Kolb interview, 2000. Marcia was Larry's second wife.

75 **"Jesus, the tall tales we have told each other"** Larry Kimpton to Norman Maclean, December 22, 1949.

CHAPTER 7. TRAGEDY WAS INEVITABLE

78 **years after Norman died, four of the chapters** That book is *The Norman Maclean Reader*, edited by O. Alan Weltzien (Chicago: University of Chicago Press, 2008).

78 **Utley had spent his college summers working at Little Bighorn** "Edward S. Luce, Commanding General (Retired), Department of the Little Bighorn," *Montana: The Magazine of Western History* 6 (Summer 1956): 51–55.

79 **"how kindly and gently Norman handled our 'collaboration'"** "Professor Maclean and General Custer," *Montana: The Magazine of Western History* 43 (Summer 1993): 75–77.

79 **Custer was never far from Norman's thoughts** Interview and emails with Michael Fixler, fall 1999.

79 **Fixler researched the proceedings of the US Army court of inquiry** Marcus A. Reno, *The Official Record of a Court of Inquiry Convened at Chicago, Illinois, January 13, 1879, by the President of the United States upon*

the Request of Major Marcus A. Reno, 7th U.S. Cavalry, to Investigate His Conduct at the Battle of the Little Big Horn, June 25–26, 1876 (Pacific Palisades, CA, 1951), History Collection, University of Wisconsin–Madison Libraries, https://search.library.wisc.edu/digital/AVS3OXJ4IU3VTA8P.

79 **"there isn't any doubt: Benteen screwed Custer"** Michael Fixler to Rebecca McCarthy, September 19, 1999.

80 **"I'm getting pretty old to write a book"** Weltzien, *Norman Maclean Reader*, 194.

81 **the editor-in-chief of Chicago-based Swallow House found the story "delightful and stunning"** Allen Fitchen interview with Rebecca McCarthy, 2000.

83 **"I find it somewhat ironical, Bud"** Norman Maclean to Bud Moore, July 7, 1974, Archives and Special Collections, Mansfield Library.

83 **Norman tried to impart confidence to Bud** Norman Maclean to Bud Moore, March 7, 1974. Archives and Special Collections, Mansfield Library, University of Montana Missoula.

85 **He had been grieving for that man since they were children** Maclean Papers, box 16, folder 6.

86 **he said he planned to buy new clothes** Maclean Papers, box 3, folder 1.

86 **Paul wouldn't have been walking around the neighborhood south of the Midway** "College Writer Found Slain," *Albuquerque Journal*, May 3, 1938.

86 **He also majored in English** Dartmouth College, Registrar's Office.

87 **Clack recalled how the three friends spoofed officials** W. Turner Clack to Norman Maclean, May 3, 1976.

88 **Norman encouraged Paul to move to Chicago** Story shared by Joel M. Snyder.

88 **Paul had left Helena the previous Friday** *Billings Gazette*, March 16, 1937.

88 **she was an intelligent and well-rounded student** *Maroon*, Champaign High School yearbook, 1925, 1926.

88 **she told authorities that she and Paul had been planning to marry** *Missoulian*, May 5, 1933.

88 **He mentioned being in "tip top physical condition"** Maclean Papers, box 3, folder 1.

91 **If only Paul hadn't died in the spring of 1938** A few months after Paul
Maclean was murdered, Norman and Jessie, along with the entire Burns
family, experienced another devastating loss. On September 2 Jessie's
younger sister Marjorie was riding in a car near Livingston when the
driver lost control of the vehicle and wrecked, killing Marjorie. She was
twenty-two and was working in the Montana headquarters of the Works
Progress Administration, whose office had moved from Helena to Butte.
The Reverend Maclean conducted the funeral service. I can't imagine
how Florence and John Burns handled the loss of their daughter or how
the other Burns children, including Marjorie's twin, Margaret, handled
the loss of their sister. Jean Maclean Snyder said her mother never spoke
about Marjorie, just as Norman never spoke about Paul.

91 **Gene Davis immediately sent Norman a note** Gene Davis to Rebecca
McCarthy, June 21, 2000.

91 **Norman was so distraught at the funeral parlor** Interview with Joel
Snyder.

91 **Hundreds of people jammed into First Presbyterian in Missoula**
Helena Independent Record, May 7, 1938.

92 **After the funeral, Norman and his parents went to their Seeley Lake
cabin** Maclean Papers, box 31, folder 2.

92 **A coroner's inquest later in May** *Billings Gazette*, May 25, 1938.

92 **the Reverend wrote Norman a letter describing the Christmas celebration** Reverend J. N. Maclean to Norman Maclean, December 28, 1941.

CHAPTER 8. CREATING THE COMMITTEE

94 **he was "trying to take old western bear stories and turn them into
art"** Norman Maclean to Bud Moore, January 23, 1973, Archives and
Special Collections, Mansfield Library.

94 **the highlight of his summer** Norman Maclean to Bud and Janet
Moore, September 18, 1974, Archives and Special Collections, Mansfield
Library.

95 **"Shortly before my retirement I began to write reminiscent stories."**
Maclean Papers, box 33, folder 13 (A).

95 **Norman delivered a revised version of "A River Runs Through It"**
From an essay Allen Fitchen shared with me, September 8, 1999.

97 **"The story means more to me personally"** Norman Maclean to Bud
and Janet Moore, January 22, 1975, Archives and Special Collections,
Mansfield Library.

98 **"I spent a year and a half (nearly) writing it."** Norman Maclean to Bud
and Janet Moore, February 17, 1975, Archives and Special Collections,
Mansfield Library.

98 **Norman sent the complete manuscript to Kenneth Pierce** Maclean
Papers, box 39, folder 8.

99 **Norman bemoaned that he had missed the chance to write a fuck-
you response** Norman Maclean to Charles Elliot, December 7, 1981.

100 **Norman showed the contract to Stuart Tave** Interview with Stuart
Tave, July 1999.

100 **Fitchen had to "standardize" punctuation, capitalization, and
hyphenation** George Jensen and Heidi Skurat, "Norman Maclean: A
Search for Beauty," unpublished book manuscript, 33.

100 **"I have already partly accomplished two things that I wanted to do"**
Weltzien, *Norman Maclean Reader*, 210.

101 **Norman published two scholarly articles** R. S. Crane, editor, *Critics
and Criticism, Ancient and Modern* (Chicago: University of Chicago
Press, 1952).

102 **In 1950, the same year she went to work** Personal communication from Norman Maclean to Rebecca McCarthy; and Jessie Burns
Maclean's memorial service, December 17, 1968, Maclean Papers, box 3,
folder 14.

102 **She was forty-five** Information from Dottie Burns to John Roberts,
1972.

102 **Friends of the Macleans remembered** Peg Rosenheim and Ruth Kolb
interviews, July 1999.

103 **Along the way, she became the effective housemother** Jessie Burns
Maclean Memorial Service, December 17, 1968. Jessie was "someone
everyone knew because Jessie was someone worth knowing," said Stuart Tave, former head of the University of Chicago English department.

Jessie was friends with the critic Morton Zabel, who had been an editor at *Poetry Magazine*. Norman didn't particularly like Zabel, but those in the English department said Zabel was devoted to Jessie.

103 **At the end of the year, Hutchins revealed he was leaving** Norman relayed this information to me with a laugh.

103 **The board of trustees announced in April 1951** "Lawrence A. Kimpton, 1951–1960," University of Chicago Office of the President, accessed November 1, 2023, https://president.uchicago.edu/directory/lawrence -kimpton.

103 **"Larry had to come in looking like a damn Rotarian"** Ned Rosenheim interview, July 1999.

103 **Kimpton found an institution with disaffected alumni** "Lawrence A. Kimpton, 1951–1960."

103 **It's a testament to Norman's loyalty** Wayne Booth interview, July 1999.

104 **Kimpton launched the Boy Scout campaign** *Chicago Tribune*, January 10, 1952.

104 **Julian Levi was known as "a tough-minded, virtuoso political charac-ter"** John W. Boyer, "A Hell of a Job Getting It Squared Around," *Occasional Papers on Higher Education* (Chicago: College of the University of Chicago, October 31, 2012).

104 **There had been talk about moving the university** Maclean Papers, box 11, folder 29.

104 **The commission and city officials plowed under historic buildings** Under the 1958 renewal plan, substandard buildings were demolished that housed 4,371 families, 1,837 of them white and 2,534 Black. Most of those forced to move were poor.

104 **"Norman wrote most of Kimpton's speeches"** Interview with Richard Stern, July 2000.

104 **NBC Radio broadcasted the *University of Chicago Round Table*** Laura Demanski, "Radio Days: Reviving the Spirit of the University of Chicago Round Table of the Air," *University of Chicago Magazine* (Summer 2017), https://mag.uchicago.edu/university-news/radio-days.

105 **he used Shakespeare to reveal some of his beliefs** Maclean Papers, box 22, folder 8.

105 **Norman and other faculty members welcomed fourteen graduate students** Norman Maclean to Chester Neudling, Division of Higher Education, Department of Health, Education and Welfare, Washington, DC, [1951].

106 **professional writer Richard Stern was put in charge** Norman Maclean to Chester Neudling, [1951].

106 **Stern . . . is remembered as "the best American author"** *New York Times*, January 24, 2013.

106 **They crowded into the Maclean apartment** Art Geffen, who worked at University Tavern, said he delivered a case of Old Underroof whiskey to the Maclean household every week in the 1950s.

106 **Clara Maclean wondered about the "finality"** Maclean Papers, box 3, folder 1.

107 **Students recall spending happy evenings** Interviews with many former students from the Committee on General Studies.

107 **the committee was built "on close personal relations"** Norman Maclean to Chester Neudling, Division of Higher Education, Department of Health, Education and Welfare, Washington, DC.

CHAPTER 9. SEARCHING FOR A STORY

117 **he did take a lot of photographs** *University of Chicago Convocation Record*, 1940.

117 **he received a letter from Dudley Meek** Dudley Meek to Norman Maclean, December 17, 1940.

118 **PhD candidate Robert Cantwell** Bob Cantwell email to Rebecca McCarthy, August 4, 1999.

118 **during his exam, he "ran into problems"** Terry Myers email to Rebecca McCarthy, July 21, 1999.

121 **"The essay marches steadily to your conclusion."** James Dowd McCallum to Norman Maclean, June 28, 1951.

121 **"What I want to convey to you now"** Ronald S. Crane to Norman Maclean, August 14, 1945.

121 **Little that Norman wrote was good enough for him** Richard Stern

Papers, box 33, folder 3, Hanna Holborn Gray Special Collections Research Center, University of Chicago Library.

122 **Younger faculty members, including Norman, embraced Crane's ideas** Gwin Kolb interviews, 1999–2001.

122 **"not a mass of facts but a narrative"** When Crane was dying, Wayne Booth went to visit him. He told Crane, "You're looking better," and Crane shot back, "What's your evidence?" Wayne's wife, Phyllis Booth, says this is a true story.

123 **Norman used the Socratic method in his teaching** *Hypotheses: Neo-Aristotelian Analysis*, no. 8 (Winter 1994).

CHAPTER 10. STUDENT AND TEACHER

126 **The oldest of seven children** The brother "Neal" who appears in "A River Runs Through It" is very loosely based on Doug, Jessie's brother, who lived on the West Coast, and her brother Art.

126 **Jessie was a lively, well-liked, attractive young woman** *Helena Independent-Record*, September 24, 1923. Jessie was a member of Kappa Kappa Gamma at Montana. *Missoulian*, November 2, 1924.

126 **After finishing her second year of college, she returned to Helena** *Missoulian*, November 2, 1928.

126 **Those dreams went up in smoke** *Dartmouth*, February 25, 1925.

126 **Norman and Paul "barely escaped"** "Norman, Paul Maclean Have Narrow Escape," *Daily Missoulian*, February 26, 1925.

127 **"Unlike Thomas Carlyle"** Lathem, *Beginnings of Dr. Seuss*.

127 **Mrs. David Lambuth had invited Norman to work on a second draft** Imbs, *Professor's Wife*, https://babel.hathitrust.org/cgi/pt?id=mdp .39015031500278&seq=291&q1=Douglas.

128 **Norman would make his way to the Quadrangle Club** Norman Maclean, "Billiards Is a Good Game: Gamesmanship and America's First Nobel Prize Scientist," *University of Chicago Magazine* (Summer 1975).

128 **No doubt there were some pretentious professors** Norman was proud to be a member of the "I Never Had Manly" club. John Matthew Manly

was said to be a brilliant and imperious scholar at Chicago who, with Edith Rickert, produced an eight-volume edition of the text of Chaucer's *Canterbury Tales*.

129 **Jessie traveled to Chicago by train** *Helena Independent-Record*, June 19, 1929.

130 **The cells housing the monks were cold** Maclean Papers, box 16, folder 1.

130 **Norman traveled to Montana in August** *Great Falls Tribune*, August 3, 1930.

130 **Jessie came home to Wolf Creek** *Great Falls Tribune*, September 2, 1930.

131 **the course was designed to generate "straight and independent habits of thinking"** John W. Boyer, *A Twentieth Century Cosmos: The New Plan and the Origins of General Education at Chicago* (Chicago: College at the University of Chicago, October 31, 2006).

131 **To lead the discussion sessions, Schevill hired Jimmie Cate** Maclean Papers, box 6, folder 8.

131 **Jessie and he married in Helena at her parents' home** *Helena Independent*, September 27, 1931.

131 **Norman's new position meant he earned more than slave wages** *Helena Independent*, September 27, 1931.

132 **Norman liked to tell a story about meeting Sherwood Anderson and Carl Sandburg** Kittredge and Smith, "Two Worlds of Norman Maclean."

132 **Norman and Jessie rode the train to Michigan City to be Schevill's guests** Kittredge and Smith, "Two Worlds of Norman Maclean."

CHAPTER 11. A CHOICE SOUL

133 **Dean of the College Chauncey Boucher described Maclean's work** Boucher's evaluation, dated 1935, is in the Presidents' Papers, 1925–40, box 42, folder 1, HHGSC, UC Library.

134 **The class of 1937 adopted him as an honorary member** Maclean Papers, box 33, folder 7.

134 **Jessie described Norman giving a 1935 lecture on *The Song of Roland*** Maclean Papers, box 2, folder 32.

135 **The family had its roots in the Scottish island of Coll** The Maclean male line of descent has been traced back at least as far back as the early 1700s. John Norman's father, Norman, was the son of Lachlan, son of Neil, son of Lachlan, son of Angus, son of Angus. John Norman's great-grandfather Neil lived on an estate on the Isle of Coll. When the kelp market collapsed after the Napoleonic Wars, hardship was widespread on the island. Neil's son Lachlan (1791–1855), John Norman's grandfather, left for Nova Scotia in 1821 with his second wife, Elizabeth Campbell, and their infant son, Neil (b. 1820). They landed at Cape Breton and traveled on to Pictou in an open boat. From there, they walked sixteen miles to Cape John, where Lachlan's sister Isobel lived on a farm. Thereafter, he worked at his trade and was called "Lachainn Saor" (Gaelic for "Lachlan the carpenter"). Lachlan and his family eventually settled on a farm at a place called Keppock in Antigonish County. He is buried at Glenbard Cemetery, Pictou County. Genealogy of the McLean Family, Norman McLean, Vancouver, 1924.

136 **he wrote for a monthly humor magazine** John Norman had a youthful flair for writing poetry and was the darling of his sisters and mother, who gave him a proper Presbyterian upbringing, with a strong emphasis on education. He finished Pictou Academy in Antigonish and briefly taught at the Marshy Hope School, before going on to Dalhousie University in Halifax in 1885. There he led a very active life as a student: he served as editor of the school newspaper, joined the rugby club, and took classes in Latin, Greek, and English. John Norman also wrote for the *Dalhousie Gazetteer*, a monthly humor magazine, producing articles and funny poems about fishing. He was known to spend his free time casting for salmon and trout along the rivers of North Umberland. While he wasn't an honors student, he was immensely popular, often giving witty toasts at student dinners. Even after he left Dalhousie, without a degree, in 1889, the campus newspaper continued to mention him, which was unusual for a person of no great means.

136 **They were all proud of John Norman and his career as a minister** Personal communication from Norman Maclean, n.d.

136 **Mowbray School in southern Manitoba** "Historic Sites of Manitoba:

Mowbray School No. 245 (Municipality of Pembina)," Manitoba Historical Society, Winnipeg, last updated November 4, 2021, http://www.mhs.mb.ca/docs/sites/mowbrayschool.shtml.

136 **San Francisco Theological Seminary in San Anselmo, California** "Celebrating 150 Years of Theological Education," University of Redlands, accessed November 1, 2023, https://www.redlands.edu/study/schools-and-centers/gst/sfts/history.

136 **He and Clara were married on August 1** "Maclean Family Record," researcher Dr. Jim Habeck, IAGenWeb Project, accessed November 1, 2023, http://iagenweb.org/page/famrecd/maclean/page1.html.

137 **Clarinda was laid out in a grid** "History," Clarinda Chamber of Commerce, accessed November 1, 2023, https://clarinda.org/history.

137 **Chestnuts and Dutch elms shaded the town's streets.** Nodaway Valley Historic Museum, Clarinda, IA.

137 **The town had two schools** *Iowa: A Guide to the Hawkeye State*, compiled and written by the Federal Writers' Project of the Works Progress Administration for the state of Iowa, reprint of 1949 Hastings House edition (St. Clair Shores, MI: Scholarly Press, 1977).

137 **Clarinda hosted a Chautauqua assembly at its fairgrounds** Nodaway Valley Historic Museum, Clarinda, IA.

137 **like the rest of Iowa, Clarinda was dry** "Early Temperance Activity in Iowa," Iowa Pathways, PBS, accessed November 1, 2023, https://www.iowapbs.org/iowapathways/mypath/2631/early-temperance-activity-iowa.

137 **Clara was a lifelong teetotaler** Interview with Jean Maclean Snyder.

138 **a welcoming reception at which the Reverend's parishioners "invoked his work and help"** *Clarinda (IA) Herald*, April 11, 1902.

138 **he took the pulpit at First Presbyterian** Though it was named First Presbyterian when the Macleans were in Iowa, the church later became Westminister Presbyterian.

138 **a friend and fellow Presbyterian minister told the Reverend about a pastoral position** The friend was the Reverend John H. McJunkin (1869–1915), an Iowa native and a graduate of Parsons College in Fairfield, founded and staffed by Presbyterians, and of the McCor-

mick Theological Seminary in Chicago. The two men probably met in Iowa at a Presbytery meeting. McJunkin served as interim pastor at Presbyterian churches throughout Iowa and in much of the Northwest, including First Presbyterian in Missoula, where Reverend Maclean was later pastor. It's likely McJunkin both recommended Maclean for an honorary doctorate from Parsons and alerted him to the job opening in Missoula. Reverend McJunkin died of pneumonia in Helena when he was forty-five. John Norman said of his friend: "He was genial, witty, the life of every company in which he found himself, always ready with a good story, which was always a clean story. He was a staunch friend, clean, never compromising himself as a Christian gentleman, although he lived for 20 years without a home with all classes and all conditions of people. Children loved him, old men and young men made him a comrade, and women trusted him. He was of splendid stock, his father being attorney general of Iowa, and of high rank as a statesman."

138 **"Mr. Maclean formerly lived in Bozeman"** *Clarinda Herald*, July 19, 1907.

138 **he had vacationed in Yellowstone National Park with another Presbyterian minister** *Adams County Free Press* (Corning, IA), July 24, 1907.

139 **the family was heading to Montana** *Clarinda Herald*, January 28, 1909.

139 **Clara received gifts from the church's Young People's Society** *Clarinda Herald*, February 11, 1909. She had worked closely with both groups since her arrival.

139 **the Amalgamated Copper Company, later the Anaconda Mining Company, was expanding its grip** "1870s–1900s: Copper and Development," Clark Fork Watershed Education Program, accessed November 1, 2023, https://cfwep.org/clark-fork-info/history/1870s-1900s-copper -and-development.

139 **It owned newspapers and legislators across the state** "The Press: The Chain of Copper," *Time*, June 1, 1959, https://content.time.com/time /subscriber/article/0,33009,811163,00.html.

139 **South of the train station was Higgins Avenue** National Register of Historic Places, National Park Service, March 19, 1990, https://mhs.mt .gov/Shpo/docs/MPDs/Historic-Resources-of-Missoula-MPD.pdf.

140 **Members of First Presbyterian, who had called Reverend Maclean to his new pastoral position, welcomed the family** *Missoulian*, September 11, 1910.

140 **From their home, the Macleans could hear the whistle of the Northern Pacific trains** The Higgins Street Bridge was washed away during a flood on the Clark Fork in June 1908 and was replaced by a temporary swinging bridge that was very rickety. Stan Cohen and Frank Houde, *Missoula-Bitterroot Memory Book: A Picture Postcard* (Missoula: Pictorial Histories, 1979); and *Missoulian*, June 8, 2008.

140 **it still had vestiges of a wide-open western town, with ample opportunities for vice and sin** Lenora Koelbel, *Missoula the Way It Was: Portrait of an Early Western Town* (Missoula: Gateway Printing and Lithography, 1972).

140 **Missoula was to become the setting for a free speech struggle that October** Percy Stickney Grant, *Fair Play for the Workers* (New York: Moffat, Yard and Company, 1919), 267, Google Books, https://tinyurl.com/y7tc9e9b.

140 **the biggest forest fire of the twentieth century** Information about the 1910 fire is drawn from several sources, including Elers Koch, Joe B. Halm, and Mr. Swaine, *When the Mountains Roared: Stories of the 1910 Fire*, R1-78-30 (US Department of Agriculture, Forest Service, Idaho Panhandle National Forests, 1978), http://npshistory.com/publications/usfs/region/1/idaho-panhandle/r1-78-30/sec1.htm; Elers Koch, "History of the 1910 Forest Fires—Idaho and Western Montana," in Koch, Halm, and Swaine, *When the Mountains Roared*; Stan Cohen and Don Miller, *The Big Burn: The Northwest's Forest Fire of 1910* (Missoula: Pictorial Histories, 1978); Timothy Egan, *The Big Burn: Teddy Roosevelt and the Fire That Saved America* (New York: Houghton Mifflin Harcourt, 2009).

142 **a gathering where the Reverend and other Scotsmen were telling stories** George Wiesel to Rebecca McCarthy, June 12, 1999. Scotty Brown, a wool merchant, was the Reverend's best friend. When they were together and imbibing even slightly, their brogues became so thick that few could understand them, according to many in attendance.

142 **Sawn from the lake's shores, the notched logs formed a box** David Roberts, "A Journey to Montana: Old Scenes, Old Friends," *Cincinnati Post*, July 21, 1975, Maclean Papers.

143 **Clara "was one of those chipper ladies who was always pleasant"** C. W. Leaphart to Rebecca McCarthy, December 15, 1999.

143 **a friend and fellow Presbyterian minister** The friend was the Reverend John H. McJunkin (1869–1915).

143 **Parsons College in Fairfield conferred on John Norman an honorary Doctor of Divinity degree** *Ottumwa (IA) Tri-Weekly Courier*, June 11, 1910.

144 **Norman served as an usher** Maclean Papers, box 8, folder 16.

146 **C. W. Leaphart knew "both of those boys could fight like the devil"** C. W. Leaphart to Rebecca McCarthy, December 15, 1999.

146 **The Reverend knew something about fighting** John Norman's father, Norman, and his four brothers were renowned for their practical jokes, their abilities to thrash their opponents, and their sense of loyalty to the clan.

147 **Norman later said his father's reading aloud "was very good for me"** Maclean Papers, box 30, folder 7.

147 **the Reverend "had heard of another Scot, James Mill, who had achieved some spectacular effects** Weltzien, *Norman Maclean Reader*, 193.

CHAPTER 12. TRAGEDY AND ACCIDENT

149 **Dotty Burns, Norman's beloved sister-in-law, had died** *Helena Independent Record*, June 26, 1975.

149 **Kenny and Dotty in the cabin—cleaning, buying groceries, fixing meals** Maclean Papers, box 55, folder 11. During his research and writing on a manuscript that became *Young Men and Fire*, Norman kept notebooks on which chapters he needed to work on and what he needed to do. At times, he was despairing; at other times, he was giving himself a pep talk about getting back to work and doing a good job.

150 **He also wanted to learn about the character of the firefighters** Maclean Papers, box 55, folder 11.

151 **Norman wasn't reporting a story; he was telling one.** Norman Maclean, *Young Men and Fire* (Chicago: University of Chicago Press, 1992), 113.

152 **Norman was trying to reconcile history with imagination** Interview with John Cawelti, July 2021.

152 **he hadn't written "a line since last September"** Weltzien, *Norman Maclean Reader*, 198.

152 **after 1960, Jessie no longer accompanied him to Seeley Lake** Interview with Jean Maclean Snyder.

153 **In early March 1963, Jessie lost Marcia Kimpton** *Chicago Tribune*, March 7, 1963.

153 **Muriel McKeon, Jessie's other close friend, died of cancer** *Chicago Tribune*, May 23, 1964.

153 **People remember Jessie sitting with Muriel nightly** Interview with Ruth Bowen, July 1999.

153 **he confessed to Robert Utley that he seemed "to be defeated by the defeat"** Weltzien, *Norman Maclean Reader*, 201.

153 **Norman was walloped by chronic health problems** Interview with Jean Maclean Snyder.

153 **he tried not to be depressed about a lack of progress on the Custer book** Weltzien, *Norman Maclean Reader*, 205.

153 **he continued to compile his annual chairman's letter** Norman Maclean to the Committee on General Studies in the Humanities, September 6, 1963.

154 **Jessie also was periodically hospitalized** Personal communication with Jean Maclean Snyder and Joel Snyder.

154 **"It was a horrible disease"** Interview with Ruth Bowen, July 1999.

154 **That year found Norman in the hospital four different times** Norman Maclean wrote on July 10, 1966, to Robert Utley, cited in "Professor Maclean and General Custer," in *Montana: The Magazine of Western History*, Summer 1993, pages 75–77; and in O. Alan Weltzien's "A 'Mail-Order Marriage': The Norman Maclean–Robert Utley Correspondence," *Montana: The Magazine of Western History*, Winter 1998.

154 **Norman wrote that he had spent half of 1964 in the hospital** Norman Maclean to Lois Applebaum, January 13, 1965.

154 **"It is a good time to resign"** Norman Maclean to Robert Streeter and
Wayne Booth, November 8, 1965, Hanna Holborn Gray Special Collections Research Center.

155 **"Suddenly all of us realized that the emperor had no clothes"** John
Cawelti, letter upon Norman's leaving the Committee on General Studies, undated letter from 1965–66, Maclean Papers, box 18. This letter
is in a little book of letters of appreciation and remembrance about
Norman and the committee from students and colleagues, compiled by
Richard Stern. The dedication says: "Dear Norman, this is an edition of
one. It is for an edition of one."

155 **Norman had read the book while he was hospitalized** William
McNeill, undated letter from 1965–66, in little book of letters compiled
by Stern. Maclean Papers, box 18.

156 **"Everyone who spoke had his own style and was good"** Norman
Maclean to Jessie Burns Maclean, July 1966, Hanna Holborn Gray Special Collections Research Center.

156 **he thanked Jessie for adding staff to her medical school office** Norman Maclean to Jessie Burns Maclean, August 26, 1966, Hanna Holborn
Gray Special Collections Research Center.

156 **He missed Jessie, and he hoped she would come to Montana** Norman
Maclean to Jessie Burns Maclean, September 1966, Hanna Holborn
Gray Special Collections Research Center.

156 **He was also deluding himself** Maclean Papers, box 3, folder 5.

157 **Norman told him he wanted to write a book about the Sage Motel**
Interview with John Cawelti, July 10, 2021.

157 **he wouldn't be spending any more time on his Custer project** Weltzien, *Norman Maclean Reader*, 206.

157 **He had written at least four chapters** Some of Norman's writing on
Custer is found in Weltzien, *Norman Maclean Reader*.

CHAPTER 13. THE CRUX OF IT ALL

159 **Jessie Maclean received the Gold Key Award for Distinguished Service by the Medical Alumni Association** Memorial service program for

Jessie Maclean, December 17, 1968, Maclean Papers, box 3, folder 14.

160 **Masur remembers taking a Shakespeare course with Norman during fall quarter** Interview with Howard Masur, Spring 2021.

160 **she didn't want to live in a country that had elected Richard Nixon** Interview with Joel Snyder.

160 **Ned Rosenheim told me about that day** Norman Maclean to Marie Boroff, June 10, 1969.

161 **Nadel also took a Shakespeare course with Norman** Interview with Larry Nadel, spring 2021.

161 **Norman and he sometimes took walks, during which Levi told Norman he was thinking of studying history** Interview with David Levi, spring 2021.

162 **During the quarter, Elise said, she dropped in on a Shakespeare class Howard was taking** Interview with Elise Frank, spring 2021.

162 **Sometime in early 1970, Norman collapsed and was hospitalized** Weltzien, *Norman Maclean Reader*, 222.

163 **Gwin told me he called Joel Snyder** Gwin Kolb and Ruth Godbold Kolb interviews.

163 **Gwin and Ruth were alarmed by Norman's behavior** Personal communication from Jean Maclean Snyder.

165 **For Alm, that definition captured Norman perfectly** Brian Alm to Rebecca McCarthy, August 21, 1999.

165 **Joel thought Norman had had a stroke** Personal communication from Joel Snyder.

CHAPTER 14. THE WORK NEVER ENDS

167 **Norman had returned to Hyde Park after spending a week fishing** Maclean Papers, box 55, folder 11.

168 **I don't think he was prepared to learn how the federal government had mishandled its investigation** Weltzien, *Norman Maclean Reader*, 253.

168 **Weeks before the book's April release, the first review ran** *Publishers Weekly*, February 3, 1976.

169 **"a stunning debut by MacLean [*sic*]"** Red Smith, New York Times News Service, February 22, 1976.

169 **Norman wrote an essay, "Black Ghost"** Maclean Papers, box 55, folder 11.

169 **He sent a letter and a copy of the *Publishers Weekly* review** Norman Maclean to Bud and Janet Moore, February 27, 1976, Archives and Special Collections, Mansfield Library.

169 **Larry Kimpton read his early copy of *A River Runs Through It* and wrote Norman** Maclean Papers, box 11, folder 8.

170 **In early March, Norman got more advance copies** My copy of *A River Runs Through It and Other Stories* is inscribed with: "Dear Rebecca, I wish I could write poems. Maybe I'll try some day."

170 **Nick Lyons in the spring issue of *Fly Fisherman* said the book would become a classic** *Flyfishing Magazine*, Spring 1976.

170 **Ken Pierce reviewed the book for the *Village Voice*** *Village Voice*, May 17, 1976.

170 **"But it looks so much worse in print"** Personal communication from Joel and Jean Maclean Snyder.

170 **there was a reception for Norman's book at a crowded Ida Noyes Hall** Norman Maclean to Bud and Janet Moore, April 9, 1976, Archives and Special Collections, Mansfield Library.

170 **He was also continuing to nudge Bud Moore** Norman Maclean to Bud Moore, March 20, 1976, Archives and Special Collections, Mansfield Library.

171 **Studs Terkel brought Norman on his syndicated show, *Art of Conversation*** "Norman Maclean Reads from and Discusses His Book 'A River Runs Through It,'" audio recording and transcript, Studs Terkel Radio Archive, June 8, 1976, https://studsterkel.wfmt.com/programs/norman-maclean-discusses-his-book-river-runs-through-it.

171 **Norman wrote to me about Mrs. Heiserman's visit** Norman Maclean to Rebecca McCarthy, July 17, 1976.

171 **Heiserman later recalled . . . that she and Norman went fishing** Interview with Virginia Heiserman, summer 1999.

171 **Virginia told him she wished there was a phone in his Seeley Lake cabin** Maclean Papers, box 41, folder 20.

172 Norman continued working on the Mann Gulch story Maclean Papers.

172 "I get a good deal of pleasure spending hours talking to some of the big shots" Maclean Papers, box 4, folder 13.

173 Norman said he remembered Roberts's mother and father Maclean Papers, box 17, folder 7.

173 he wrote to Mann Gulch survivor Robert Sallee Maclean Papers, box 55, folder 2.

173 his son said he had never talked about the fire *New York Times*, May 31, 2014.

173 Norman traveled by truck to the top of Meriwether Peak Maclean Papers, box 54, folder 6.

173 "working for Sliman was something like working for Morris Philipson" Norman Maclean to Jean Maclean Snyder, September 8, 1976.

173 He told David Roberts he was "enraged" Maclean Papers, box 17, folder 7.

174 In early November, he wrote to Walter Rumsey Maclean Papers, box 55, folder 2.

174 He was having a hard time settling down Norman Maclean to Bud and Janet Moore, December 22, 1976, Archives and Special Collections, Mansfield Library. Norman wrote, "I would jump on you about your writing, but I'm having a hard time settling down to my second book—and I don't have to stop every now and then to run a trap line."

174 Sales of *A River Runs Through It and Other Stories* were increasing Norman Maclean to Bud and Janet Moore, December 22, 1976.

174 he wanted advice from Virginia and from Allen Fitchen Maclean Papers, box 48, folder 20.

174 Norman had been "hung up with a scriptwriter from Paramount" Maclean Papers, box 4, folder 13.

175 Larry's declining health worried Norman Maclean Papers, box 4, folder 13.

175 all traveled with Norman once again to Jasper-Pulaski Woods Personal communication with Nick Rudall.

176 It was one of the first things he talked about with me Maclean, *Young Men and Fire*, xix.

176 **He told the Billings audience, "So when I went about writing my first book"** Maclean Papers, box 30, folder 9.

176 **Norman also returned to Washington, DC** Maclean Papers, box 4, folder 13.

176 **The fiction committee "enthusiastically" recommended giving the prize** Francis Ward, "Near Miss for a Pulitzer Prize," *Los Angeles Times*, April 22, 1977.

177 **Norman said he wasn't happy about the situation** Maclean Papers, box 55, folder 2.

CHAPTER 15. LOOSE ENDS AND LONG FRIENDSHIPS

179 **A letter from Virginia Heiserman** Maclean Papers, box 41, folder 20.

179 **Norman was more than a little steamed** Maclean Papers, box 45, folder 19.

179 **His distress grew into fury** Interview with Wayne Booth, July 1999.

179 **the situation would give him a chance to ride in** Throughout his life, Norman was always an advocate for whomever he deemed to be the underdog, said his friends and family. That advocacy is also front and center in a June 10, 1949, letter he wrote to James A. Cunningham, the university's new vice president of business affairs. The vice president had fired a Mrs. Nellie Morrisey, a cleaning woman who had worked for the university for forty-five years, with no complaints about her competence. She had told faculty members about the man's actions. Norman, who was then a member of the faculty senate and a friend of university president Ernest Colwell, charged, spraying the man with sarcasm: "I swear that I belong to the school of economics that regards economics, like politics, as the art of the possible which may not be the same as the ideally just, and, that, therefore, I understood one of your major arguments. The other, that Mrs. Morrissey is and has been incompetent, I did not understand so well. I swear that I believe that after a person has worked 45 years for the same institution and then is discovered to have been incompetent all that time, the question of who has been incompetent is a very wide one." Mrs. Morrisey kept her custodial position. Maclean Papers.

179 **Norman was still making the fifty-two-mile trip** Personal communication with Joel Snyder; and recounted in Maclean, *Young Men and Fire.*

180 **Decades earlier, fire scientist Harry Gisborne had made the same climb** *Norman Maclean*, edited by Ron McFarland and Hugh Nichols, American Authors Series (Lewiston, ID: Confluence Press, 1988), 106.

180 **Norman occasionally told friends he would be happy** Norman said this to Ned Rosenheim, Gwin Kolb, Richard Stern, Bud Moore, and me.

180 **Norman's dealings with officials from Paramount** Maclean Papers, box 45, folder 19.

180 **He found his dealings with Paramount to be so humiliating** Maclean Papers, box 45, folder 18.

181 **"I've sold everything I've written or talked"** Maclean Papers, box 45, folder 19.

181 **Part of Norman's eulogy mentions Kimpton's writing style** *University of Chicago Record* 12, no. 2 (February 28, 1978).

181 **January 1978 was very harsh in Chicago** In the winter of 1977–78, Chicago received eighty-two inches of snow, the second highest amount of snow since city officials started keeping records.

182 **"I try to work every morning"** Norman Maclean to Bud and Janet Moore, February 1, 1978, Archives and Special Collections, Mansfield Library.

182 **he had seen no prints in the snow** Norman Maclean to Bud and Janet Moore, February 1, 1978.

182 **dealings with Paramount continued to exasperate him** Maclean Papers, box 45, folder 18.

182 **a script he received in May was "so distended now"** Maclean Papers, box 45, folder 18.

182 **he regretted "that you see me as the culprit"** Morris Philipson to Norman Maclean, May 8, 1978. Maclean Papers.

183 **the ties between Norman and the press were further loosened** Allen Fitchen to Norman Maclean, May 31, 1978.

183 **the press granted "all rights related to broadcast, performance, and dramatization"** Morris Philipson to Norman Maclean, April 14, 1980.

183 **Norman thanked Philipson for the letter** Norman Maclean to Morris Philipson, April 22, 1980.

183 A letter at the end of May to Robert Sallee and Walter Rumsey seems almost optimistic. Maclean Papers, box 55, folder 15.

183 Norman and Laird, along with Sallee and Rumsey, went by boat and foot to Rescue Gulch Maclean Papers, box 45, folder 15.

183 Sallee and Rumsey spent hours that hot July day Maclean, *Young Men and Fire*, 210.

184 Norman wrote a blistering letter to his longtime friend Wayne Booth Maclean Papers, box 5, folder 14.

185 it was time to "put an end to the whole proceedings" Maclean Papers, box 41, folder 20.

185 Early in 1979, Norman contracted shingles Maclean Papers, box 11, folder 12.

185 Grateful for a ticket to Missoula, Norman said yes Maclean Papers, box 12, folder 12.

185 There was nothing for Norman to do but write Norman Maclean to Bud and Janet Moore, March 9, 1974, Archives and Special Collections, Mansfield Library.

185 Norman told Bud and Janet he wasn't "taking any more shit" from the Forest Service Norman Maclean to Bud and Janet Moore, April 22, 1979, Archives and Special Collections, Mansfield Library.

186 "It enrages me to think of the time, money and pride we sacrificed" Maclean Papers, box 45, folder 19.

186 he had received a request from novelist Richard Ford for permission to include the story Maclean Papers, box 41, folder 18.

186 Norman wanted his story in Ford's anthology Maclean Papers, box 45, folder 19.

186 Norman had an answer for Ford Maclean Papers, box 45, folder 18.

186 sales of their newly published paperback edition The cover of that book features a photo of Seeley Lake, which is so long that it looks like a river, taken by my brother John B. Roberts Jr., from Double Arrow Lookout.

186 Ford didn't give up easily. Maclean Papers, box 41, folder 18.

187 Gisborne had a heart attack and died Maclean, *Young Men and Fire*, 154, 155.

187 "It was worth the trip out to see you" Norman Maclean to Bud and Janet Moore, November 4, 1979, Archives and Special Collections, Mansfield Library.

187 he wrote them a Christmas note Norman Maclean to Bud and Janet Moore, Christmas 1979, Archives and Special Collections, Mansfield Library.

CHAPTER 16. NO TIME TO TARRY

189 he talked about the time after the funeral Maclean Papers, box 18, folder 4.

190 one featuring beautiful photographs by Joel Snyder Maclean Papers, box 39, folder 15. Joel Snyder was for many years a full-time professional photographer before becoming an art professor at the University of Chicago.

190 Norman wanted to turn his full attention to his second book Maclean Papers, box 55, folder 1.

190 Forest Service engineers had constructed a sewage treatment facility Norman Maclean to Bud and Janet Moore, February 20, 1980, Archives and Special Collections, Mansfield Library.

190 Norman fired off a barrage of letters Norman Maclean to Bud and Janet Moore, February 18, 1980, Archives and Special Collections, Mansfield Library.

191 Norman told friends he intended to leave Montana Norman Maclean to Bud and Janet Moore, April 11, 1980, Archives and Special Collections, Mansfield Library.

191 The stinky facility was open Maclean Papers, box 6, folder 15.

191 Norman flew to Bozeman to receive an honorary doctorate Maclean Papers, box 55, folder 1.

192 a fellow graduate sent him a class memento Letter from Dartmouth classmate (class of '24).

192 Exactly what occurred isn't certain. Personal communication with Bud Moore, September 1987.

192 **Pete Dexter visited Norman in Seeley Lake** Pete Dexter, "The Old Man and the River," *Esquire*, June 1981. He visited Norman in Seeley Lake in October 1980.

193 **Norman struggled to know exactly what had transpired at Mann Gulch** Norman Maclean to Bud and Janet Moore, January 5, 1981, Archives and Special Collections, Mansfield Library.

193 **Walter Rumsey and Robert Sallee had relied on their memories and landmarks** *Los Angeles Times*, May 29, 2014.

193 **"the problem of what men who have escaped death remember"** Maclean Papers, box 55, folder 1.

194 **Sallee resented Norman saying that he and Rumsey couldn't remember** Mark Matthews, *A Great Day to Fight Fire* (Norman: University of Oklahoma Press, 2007), 229.

194 **"I have worked way too long on [my forest fire story] already"** Weltzien, *Norman Maclean Reader*, 244.

194 **he wrote a detailed analysis, chapter by chapter** Maclean Papers, box 60, folder 11.

195 **She had heard from others that Norman could "be a mean SOB"** Personal communication with Dorothy Pesch, October 2010.

195 **Norman was finished with Hurt** Maclean Papers, box 44, folder 24.

196 **Norman began seeing Jean Block on a regular basis** Maclean Papers, box 5, folder 12.

196 **"Right now, I am in the state of revision"** Maclean Papers, box 6, folder 15.

197 **She finally asked him to stop.** Personal communication from Joel Snyder, October 2010.

197 **he might have the car brought to Chicago** Maclean Papers, box 5, folder 12.

197 **Norman asked if he could see her before he left** Maclean Papers, box 5, folder 12.

198 **The two men met at Redford's Sundance Institute** According to its website, the Sundance Institute is a nonprofit agency, founded by Robert Redford, that "advances the work of independent storytellers in film

and theatre." "Our Story," Sundance Institute, https://www.sundance.org/about/us.

198 Redford was "pleased to hear the progress on 'A River Runs Through It.'" Maclean Papers, box 47, folder 7.

198 after Norman sent him a revised script Maclean Papers, box 47, folder 4.

198 Norman was irate Letter provided to me by the General Learning Corporation in Northbrook, Illinois.

199 The Christmas letter Norman sent in 1986 said Robert Redford was coming to Chicago Maclean Papers, box 48, folder 6.

199 Redford wrote Norman a letter detailing some of the problems he found Maclean Papers, box 48, folder 8.

199 Redford thought that Kittredge's script "has tried hard to be reverent to your wishes" Richard Friedenberg, *A River Runs Through It: Bringing a Classic to the Screen* (Livingston, MT: Clark City Press), 1, 2.

199 Norman battled his way through bad weather and sketchy flight connections Maclean Papers, box 33, folder 2.

200 Redford returned to Chicago in early February and met with Norman Maclean Papers, box 48, folder 8.

200 Redford read the working script in detail Maclean Papers, box 48, folder 8.

200 Norman began to regret ever having formed a partnership with Annick Smith and Bill Kittridge Maclean Papers, box 44, folder 8.

200 Norman received an honorary doctorate from Dartmouth Interview with Dorothy Pesch.

200 Norman was diagnosed with prostate cancer Maclean Papers, box 49, folder 9.

200 he traveled to Lewiston, Idaho, where he delivered a lecture at Lewis and Clark State College That lecture, along with others Norman gave, is found in *Norman Maclean*, edited by Ron McFarland and Hugh Nichols and published in 1988 as part of the American Authors Series by the short-lived Confluence Press in Lewiston. The collection also includes some of Norman's essays as well as criticism of *A River Runs Through It*.

200 "at the confluence of two of the mightiest tributaries of the mighty Columbia" Maclean Papers, box 49, folder 9.

200 "no matter what is ahead of me, I cannot afford to let the next eight months pass" Maclean Papers, box 49, folder 9.

201 Redford assured Norman that he was serious about making a movie with him Maclean Papers, box 49, folder 9.

201 Redford wrote in early November Maclean Papers, box 49, folder 9.

202 Friedenberg wanted to visit Norman in 1988 Friedenberg, *River Runs Through It: Bringing a Classic to the Screen*, 5, 6.

203 Dorothy Pesch and Jim Chandler, a Wordsworth scholar and a member of the English department, did visit Norman regularly Personal communication with Jim Chandler, June 1999.

203 Norman had such loving assurance from his children and his two Chicago grandsons Jacob Snyder says the name "Moose" originated in Seeley Lake, when he was a little boy. One morning, Joel, Jean, and Jacob had walked up from the lower cabin for breakfast. Norman was in the kitchen and said with great delight, "When I woke up this morning and looked down at the lake, I saw a big moose standing right on our rocky beach." Jacob was impressed. They started making breakfast, and Norman walked outside. A minute later, the Snyders heard a bellowing call. Norman walked into the cabin and asked Jacob, "Did you hear that moose?" Jacob said, "You the moose."

CHAPTER 17. HONORS AND UNFINISHED WORK

206 They entrusted the unorganized and unfinished sections to Alan Thomas Alan Thomas describes the process in a 2015 essay, "The Achievement of 'Young Men and Fire,'" *LA Review of Books*, September 10, 2015, https://lareviewofbooks.org/article/the-achievement-of-young -men-and-fire.

206 "There's a lot of tragedy in the universe" Maclean, *Young Men and Fire*, 156.

INDEX

Adler Planetarium, Chicago, 16
administrative work, 48–49, 51,
    101–2, 117–18, 152, 155
Aegis (yearbook), 62
Aeschylus, 118
Alfred A. Knopf, 97, 98, 99, 182
Alm, Brian, 164, 165
"Almost Duck Dogs" (Maclean), 181
Amalgamated Copper Company, 139
American Baptist Education Fund,
    128
Anaconda Mining Company, 59, 125,
    139
Anderson, Eugene, 131
Anderson, Sherwood, 132
Aristotelians, neo-, 43, 50, 119, 122, 123
Armour, A. Watson, 130
Arnold, Matthew, 95, 130
Art Institute of Chicago, 134
Art of Conversation (Terkel), 171
Associated Press, 90
awards, 49, 159, 191–92, 199, 200,
    205–6

Bailey, Dan, 191–92
Bailey, Helen, 191–92
Barnswallow (Schevill's vacation
    home), 131

Baxter Labs, 51
Beaver Mountain, 135
Benteen, Frederick W., 79
Berwanger, Jay, 47
Best, Charles, 44
Beta Theta Pi, Norman and, 61–62,
    85, 91, 155
"Big Two-Hearted River" (Heming-
    way), 211
Billings Hospital, 14, 41, 153, 160, 163
Bitterroot Mountains, 61, 169, 170
Blackfoot River, 31, 125, 195, 207, 211;
    fishing on, 169, 180, 212; photo of,
    112
"Black Ghost" (Maclean), 169
Bleak House (Dickens), 123
Block, Elizabeth, 197, 198
Block, Jean, 196, 197–98
Blunt, Judy, 207
Bob Marshall Wilderness, 32
Bond Chapel, Univ. of Chicago, 38
Booth, Phyllis, 162, 163, 185
Booth, Wayne, 71, 95, 99, 162, 163,
    206; on Norman/Virginia, 184;
    relationship with, 184, 185
Borns, Leslie, 116
Boucher, Chauncey, 133
Bowen, Ruth, 152–53, 154

Boyer, John, 131
Breaking Clean (Blunt), 207
Brown, Scotty, 237n
Browning, Robert, 95, 96, 97, 147
Browning Society, 95–96
Buckingham Fountain, Chicago, 16
"Burning Bright: The Life Story of a Tragedy" (Maclean), 167
Burns, Art, 232n
Burns, Dotty, 29, 30, 94, 149
Burns, Doug, 232n
Burns, Florence, 46, 228n
Burns, John, 228n
Burns, Kenny, 29, 30, 94, 149, 171; hunting with, 23, 31; Mann Gulch and, 52, 150
Burns, Margaret, 228n
Burns, Marjorie, 228n
Burns, Neal (fictional character): basis for, 94, 232n
Burns, Robert, 168
Burton-Judson residence hall, Univ. of Chicago, 196
Bush, Earl, 51
Byron, Lord, 130

Cainan, Daisy, 81
Cameron, Angus, 97, 98
Cameron, E. R., 46
Canterbury Tales (Chaucer), 233n
Cantwell, Robert, 118
Capone, Al, 12, 127
Carlyle, Thomas, 127
Carnegie Library, Clarinda, 137
Carrie, Sister (fictional character), 12
Carver, Raymond, 186

Catch-22 (Heller), 31
Catcher in the Rye, The (Salinger), 31
Cate, Frances, 131
Cate, Jimmie, 75, 131
Cawelti, John, 70, 151, 152, 157, 175; on General Education revision, 155; Norman and, 155–56
Chandler, Jim, 203
Chautauqua assembly, Clarinda, 137, 145
Chicago, 95, 117, 152, 163, 185, 211; Norman and, 10–11, 14–15, 127; violence in, 86, 159; visiting, 12, 15–17, 19; winter in, 37, 181–82, 245n
Chicago, Milwaukee & Puget Sound Railway, 140
Chicago Magazine, 175, 181
Chicago Manual of Style, 100
Chicago Metallurgical Lab, 73, 74, 114
Chicago Nuclear Experimentation Lab, 73
Chicago Sun-Times, 177
Chicago Symphony, 51, 56
Chicago World's Fair (1893), 40, 44, 55
Civilian Conservation Corps, 116
Clack, W. Turner, 87
Clarinda, IA, 136, 137, 138, 139; described, 144–45
Clarinda Herald, 138, 141
Clark Fork River, 140, 144, 146, 211, 237n
Clearwater River, 31, 200, 211
Cobb, Henry Ives: design by, 128
Cobb Hall, Univ. of Chicago, 38
Columbian Exposition (Chicago, 1893), 40, 44, 55

Columbia River, 200

Colwell, Ernest, 244n

Committee on General Studies in the Humanities, 56, 105, 153, 154, 155; courses of study and, 102; Kimpton and, 103; work with, 80, 106, 122, 152

Compton, Arthur Holly, 73

Court Theatre, Chicago, 34, 175

Crane, Ronald S., 50, 118, 122, 232n; on Maclean dissertation, 121; tragedy and, 152

Crane and Company (publisher), 117, 209

Critics and Criticism, Ancient and Modern (Crane), 101, 119

Croonenberghs, George, 94, 195

Crow Indians, 157

Cullen, Countee, 20

"Cumberland Cowboy," 209

Cunningham, James A., 244n

Curley, Michael, 163–64, 165

Custer, George Armstrong, 61, 157, 209; interest in, 77, 79, 80, 151, 152, 153; writing about, 78

Daily Missoulian, 126, 143

Daley, Richard J., 51

Dalhousie Gazetteer, 234n

Dalhousie University, 136, 234n

Dan and Helen Bailey Award, 191

Darrow, Clarence, 56

Dartmouth (newspaper), 62

Dartmouth Bema (literary magazine), 20–21, 62, 126

Dartmouth College, 94, 125, 128; caste system at, 64; honorary doctorate from, 192, 200; Norman at, 10, 59–63, 65, 91, 120–21; Paul at, 86–87, 91, 126

Dartmouth Jack-O-Lantern (humor magazine), 62–63, 126, 224n

Darwin, Charles, 123

Davis, Gene, 91

Decline and Fall of the Roman Empire (Gibbon), 123

Deep Springs College (California), 73, 74

Democratic National Convention (Chicago, 1968), 159

Department of Agriculture, 170

depression, suffering from, 11, 12, 163, 209

Dexter, Pete, 192

Dial (magazine), prize from, 20

Dickson, William, 92

Distinguished Professor Lecture (Stanford), Norman and, 192

Division of Fire Control and Air Operations (USFS), 11

Dodge, Wagner "Wag," 150, 177–78, 193

Double Arrow Lookout, 81, 116, 246n; photo of, 116

Duke University, 7, 12, 161, 176

Dunham, Bertrand, 51

Dunham, Joe, 51, 144

Dunham, Joyce, 51

Eliot, T. S., 20

Emerson, Ralph Waldo, 17, 132

emphysema, Jessie's, 1, 15, 102, 103, 154

"Energy and Montana Memory"
(Maclean), 176
"Episode, Scene, Speech, and Word:
The Madness of Lear" (Maclean),
101, 119, 121; quote from, 120
Esquire magazine, 181, 192

Fermi, Enrico, 73, 74, 75
Finnegan, William, 208
fire. *See* Mann Gulch Fire
firefighting, Norman's, 61, 169
First Presbyterian Church, Missoula,
20, 125, 141, 142; fifty-year celebra-
tion of, 156; influence of, 144; John
Norman and, 138, 216; memorial
service at, 46, 91; Paul at, 87; wel-
come to, 140
Fish Creek, MT, 169
Fiske, Horace Spencer, 222n
Fitchen, Allen, 71, 72, 83, 98; docket
by, 182; editing by, 100; Mann
Gulch and, 180, 181, 183; Norman
and, 80, 97, 167, 172, 175, 181; *River*
and, 95, 99
Fixler, Michael, 79, 80
Flathead Indians, 144
Flathead Lake, MT, 82
Florence Hotel, Missoula, 173
Fly Fisherman (Lyons), 170
"Fly Fishing" (Maclean), writing, 30
Flynn, Elizabeth Gurley, 140
Ford, Kristina, 186
Ford, Richard, 186, 208
Ford Foundation, 103
forest fire. *See* Mann Gulch Fire
forest fires, Norman fighting, 61, 169

Forest Service. *See* US Forest Service
"Forever" (Maclean), text of, 204
Fountain of Time (Taft), 41
Franck, James, 74
Frank, Elise, 162
French, Arthur, 224n
Friedenberg, Richard, 202
"From Action to Image: Theories of
the Lyric in the Eighteenth Cen-
tury" (Maclean), 101, 118
Frost, Robert, 61
Fulk, Phyllis, 138

Gallatin River, 136
gambling, 85, 89, 90, 140
Gans, Herbert J., 48
Gates-Blake Hall, Univ. of Chicago,
96
Geffen, Art, 231n
Geisel, Theodor "Ted" Seuss, 10,
62–63, 64, 127
"General Custer and the Battle
of the Little Big Horn: A Study
in Historiography and Literary
Method" (Maclean), 79
GI Bill, Gans and, 48
Gibbon, Edward, 123
Gibson, Mary Ellis, 120
Gisborne, Harry T., 180, 187
Glenbard Cemetery, Pictou County,
Nova Scotia, 234n
"God's Grandeur" (Hopkins), 67
Golden Book on Writing, The (Lam-
buth), 121
Gold Key Award for Distinguished
Service, 159

Good Day to Fight Fire, A (Matthews), 194

Gothic architecture, Univ. of Chicago, 38, 40, 196

Governor's Arts Award for Literature, 199

Grande Chartreuse (monastery), 130

Great Falls Leader (newspaper), 87

Great Falls Tribune, 87

Great Northern Railway, 126

Greer, Andrew Sean, 208

Groves, Leslie, 74, 75

Guggenheim smelter, Norman's work on, 125

Hamlet (Shakespeare), 105, 160

Hamm, Catherine, 163

Handel, Friedrich, 56

Harcourt, Brace and Company (publisher), 117

Hardy, Thomas, 102

Harmon, Bill, 13, 176

Harper, William Rainey, 32

Harper Library, Univ. of Chicago, 32, 34, 70

Hawley's Opera House, Clarinda, 136

Heiserman, Arthur, 17, 71

Heiserman, Virginia, 167, 180–81; Norman's relationship with, 71, 170–72, 174, 179, 184–85; *River* and, 183

Helena Independent, 87, 88, 129

Helms, Helen, 143

Hemingway, Ernest, 211

Higgins Street Bridge, Missoula, 139, 146, 237n

Hill & Wang (publisher), 70

Holland Lake, MT, 32

Hopkins, Gerard Manley, 67

hospitals: Billings, 14, 41, 153, 160, 163; Michael Reese, 165; Woodlawn, 89, 154

humanities: Norman on, 104–5; Norman's classes, 133, 134, 213; Norman's lectures, 45, 50; Schevill and, 130–31, 132. *See also* Committee on General Studies in the Humanities

humor: sardonic sense of, 61; in writing, 119, 126, 136, 234n. See also *Dartmouth Jack-O-Lantern*

Hurt, William: letters to, 195

Hutchins, Marcia, 75

Hutchins, Robert Maynard, 44, 47, 103, 129–30; changes by, 121; Kimpton and, 74; relationship with, 50–51, 52, 221n

Hutchins College, Univ. of Chicago, 103, 105, 112, 129, 131, 134

Hyde Park (Chicago neighborhood), 32, 41, 42, 74, 77; changes to, 1; described, 38; living in, 37, 56, 85, 164, 196, 202; structures in, 220n

Ida Noyes Hall, Univ. of Chicago: reception at, 170; story about suicide at, 70

Imbs, Bravig, 63

Industrial Workers of the World (Wobblies), 61, 140

"I Never Had Manly" club, 232n

Institute of Military Studies, Univ. of Chicago, 45, 47, 48

Institute of the Rockies, Billings, 176
Isle of Coll, Scotland, 135, 234n
Ivy League, criticism of, 10, 223n

Jacko. See Dartmouth Jack-O-Lantern
Jackson, David E., 91
Jackson Park, Chicago, 40, 55, 56, 116, 182
Jansen, Robert, 187
Jasper-Pulaski Woods, IN, 151, 175
Jensen, George, 29, 30, 33, 100
Jimmy's Woodlawn Tap (bar, Chicago), 38, 59
John Billings Fiske Poetry Prize, 49, 222n
Johnson, Samuel, 118, 162
"Joke of the Stars, The" (Maclean), text of, 19
Joseph Regenstein Library, Univ. of Chicago, 33, 39, 98, 149, 163, 171; sculpture at, 42

Keast, W. Rea, 122
Keats, John, 161, 162
Keller, Martha, 20
Kimpton, Eleanor, 72, 153, 175
Kimpton, Lawrence A., 19, 24, 51, 103, 160, 169; Boy Scout campaign of, 104; death of, 181; described, 72, 73, 74; health problems of, 75, 175; Hutchins and, 74; Marcia and, 153; Norman and, 74, 75, 167; photo of, 114; *River* and, 169; speeches by, 104; on Sterling, 52–53; as Univ. of Chicago chancellor, 53
Kimpton, Marcia, 75, 153

Kimpton, Mary, 167, 175
King Lear (Shakespeare), 120. *See also* Lear, King
Kittridge, William "Bill," 185, 187, 196; Redford and, 199; Smith and, 198, 199, 200
Koelbel, Lenora, 140
Kogan, Herman: on *River*, 177
Kolb, Gwin, 61, 101, 106, 162, 163, 204; on Norman, 99, 118, 160
Kolb, Ruth, 162

Lakeside, MI, 72
Lambuth, David, 63, 65, 121, 225n; character based on, 64
Lambuth, Myrtle, 63, 64, 127
Leaphart, C. W., 143, 146
Lear, King (Shakepearean character), 101, 119–20
Leopold, Richard, 56
Levi, David, 161
Levi, Edward, 14, 104, 160, 161
Levi, Julian, 104
Levi, Kate, 161
Lewis and Clark State College (Lewiston, ID), lecture at, 192, 200
Lewisohn, Ludwig, 224n
libraries: in Clarinda, 137; Norman and, 121, 144; Maclean papers at, 214; speech at, 32, 34; visiting McCarthy at, 56
Little, Brown & Company (publisher), 98
Little Bighorn, 135, 152, 183; interest in, 77, 78, 79, 80, 151, 209; visits to, 78, 153, 157

Llewellyn John and Harriet Manchester Quantrell Award for Undergraduate Teaching, 4

Lochsa, MT, 170, 186, 187

Loeb, Nathan, 56

"Logging and Pimping" (Maclean), 80, 94, 100; reading, 34–35; writing, 149

Los Angeles Times, 192

Luce, Edward, 79

Lynn, Teddy, 117

Lyons, Nick, 170, 174

Maclean, Angus (ancestor), 234n

Maclean, Clara Davidson (mother), 45, 106; cabin and, 47, 49–50, 142; Chautauqua and, 137, 145; church work and, 143; Clarinda and, 137; death of, 50; letter to, 134–35; marriage of, 136; Missoula and, 46, 140; Paul's death and, 91–92; teaching by, 144, 147

Maclean, Elizabeth Campbell (great-grandmother), 234n

Maclean, Isobel (great-aunt), 234n

Maclean, Jean (daughter). *See* Snyder, Jean Maclean

Maclean, Jessie Burns (wife), 37, 56, 129, 130, 165, 202; award for, 159; brothers of, 232n; caretaking by, 50; children of, 42, 47, 49; death of, 1, 14, 83, 160, 161, 190; drinking and, 137; friends and, 51, 75, 153; health problems of, 22, 102–3, 106, 152, 153, 154, 156; Kimptons and, 19, 153; lamb roast tradition

and, 56–57; marriage of, 125, 131; movie version of, 207; on Norman, 134–35; Paul's murder and, 91, 228n; photo of, 110, 111, 115; politics of, 61; pregnancy of, 46; sister's death, 228n; traveling and, 84; youth of, 126

Maclean, John Norman (father), 45–46, 139, 175, 234n, 236n, 237n; death of, 42, 46, 91, 92; described, 141–42, 143, 146–48; honorary doctorate for, 143; marriage of, 136; on McJunkin, 236n; Missoula and, 140, 141; outdoor life and, 138; photo of, 109, 111; youth of, 135–36

Maclean, John Norman (son), 47, 71

Maclean, Lachlan (ancestor), 234n

Maclean, Neil (ancestor), 136, 234n

Maclean, Norman: birth of, 136–37; death of, 203–4, 205, 206; described, 1–2, 5–7, 146–47; drinking with, 7–9, 57–58, 59, 69, 106, 164; family of, 134–35, 196; health problems of, 102, 152–53, 163, 180, 185, 192–93, 200-201; marriage of, 125, 131; Paul's murder and, 89–90, 94, 228n; photo of, 109, 115, 116; silhouette by, 110 (fig.); teaching by, 101–2, 117–18, 122–24, 127–29, 130, 133–34; youth of, 142, 144, 147–48

Maclean, Norman (grandfather), 234n, 238n

Maclean, Paul (brother): apartment fire and, 126; birth of, 136–37; career of, 87–88; Chicago and, 9, 86, 88; described, 85, 90, 146–47,

Maclean, Paul (brother) (*continued*) 210; fighting and, 146; fishing and, 171, 211, 212; grieving for, 2; movie version of, 101, 199, 207; murder of, 46, 84–90, 91–92, 101, 164, 228n; photo of, 112, 113; youth of, 142, 143, 144, 147–48

Maclean House, naming of, 205

MacNeil, Douglas (fictional character), 63, 64

Madison Park area, Chicago, 106, 163, 164, 165

Madison River, 136

Manchester (NH) Union Leader, 90

Mandel Hall, Univ. of Chicago, 45, 104, 134

Manhattan Project, 73

Manly, John Matthew, 232–33n

Mann Gulch, 90, 176, 185, 187, 193; history of, 150, 151, 152

Mann Gulch Fire, 51, 167, 173; fighting, 177; lessons from, 168, 169, 206, 207; research on, 181–82; story of, 196–97; USFS files on, 170; writing about, 172, 174, 177, 179–80, 182–83, 186, 189

Mann Gulch manuscript, 187, 201, 205, 206; reworking, 194–95. See also *Young Men and Fire*

Manual of Instruction in Military Maps and Aerial Photographs (Olson), 47

Marshall Field (retailer), 128

Masur, Howard, 159–60, 162

Matthews, Mark, 194

Maxwell House coffee company, 87

McCallum, James Dowd, 64, 121

McCormick Theological Seminary, Chicago, 38, 235n

McElroy, George, 43, 91

McGuane, Tom, 198

McJunkin, John H., 235–36n, 238n

McKeon, Muriel, 153

McKeon, Richard, 34, 51, 104, 121

McNeill, William, 155

McPhee, John, 208

McTeague, Gordon, 48

Medical Alumni Association, Jessie's award from, 159

Medical Alumni Bulletin, Jessie and, 153

Medici (coffee shop, Chicago), 202

Meek, Dudley, 117

Meriwether Peak, MT, 173

Michael Reese Hospital, Chicago, 165

Michelson, Albert, 128

Michigan, Lake, 38, 55, 56, 131, 163, 165

Michigan City, IN, 131, 151, 175; traveling to, 77, 132

Middle East Club, Chicago, 68

Midway (Midway Plaisance), Chicago, 40, 44, 84, 90, 101

Midway Airport, Chicago, 48

Midway Studios, Chicago, 41

Mies Van der Rohe, Ludwig, 40

Milagro Beanfield War, The (film, dir. Redford), 198

Mill, James, 147

Mill, John Stuart, 147

Millay, Edna St. Vincent, 62

Milwaukee Raiload tracks, 145

mining, in Montana, 135, 139–40

Mission Mountains, MT, 24, 32, 42, 84, 173, 204
Missoula, Lake, 144
Missoula, MT, 91, 93, 106, 138; described, 145, 146; Norman and, 125, 139, 140; pastimes in, 144, 145
Missoula City Cemetery, 46, 172
Missoula Mercantile, 139
Missoula Stampede, 145
Missoulian (newspaper). See *Daily Missoulian*; *Weekly Missoulian*
Missouri River, 142, 177, 180
Moby-Dick (Melville), 123
Montana Fish and Game Commission, 88
Montana Fish and Game Notes, 87–88
Montana State University, honorary doctorate from, 191
Montana State University (later University of Montana), 63, 126
Moore, Henry, 42
Moore, Janet, 83, 93, 182, 185, 187, 197; fishing with, 171; Mann Gulch and, 150, 169; "River" and, 97–98
Moore, William R. "Bud," 93, 170, 182, 185–87, 192–93, 197; correspondence with, 11, 19, 33; fishing with, 171; Mann Gulch and, 150, 169; Norman and, 71, 182, 206; "River" and, 33–34, 97–98; sewage treatment plant and, 190; "USFS 1919" and, 72, 83
Moran, Bugs, 127
Morgenstern, William, 88
Morris, Don, 94
Morrisey, Nellie, 244n

Mount Sentinel, MT, 145
Mowbray School, Manitoba, Canada, 136
Much Ado about Nothing (Shakespeare), 162
Muir, Edward, 49
Museum of Science and Industry, Chicago, 55–56
Myers, Terry, 118

Nadel, Larry, 161
Nader, Ralph, 191
Nash, Lois, 88, 89, 90, 92
Nasser, Gamal Abdel, 68
Nasser, Sliman, 173
National Book Critics Circle Award, 206
National Park Service, US, 79
National Scholastic Creative Writing Award for Poetry, 22, 23
National Society of Colonial Daughters, 145
NBC Radio, 104
neo-Aristotelians, 43, 50, 119, 122, 123
New York Times, 169
Nixon, Richard, 160
Nodaway River, 136, 138
Norman, Geoffrey, 208
Norman Fitzroy and Jessie Burns Maclean Scholarship, 205
Norman Maclean Faculty Award, 205
Northcott, Kenneth, 33, 151, 175
Northern Cheyenne Indians, 78
Northern Pacific trains, 139, 140
Northey, Dorcus, 143
Northwest Airlines, 28

O'Connell, Chuck, 196, 206

"Ode on Imitations of Immortality from Recollections of Early Childhood" (Wordsworth), 67, 209–10

O'Hare Airport, 23, 27, 163

Olmsted, Frederick Law, 40, 127

Olsen, Elder, 118, 122

Olson, Everett C., 47

"On First Looking into Chapman's Homer" (Keats), 161

"On the Concord and Merrimack Rivers" (Thoreau), 211

On the Edge of Swirls (Maclean and Snyder), 190

Origin of Species (Darwin), 123

Orwell, George, 118

Palace of Fine Arts, Chicago, 55

Palos Park, IL, 48, 56

Paramount, contract with, 174, 180, 182, 186

Parsons College, Fairfield, IA, 143, 235n, 236n

Pei, I. M., 38

People, story in, 174

Pesch, Dorothy, 193, 195, 203, 204

Philipson, Morris, 71, 97, 98, 173, 179; relationship with, 180–81, 182, 183, 184

photography, Norman and, 117, 133–34

"Pied Beauty" (Hopkins), 67

Pierce, Kenneth, 98, 169, 170

Pierce Tower, Univ. of Chicago, 32–33, 38, 124

Pine Needles (magazine), 23, 24

Pittsburgh Press, 170

Plato, 39

Poetics (Aristotle), 123

poetry, 61, 62, 64, 93, 132; British, 95, 98; critiquing of, 6, 12–13, 19–20; lyric, 43, 44, 47, 118, 119; Norman and, 6, 19–20, 21–22; technical aspects of, 96; writing, 10, 13, 19. *See also* sonnets

Poetry Magazine, 230n

Poetry Society of America, 20

poker, 10, 62, 63, 85, 89

Popular Photography, 110

Priest River, 30

Professor's Wife, The (Imbs), 63

Prohibition, 88–89, 131

Publishers Weekly, 168, 169

Pulitzer Prizes, 176, 177, 208

Quadrangle Club, Univ. of Chicago, 14, 35, 96, 128, 161

Quantrell Award for Excellence in Undergraduate Teaching, 24, 44, 225n

"Race That Couldn't Be Won, The" (Rothermel), 193

Rattlesnake Creek, 145

Redford, Robert, 4, 207; Kittridge and, 199; McGuane and, 198; Norman and, 198, 199, 200–201, 201–2; Sundance Institute and, 248n

Regional Fire Lab (USFS), 185, 193, 206

Republic, The (Plato), 39

Rescue Gulch, 183

"Retrievers Good and Bad" (Maclean), 181

Rich, Mabel, 145–46

Rickert, Edith, 233n

Rise of the West, The (McNeill), 155

River Runs Through It, A (film, dir. Redford), 4, 207; scriptwriting and development of, 198, 199–201

"River Runs Through It, A" (story, Maclean), 46, 121, 147, 164, 186, 232n; critique of, 34; film rights, 100, 190; Paul and, 84–85, 91; reading, 138; revision of, 95, 97; writing, 29, 33–34, 85, 93, 209

River Runs Through It and Other Stories, A (Maclean), 34–35, 48, 94, 97, 210; interviews about, 189, 190; promoting, 183; publication of, 3, 4, 99–100, 127, 167–69, 174; reading, 200; reception for, 168–69, 170, 174, 176–77; royalties for, 173; study guide for, 211; themes/characters of, 171; writing, 29, 208–9; *Young Men and Fire* and, 208–9

Roberts, David, 173–74, 211

Roberts, Frank, 173

Roberts, John B., Jr., 5–7, 10–13, 15, 84, 149; drinking with, 8–9; hunting with, 23; job for, 81; Meg and, 27, 28; photos by, 116, 246n; praying for, 22; second marriage of, 81; struggles of, 23, 28–29, 30, 31–32

Roberts, Marilyn, 5, 10, 11, 15, 30, 81; death of, 22–23, 27, 28, 29; illness of, 6, 7, 12, 22; respect for, 32; talents of, 31; writing about, 22

Roberts, Meg, 5, 6, 7, 15, 23, 24; caring for, 22, 27, 28, 29, 30–31, 81

Robie House, Chicago, 38

Robinson, Laird, 172, 179–80, 183, 184, 193, 206

Rockefeller, John D., 32, 44, 128

Rockefeller Chapel, Univ. of Chicago, 24, 129, 181, 205, 219n

Romeo and Juliet (Shakespeare), 151

Roosevelt, Franklin D., 56, 134, 160

Rosenheim, Edward "Ned," 22, 95–96, 99, 101, 103, 160

Roth, Marty, 79

Rothermel, Richard, 193, 206

R. S. Crane and Company (publisher), 117, 209

Rudall, Nick, 34, 100, 151, 175

Rumsey, Walter, 183–84, 193, 194; survival of, 178; testimony of, 185

Russell, Bertrand, 51

Russell, Charlie, 28, 51, 72, 114, 169

Saarinen, Eero, 40

Sadat, Anwar, 69

Sage Motel (near Little Bighorn Battlefield), 157

Sallee, Robert, 173, 183–84, 193, 194; survival of, 178; testimony of, 185

Sandburg, Carl, 20, 35, 132, 219n

San Francisco Theological Seminary, 136

Sapphire Range, 145

"Saul" (Browning), paper on, 96

Scarry, Richard, 15

Schevill, Ferdinand, 130–31, 132; photo of, 112

Schulman, Sidney, 159

Scott, Arthur, 131

Sears building, Chicago, 16

Seeley Campground, 13

Seeley Lake, MT: cabin at, 49–50, 92, 95, 142–43, 172, 185; photo of, 111, 116; saloon at, 31; traveling to, 81, 83, 84, 149, 168, 179; visiting, 171–72

Seeley Lake Inn, 81, 83

Seeley Swan High School, 31

Sevareid, Eric, 208

Seven-Up Ranch restaurant, Lincoln, MT, 5, 6

Shakespeare, William, 6, 120, 151, 160, 162, 208; reading, 13; teaching, 11, 79, 105, 118, 161

Shelley, Percy Bysshe, 130

silhouette, 110 (fig.)

Sinaiko, Herman, 122

Sioux Nation, 135; Sioux Indians, 78

Sister Carrie (fictional character), 12

Skurat, Heidi, 29, 30, 33, 100

Slaughterhouse 5 (Vonnegut), 31

smelter, Norman's work on, 125

Smith, Annick, 196, 198, 199, 200

Smith, Red, 169

Smokejumper Base, 185

Smokejumpers, 51, 150

Smokejumper Visitor Center, 172

Snake River, 200; wildfire along, 141

Snyder, Jacob (grandson), 200, 250n

Snyder, Jean Maclean (daughter), 59, 115; birth of, 47; cabin and, 71; criticism and, 24; on emphysema, 102, 154; Little Bighorn and, 78, 79; Mann Gulch manuscript and, 205;

Norman and, 49, 160, 163, 197; on Paul, 85; Redford and, 200, 202; River and, 94; royalties for, 173; travels and, 84

Snyder, Joel (son-in-law), 33, 61, 162, 190, 200, 202, 203–4; cabin and, 71; Norman and, 163, 164, 165, 171, 201; on River, 93

Snyder, Noah (grandson), 203

Socratic method, 123

Song of Roland, The: lecture on, 134–35

sonnets, 12, 71, 119, 209–10. See also poetry

South East Chicago Commission, 104

South Side, Chicago, 85, 88, 90, 116, 128

Spokesman-Review (newspaper), 170

Spring Gulch, 145

Stagg Field, Univ. of Chicago, 73

Standard Oil Building, 16

Standard Oil Company, 73, 153

Stanford University, 51, 103, 192

"Stanzas from the Grande Chartreuse" (Arnold), 130

Steinspring, Estelle, 186

Sterling, J. E., 52–53

Stern, Richard, 104, 106, 121, 240n

Stevens, John Paul, 44

Stevenson, Adlai, 56

Stochastics (faculty group, Univ. of Chicago), 35, 70, 80

Stowe, Ben, 173

Stromnes, Einar, 87

Sullivan, Bert, 81, 82, 150

Sullivan, John L., 224n
Sullivan, Louis, 151
Sundance Institute, 200, 248–49n
Swallow House (publisher), 81
Swan Range, 204; photo of, 116
Swan River, 31, 82, 197, 211; episode on, 192–93; fishing on, 180, 192
Swan Valley, 31, 187
Swift, Gustavus F., 129–30
Swift, Harold, 72
Swift, Jonathan, 35
Sylvia, Joe, 184
Szilard, Leo, 73

Taft, Lorado, 41
Tave, Stuart, 14, 100, 229n
Tennyson, Alfred, Lord, 67, 95, 118, 161
"Ten Standard Fire Fighting Orders," 177
Terkel, Studs, 171
"Theory of Lyric Poetry in England from the Renaissance to Coleridge, The" (Maclean), 43
"This Quarter I Am Taking McKeon: Some Notes on the Art of Teaching" (Maclean), 34
Thomas, Alan, 4, 206
Thoreau, Henry David, 211
Time magazine, 52
Top, Everett, 91
Trails Plowed Under (Russell), 72
Travis, Leslie: photo by, 115
Tribune Tower, Chicago, 17

University of Chicago, 88, 105, 154, 161, 167, 170; academic life at, 129; classes at, 94; considering, 12, 14, 15–17; design of, 128; fiftieth birthday of, 44; honor from, 205; World War II and, 43, 47, 48
University of Chicago Alumni Magazine, 94
University of Chicago Laboratory Schools, 44
University of Chicago Press, 4, 71, 95, 99, 186, 206; Norman and, 179, 180, 182–83, 184
University of Chicago Round Table (radio show), 104
University of Montana, 30, 185, 196, 207
University of North Carolina, 7, 118, 176; considering, 12, 13
University Tavern, 231n
"Upstream" (Lewisohn), 224n
Urey, Harold Clayton, 74
Urton, Harry, 144
US Forest Service (USFS), 51, 63, 71, 77, 83, 187; early days of, 4, 5, 7, 9, 11; forest management and, 141; John and, 28–29, 31, 81; Mann Gulch Fire and, 14, 150, 172, 176, 177, 182, 206–7; Norman and, 19, 29, 172, 190–91; problems with, 185, 190–91; sewage treatment facility by, 190; working for, 94, 125, 171, 200
USFS. See US Forest Service
"USFS 1919" (Maclean), 4, 11, 22, 33–34, 94, 100; Fitchen and, 72; publication of, 70, 149; reading, 80
US Navy, 47, 49

Utley, Robert, 80, 152, 157; Little Bighorn and, 78, 153; Norman and, 79, 95, 100, 154

Village Voice, 170

Wall Street Journal, 192
Washington Park, Chicago, 40, 41, 55, 182
"Water Music" (Handel), 56
Weekly Missoulian, 141
Weldon Arms (apartment hotel, Chicago), 89
West, Rebecca, 62
WFMT (Chicago), 171
"Who Owns the West?" (conference), 185, 187, 196
William Rainey Harper Professor of English, 225n
Williamson, George, 162
Williamson, Jehanne Behar, 162
Wilson, Patricia Morris Dodge, 150
Wilt, Napier, 49
Witter Bynner poetry contest, 20
Wobblies. *See* Industrial Workers of the World
Wolf Creek, MT, 126, 130
Women's Christian Temperance Union, 137

Wooded Isle, Jackson Park, Chicago, 55
Woodlawn Hospital, Chicago, 89, 154
Wordsworth, William, 162, 164, 203; class on, 79, 118; couplet by, 12; reading, 67, 147; sonnet by, 209–10; teaching, 165
Works Progress Administration, 228n
World's Fair: Columbian Exposition (Chicago, 1893), 40, 44, 55
World War II, 42, 43, 45, 75, 118
Wright, Frank Lloyd, 38
Wright, James, 225n

Yellowstone National Park, 138
Yellowstone River, 136
Young Men and Fire (Maclean), 52, 183, 187, 193, 206, 238n; Custer and, 78; essay anchoring, 169; impact of, 168; publication of, 3–4; repetitions in, 195; *River* and, 209; writing, 98–99. *See also* Mann Gulch manuscript
Young People's Society (church group, Clarinda), 139

Zabel, Morton, 230n